THE ROBERT E. HOWARD READER

Borgo Press Books by DARRELL SCHWEITZER

Conan's World and Robert E. Howard
Deadly Things
Exploring Fantasy Worlds
The Fantastic Horizon: Essays and Reviews
Ghosts of Past and Future: Selected Poetry
The Robert E. Howard Reader
Speaking of Horror II
Speaking of the Fantastic III

The
ROBERT E. HOWARD
Reader

Edited by

Darrell Schweitzer

THE BORGO PRESS

An Imprint of Wildside Press LLC

MMX

The Milford Series
Popular Writers of Today
ISSN 0163-2469

Volume Seventy-One

To the memory of *L. Sprague de Camp*,
the #1 Robert E. Howard fan, and Conan of Cimmeria's best friend.

Copyright © 2010 by Darrell Schweitzer
[page 6 shall constitute an extension of this copyright page]

All rights reserved.
No part of this book may be reproduced in any form
without the expressed written consent
of the author and publisher.
Printed in the United States of America

www.wildsidebooks.com

FIRST EDITION

CONTENTS

Acknowledgments 6

Introduction, by Darrell Schweitzer 7

Robert E. Howard: A Texan Master, by Michael Moorcock 11
The Everlasting Barbarian, by Leo Grin 16
Robert E. Howard's Fiction, by L. Sprague de Camp 24
The Art of Robert Ervin Howard, by Poul Anderson 39
Howard's Style, by Fritz Leiber 42
What He Wrote and How They Said It, by Robert Weinberg 46
Barbarism vs. Civilization, by S. T. Joshi 51
Crash Go the Civilizations, by Mark Hall 82
Return to Xuthal, by Charles Hoffman 94
Howard's Oriental Stories, by Don D'Ammassa 114
King Kull as a Prototype of Conan, by Darrell Schweitzer 125
How Pure a Puritan Was Solomon Kane? By Robert M. Price .. 133
Balthus of Cross Plains, by George H. Scithers 139
Fictionalizing Howard, by Gary Romeo 143
A Journey to Cross Plains, by Howard Waldrop 155
Weird Tales and the Great Depression, by Scott Connors 162
After Aquilonia, and Having Left Lankhmar...: Sword &
    Sorcery Since the 1980s, by Steve Tompkins 179

About the Contributors 195
Index 199

ACKNOWLEDGMENTS

Introduction Copyright © 2010 by Darrell Schweitzer.
Robert E. Howard: A Texan Master Copyright © 2010 by Michael Moorcock.
The Everlasting Barbarian Copyright © 2006 by Wildside Press LLC. Originally published in *Weird Tales* #341, Aug.-Sept. 2006.
Robert E. Howard's Fiction Copyright © 1985 by L. Sprague de Camp. Originally published in *Exploring Fantasy Worlds* edited by Darrell Schweitzer. Reprinted by permission of the Spectrum Literary Agency.
The Art of Robert Ervin Howard by Poul Anderson Copyright © 1959 by George Scithers, for *Amra*. Reprinted by permission of Karen Anderson.
Howard's Style by Fritz Leiber, (as "An Extended Swackle") © 1961 by George Scithers for *Amra*. Reprinted by permission of the Richard Curtis Literary Agency.
What He Wrote and How They Said It Copyright © 2010 by Robert Weinberg.
Barbarism vs. Civilization Copyright © 2010 by S. T. Joshi.
Crash Go the Civilizations Copyright © 2010 by Mark Hall.
Return to Xuthal Copyright © 2010 by Charles Hoffman.
Howard's Oriental Stories Copyright © 2010 by Don D'Ammassa.
King Kull as a Prototype of Conan Copyright © 2006 by Darrell Schweitzer. Originally published in *The New York Review of Science Fiction* #220, Dec. 2006.
How Pure a Puritan Was Solomon Kane? Copyright © 2010 by Robert M. Price.
Balthus of Cross Plains Copyright © 1971 by George H. Scithers.
Fictionalizing Howard Copyright © 2010 by Gary Romeo.
A Journey to Cross Plains by Howard Waldrop Copyright © 1984 by Howard Waldrop. Originally published (in this version) in *Mile High Futures*, Nov. 1984. Reprinted by permission of Howard Waldrop.
Weird Tales and the Great Depression Copyright © 2010 by Scott Connors.
After Aquilonia and Having Left Lankhmar: Sword & Sorcery Since the 1980s Copyright © 2007 by Steve Tompkin.

INTRODUCTION

This is neither the first nor the last book about Robert E. Howard. If it is the first that you have read, you will find a recommended reading list at the back, which may lead you to a lot more.

While Leo Grin's article herein surveys the first Howardian century—this is being written at the end of Robert E. Howard's centennial year and partway into the second, so I need not repeat much of what he says here—let me first explain why I am compiling a book about Robert E. Howard, a collection of articles about various aspects of his work, which should be comprehensible to the beginner but of interest to the more advanced student of Howard, and why I am doing it from a context that might be generally described as *outside* the pressure-cooker environment of Robert E. Howard fandom, with its feuds, orthodoxies, and heresies.

The answer is very simple. Howard is not going away. He is of interest to a *lot* of people and that number does not appear to be diminishing. S. T. Joshi has observed that Howard studies are about where Lovecraft studies were in the 1980s, and I at least see that as a good thing, as the glass being half-full and filling rapidly. That is, a new generation of Howard scholars, building on the work of earlier ones, is making significant strides. There are lively new journals, most notably, in recent years, Leo Grin's *The Cimmerian* and Seele Brent Publications's *The Dark Man,* which discuss Howard and his work from a variety of fresh perspectives. These are put out by people who grew up reading earlier, classic REH magazines, Glenn Lord's *The Howard Collector* and George Scithers's *Amra.* More importantly, precisely as was happening with Lovecraft studies in the '80s, scholars are going over the texts, cleaning up corruptions and unwanted emendations by later editors, so that future reading and scholarship may be based, for better or for worse, on *what Howard actually wrote.* This is the only sound basis from which to proceed. The new editions of Howard's works, particularly those published by Wandering Star, Ballantine Books, Wildside Press, and

Bison Books (University of Nebraska Press) inevitably supersede the old.

In fact, textual purity is one of the burning issues in Howard studies right now. I myself take a moderate view: it is okay for an editor to clean up the typos, maybe even regularize the spellings of proper names, but don't rewrite. Pastiches and completions of fragments by other hands are strictly non-canonical.

Now, a hundred years after Howard's death, Howard's works are getting more respect than ever. They are being reprinted in good, textually reliable editions. Sales have been none too shabby either.

Meanwhile Howard's works continue to penetrate the general culture. His figure of the Barbarian is a genuine archetype, like the hardboiled detective as invented by Dashiell Hammett and developed by others. Howard, too, has had quite a few successors, as Steve Tompkins demonstrates, well beyond the hacks who turned out what we used to call "fur jockstrap books" back about 1970. (You remember *those*...surely. If not, you maybe you should count yourself lucky. Cheesy paperbacks featuring improbably clad, muscle-bound heroes, with names, as Ursula K. Le Guin once expressed it, like Burp and Glorp and Clod.)

As a writer of imaginary-world fantasy, Howard is probably second only to J. R. R. Tolkien in importance and influence. (And even *that* qualification is likely to start another ruckus in the Howardian journals, but we will leave it there; this book is for a more general reader.) Howard himself has already been the subject of one biography and soon is to be the subject of another. More extraordinarily, there has already been a superb feature film, *The Whole Wide World* about his life.

Since the film does ultimate build up to Howard's suicide, let me take a moment to lay that particular ghost to rest, if I can. Yes, Robert E. Howard shot himself through the head in 1936, when he learned that his dying mother would never regain consciousness. He was thirty years old. Those are the facts. The tricky part about biography is moving from *what* someone did (which often can be determined with some accuracy) to the reasons for those actions, some sense of the subject's state of mind, and some idea of what kind of person he was in the first place. The deeds are easy; but it is very hard to know a dead man's mind, particularly after all the people who knew him have died. (There are a couple left, but time is inevitably running out.) In any case, to dismiss Howard, as some of his detractors have, as "Momma's boy, couldn't cut the apron-strings, blew his brains out," is rather like saying, "John Keats, apothecary, died of TB at 24."

It does rather miss the point. The point is that in the space of a little over ten years (his first story appeared in the July 1925 *Weird Tales*; he died in June of 1936) Robert E. Howard accomplished a great deal. He turned out an enormous volume of material, admittedly of uneven quality, but now, seventy years after his death, it cannot be questioned that his work as *lived,* that it is still vital to generations yet unborn when it was written, which is surely the definition of classic literature if there ever was one. We are still exploring him. In many ways, we've just begun. Howard is an *important* writer. To put him fairly in perspective, he may well eventually assume a position in American literature comparable to that of Jack London, Dashiell Hammett, or perhaps Jim Thompson, as one of the great pulp writers, in the best sense of the term, a popular and populist writer, who wrote fiercely individual fiction for the masses, without bothering himself over the polite critical orthodoxies he transcended.

He's not going away. This bears examination. Hence this book, published a hundred and four years after the birth of Robert E. Howard, in the fourth year of the second Howardian Century.

—Darrell Schweitzer
Philadelphia, PA
February 2010

ROBERT E. HOWARD

A Texan Master

by Michael Moorcock

There's something in the Texan air which inspires vivid prose, whether it be by Jim Thompson, Larry McMurtry, Joe Lansdale, or the cyberpunk movement which had its epicentre in Austin. Probably the most vivid prose of all was Robert E. Howard's. The ability to paint a complex scene with a few expert brushstrokes remains Howard's greatest talent and such talent can't of course ever be taught.

True, his stories were usually pretty simple, pretty repetitive, and his characters not exactly complex. He and his fellow pulp writers reacted negatively to the rise of modernism and were conservative by nature, even reactionary, looking back to the great Victorians for their literary models. Certainly Kipling and Stevenson, and before them Scott, were absorbed almost unconsciously, perhaps even at second or third hand, but Howard wrote in a tradition which combined the romantic virtues of Fenimore Cooper with the visionary power of Melville and the American Transcendentalists. What makes these Americans so good, I suspect, is their proximity to the wilderness. The wilderness resonates through the American consciousness, as does the image of the half-wild man, the noble savage, the barbarian who knows what it is to pit his wits against brutal nature on a daily basis.

Frankly, Conan isn't someone I'd like to know too well and even Solomon Kane, who is relatively complex for a Howard protagonist, wouldn't make the best companion unless you were facing lurid supernatural dangers in a gloomy forest, and I find the romanticisation of Celtic 'barbarians' a bit daft, all in all. Certainly, many of the people Howard romanticised did not consider themselves barbaric and might have been offended if they heard themselves called that. Which is probably why his greatest hero, Conan the Barbarian, is his best, created from whole cloth, with a nod to Natty Bumppo and Tarzan of the Apes, and most closely representing the kind of person Howard, home-bound, mother-worshipping, suspicious of big cities, would in his dreams most like to be.

As a teenager, I loved the Conan stories, even though I didn't like Conan much. I had nothing against effete citified culture. I was very much a part of that culture, being born and raised in London. My models were much more complex individuals, though still frequently American. The included Woody Guthrie, Howlin' Wolf, and Marlon Brando. For images of brooding rebels, I looked more to James Dean and Elvis. For heroes I preferred Philip Marlowe and Sam Spade. While I had enjoyed Edgar Rice Burroughs since I was a very small boy, I somehow didn't buy the romantic notions of wilderness and 'natural' men. I think I would have been seriously confused if I had. In many ways the real appeal of Burroughs and, later, Howard were the landscapes—the dead sea bottoms of Mars and the invented world of Conan, a kind of melange of every romantic historical tale that had ever been told since *Beowulf* and the *Arabian Nights*.

And there was no doubt in my mind that Howard's invented world, his mock history, made vastly superior fiction to the reality. If 'reality' had any meaning, of course, since by then I had also become a fan of French existentialism, especially Camus, who in a strange way also reflected any philosophy underlying Howard's work. I'm not an academic and I have no interest in drawing comparisons between the young middle-class Texan, raised in a remote small town and a young middle-class Algerian *colon* raised in a relatively remote corner of the French empire, but the resonances were there for me when I first read the Ace Double *Conan the Conqueror* (backed by the equally thrilling *Sword of Rhiannon* by Brackett) and a paperback translation of *La Chute*. As I've said before, not having much of a conventional education, I simply didn't know what was 'good' fiction and what was 'bad'. For me, both writers offered a persuasive atmosphere which sparked my imagination in ways it hadn't been sparked before!

When I came to read Tolkien's *Lord of the Rings*, which I had bought when it first appeared, I found him very disappointing in comparison. The soft landscapes of the shire were no more absorbing than the harsher landscapes over which the various characters quested. They had a second-hand feel to me which I didn't find in Howard, for all Howard had produced a scarcely-logical melange.

Tolkien felt safe in a way Howard never did, maybe because Howard himself never felt entirely safe in a world full of wild critters and deadly reptiles. The landscapes, like the landscapes of the German and English romanticists and their Gothic off-spring, sprang out of the mood and mind of the characters and were often there as a direct reflection of the temper of the characters themselves. They had something in common with the surrealism which was also becoming one of my enthusiasms.

For me, the appeal of Conan wasn't so much the appeal of a barbarian, but the appeal of a Heathcliffe, shouting against the brawling weather of the Yorkshire moors, raising a fist against the thunder and the lightning, a character whom the world would, if it could, bring to his knees. Conan, like many of Howard's other characters, was at his most attractive when he represented the romantic soul whom the prosaic world wished to reduce to its own level.

Whatever the appeal, I was soon searching second-hand bookstores for old copies of *Weird Tales* containing Howard stories (incredibly easy to find and pretty cheap in those days) and I began saving up for the Gnome Press editions when they started to appear. Soon I was in correspondence with L. Sprague de Camp, another writer whose work I enjoyed and who had become, by that time, the keeper of the lore, penning new Conan stories in collaboration with several other writers.

By then I had started my own writing career, though most of my fantasy was appearing in *Tarzan Adventures*, the boys' magazine I came to edit at the age of seventeen. De Camp suggested I might like to write my own Conan stories for Hans Stefan Santesson, then editor of a magazine called *Fantastic Universe*, and I began planning one out. This was at the end of the pulp era, when magazines were collapsing almost daily. *Fantastic Universe* folded and I gave up plans to write the Conan story. Although I had published a small amount of adult sf, I was working as a mainstream journalist and had already begun to write social fiction by 1959 when I had a chance meeting with the editor of the three main British sf and fantasy monthlies (*New Worlds, Science Fantasy* and *SF Adventures*), E. J.Carnell. He expressed nostalgia for Howard's work and I was commissioned, I thought, to write the Conan story for him. But when I delivered my chapter and outline he said that I'd got it wrong. He wanted a *new* sword and sorcery hero, to see how the form would go down with his readers.

Since I had nothing to lose, I decided to write a story as different as any other story of the kind I'd ever read, and that's how Elric of Melniboné, inheritor of ten thousand years of urban history, was born! I made him as different from Conan (or indeed any of the other heroes of supernatural adventure stories) as possible. But there is no doubt, certainly in the first few stories which, as it happened, became immediately popular with the readers, that Howard's techniques were informing my own, just as Camus had influenced the kind of world-weary character who inhabited this fiction.

I don't know whether or not I should be grateful to the Bard of Cross Plains for setting me on the course I followed off and on or so many years. I had very little in common with his general outlook and used my own work to do what, traditionally, sf writers had done, to try to confront social issues. However, I hope I had the sense, like Howard, to trust my romantic instincts over my conscious mind when it came to landscape and character and a sense of a good story. Like Burroughs, he knew that a good adventure story must not just consist of a goal, a mystery, a tight time element and a threat from behind, it had to have a high level of exoticism as well. If I did not learn everything from his fiction, I learned a great deal and for that I'll always be grateful.

Was Howard the reason, when I decided to settle in the USA, that I chose Texas, with its debilitating climate and often harsh, if beautiful, landscapes? He must have had something to do with it, along with the other writers I have mentioned. Texas and romanticism certainly go together, inspiring what many believe to be the quintessential American form, the Western. And of all the States of the Union, Texas must surely be the one where individualism, which the Founding Fathers enshrined in the Constitution, most flourishes. Just as a fine, enlightenment romanticism inspires that great, eloquent document, so the same romanticism continues to inspire me. There was certainly a strong element of romance which caused me to make my home along the Lower Colorado River, a few miles from Austin and if Howard didn't initiate that sensibility, he certainly encouraged me to develop it.

So I think it's pretty fair to say that Robert E. Howard significantly changed my life and brought me a whole variety of experience I would never otherwise have known, while the cadences of a language owing as much to Spanish as to English and even something to French, helped me find a prose style which suited my vision, as I'm sure it suited his. Many of us sometimes wonder what Howard would have done if he had continued to write for the rest of his life, whether he would have continued writing pulp stories—westerns, boxing yarns, oriental tales and supernatural adventure—or whether his ambitions would have grown. I like to think of him becoming, with Larry McMurtry, a big enough a writer to tell the story of Texas herself, in all her glorious and inglorious larger-than-life reality, maybe doing for Texas what Steinbeck did for California. But, in a moment of weariness and despair, he destroyed that future for himself and left us with yet another romantic image, worthy of Shelley or Byron—the writer who cared more for sensibility than sense, more for the grand dramatic gesture than for life itself. And for that, in spite of our disappointment and our sadness, I suppose we must respect him.

Lost Pines, Texas
April 2006

THE EVERLASTING BARBARIAN

Robert E. Howard at 100 Years

by Leo Grin

On January 22, 2006, at a desolate crossroads in the windswept cowtown of Peaster, Texas, a gathering of men stood reverently in a chill downpour. These weren't local ranch hands or mud-soaked oil riggers, they were fantasy fans—editors, scholars, and aficionados, from places as far away as Washington, DC, Chicago, and Los Angeles. Each had journeyed hundreds of miles through sleet and rain on a Quixotic quest of tribute. For exactly one hundred years earlier, in that isolated Texas hamlet, the ailing wife of a grizzled frontier doctor gave birth to a man whose name still echoes like a grim knell across the fantasy genre's dreamscape.

The father of Sword-and-Sorcery. The creator of Conan.

Robert Ervin Howard.

That same morning, sleepy-eyed readers of *The Washington Post* were treated to a book column by popular critic Michael Dirda, who seized upon the occasion of Howard's one hundredth birthday to review Del Rey's sumptuous new series of fully-illustrated, textually-restored Conan books. Dirda assured readers who harbor a dislike for pulp fantasy that "approached as guilty pleasures, [the Conan stories] can be wonderfully entertaining," then made a measured case for Howard's literary worth. "Howard's Conan chronicles," Dirda wrote, "are…studies in the clash of Barbarism and Civilization. In Howard's grim and all too realistic view, the barbarians are always at the gate, and once a culture allows itself to grow soft, decadent or simply neglectful, it will be swept away by the primitive and ruthless." He ended with a judgment that is old hat among fantasy fans, but one which many critics and academics are only now belatedly acknowledging: "Apart from Fritz Leiber's tales of Fafhrd and the Gray Mouser, sword and sorcery adventures don't come any better."

Amen. As criticism goes, Dirda's insightful analysis is a far cry from sixty years ago, when playwright H. R. Hays greeted Howard's first American hardcover appearance—the now-classic 1946 Arkham House release *Skull-Face and Others*—with a scathing review in *The New York Times* titled "Superman on a Psychotic Bender." Of course, Dirda's no long-dead, forgotten blowhard—he won the 1993 Pulitzer Prize for criticism. Clearly, time and age have been good to Robert E. Howard. The man whom H. P. Lovecraft christened "Two-Gun Bob" left us a large, fascinating body of work encompassing not only the birth of the Sword-and-Sorcery genre, but also the misery of the Great Depression, the bittersweet memory of the American frontier, and the millennial sweep of War and Time and History. Howard's work is increasingly perceived as a modern continuation of the gloomy, homegrown literature pioneered by giants such as Hawthorne, Melville, Poe, and London. For decades known as one of the Big Three *Weird Tales* writers, he is now also being studied and respected as a Texan writer, a 1930s writer, and a classic American writer.

My, how times have changed. A few decades ago, critics and reviewers dismissed Conan as adolescent fantasies for perpetually adolescent minds. Exciting and passionate and action-packed? Yes! But Art? Literature? Fuhgettaboutit. Granted, not everyone thought that way. Fritz Leiber's REH criticism was uncommonly perceptive, and remains as useful now as when it was written decades ago. And most fans have never heard the great anecdote L. Sprague de Camp relates in his autobiography *Time and Chance*, about his enjoyable afternoon spent in Tolkien's garage study, drinking and conversing with the legendary fantasist. When the subject turned to Howard, de Camp fully expected Tolkien—an infamous curmudgeon when it came to modern fantasy—to dismiss the Texan out of hand, if indeed he had read him at all. But to his surprise, Tolkien not only confirmed that he had read Howard, but admitted without shame that he "rather liked" the Conan tales—high praise indeed coming as it did from one of the harshest critics of the field. Still, the likes of Leiber and Tolkien were exceptions. According to most of Howard's fellow professionals, his work was forever marred by its pulp roots and his legendary psychological problems.

Today, such opinions are as outdated as a '59 Edsel. The cheap, gaudy paperbacks of yore are now deluxe illustrated volumes lovingly restored to match Howard's original typescripts. Fantasy authors routinely credit Howard as a seminal influence revered among their ranks. Critical books and magazines have prompted teachers to finally include Howard on reading lists and syllabi. (I recently read a feature about one such teacher in the *Antelope Valley Press*, a popular Southern California newspaper with a readership of 250,000—apparently his assigning Howard to students as extra credit caused a stampede to nearby bookstores, making Howard a sellout for miles around!)

To readers whose last experience with Howard was reading Conan as a teenager, all of this may seem shocking. But to those of us who have been enmeshed in Howard studies for a long time, getting face-time in *The Washington Post* from a Pulitzer Prize-winner is merely the latest in a string of breakthroughs for the Texan.

Back in the late 1960s, when science fiction grandmaster L. Sprague de Camp ushered the Conan saga into paperback for the first time, the resulting surge in Conan's popularity created a tidal wave known ever since as the "Howard Boom." It was a heady time for fans—virtually everything Howard ever wrote was published in one form or another. Incomplete stories, high school newspaper articles, juvenilia—nothing was too unfinished or just plain bad to stick into a paperback and foist upon Conan fanatics. Boxing tales, westerns, and detective stories were all encased in covers deceptively hinting at Sword-and-Sorcery pleasures, each emblazoned with "By the creator of CONAN!" Readers were grateful for the deluge, even while lamenting that some critics were judging Howard not by his best work but by haphazard paperbacks containing his very worst writing, stuff he never intended to publish.

As the Howard Boom died out in the early '80s, scholars quietly went through a decade of sifting through all of this new material and re-evaluating his reputation. Those who came to Howard as Conan fans often left with a newfound respect for his poetry, westerns, crusader tales, horror, and boxing stories. Crucially, a well-reviewed critical book called *The Dark Barbarian* appeared in 1984 from a respected academic press. Meticulously assembled and edited by critic Don Herron, it intelligently covered the whole of Howard's output, demonstrating that the creator of Conan could and should be taken more seriously. A few years later, several volumes of Howard's letters were published by Necronomicon Press, showing "crazy" Howard in a light few had fathomed: as a savvy businessman, a frequent, wide-ranging traveler, a good friend, and a passionate literary artist all too aware of the way people perceived him.

As time passed, Howard's hometown at long last began to preserve the legacy of their most famous resident. In 1986, a group of fans and civic leaders in Cross Plains combined forces to establish

Robert E. Howard Days, a festival that takes place the second weekend each June to celebrate Howard's life and work. Over the years it has grown into a vastly entertaining mini-convention hosting over a hundred fans, complete with tours, panels, awards, a banquet, and viewings of all the places Howard worked, traveled, and wrote about. The original house Howard lived and wrote in has been beatifically restored into one of the country's most charming literary museums, prompting its addition to the National Register of Historic Places in 1994. Once a forgotten figure in Cross Plains, Howard now is the town's shining light.

The same year Howard Days began, former girlfriend Novalyne Price-Ellis, then an elderly retired schoolteacher, published an autobiographical book called *One Who Walked Alone* about her years spent dating REH at the end of his life. The volume revealed Howard to be a much more conscientious and dedicated craftsman than even his most ardent fans had suspected. Howard's passion for the history and culture of his beloved Southwest, his trenchant explanations of the thematic threads tying together his *oeuvre*, and his insistence on the artistry underlying his pulp writing opened up new avenues of study. When in 1996 the book was made into a critically praised film titled *The Whole Wide World*, starring Renée Zellweger and Vincent D'Onofrio (the movie appeared on over fifty critics' Top Ten lists for that year), Howard's appeal broadened outside his fantasy roots yet again, sometimes attracting fans in strange places. (For instance, in recent years I have noticed a number of new women at Howard Days—apparently *The Whole Wide World* has been screened on Oprah Winfrey's Oxygen Network cable channel so often that it has made Howard a romantic figure among housewives!)

Between his letters, Novalyne's book and film, and various other interviews and evidence, Howard's personality has been radically redefined in the minds of fans. Previous generations took it at face value that Howard was, in a word, nuts—a crazed, paranoid eccentric living a schizophrenic life comprised of half reality and half fantasy, whose writing poured out in lengthy marathon fits of genius that eventually culminated in a senseless Oedipal suicide. Today, much more is known about Howard's life and motivations, and the old gossipy tales have lost their power to convince. By degrees, the dominant image of Howard the Crazed Nut has given way to Howard the Misunderstood Artist. By the time John Milius recorded his interview for a new *Conan the Barbarian* DVD in 2000, gleefully recounting all the silly old canards of a schizoid Howard haunted by the ghost of Conan and holed up in a boarded-up house with a shotgun sweating his terror-filled nights away, most fans knew better than to believe any part of the tale.

Throughout most of the '80s and '90s Howard studies was going gangbusters, yet the publishing of the actual stories was moribund, lost to legal wrangling between various parties intent on gaining control of Howard's valuable literary properties. Conglomerates with money to burn brought Conan back in a series of ill-advised projects. From a risible Saturday morning cartoon to lame comic book retreads to a wretched live-action television show, each attempt to recapture the Boom magic flopped among fans, who pined for more faithful and intelligent fare geared to match their newfound respect for the author. The Boom's pimply-faced teens had grown up, and no longer would they gobble down the latest tripe passed off as "faithful to Howard." They wanted the real thing, presented with the class that the author deserved.

Eventually, they got it. One by one the lawsuits were settled, the lawyers faded away, and it became possible to publish Howard in something resembling a principled fashion. In 1996 Baen came out with seven paperbacks containing much of Howard's non-Conan output, but scant advertising and publicity combined with corrupt texts doomed the series to only moderate success and no reprintings. Efforts by English publisher Wandering Star to produce lavishly illustrated and textually pure volumes of Howard's best work, a "Robert E. Howard Library of Classics," were more successful. Six books have been released to date, all widely praised for their scholarship and presentation. The stunning quality of these expensive collector's volumes attracted the interest of Del Rey, who is now filling bookstores with affordable trade paper and hardcover editions of each. It was this series, specifically designed to promote Howard as a classic American author worthy of critical attention, that caught Pulitzer Prize winner Dirda's attention and prompted his *Washington Post* piece.

In the wake of Wandering Star and Del Rey, other publishers began filling the marketplace with an array of riches that have fans talking delightedly of a second Howard Boom. Wildside Press is currently producing a ten-volume hardcover set encompassing all of Howard's classic *Weird Tales* output, and they have other volumes out dedicated to his detective, crusader, humorous boxing, and western tales. Last year Bison Books, a prestigious academic press based at the University of Nebraska, released five elegant hardcovers of Howard's best non-Conan work, each edited and introduced by a longtime Howard scholar. Girasol Books, a pulp reprint house based in Canada, has released two massive books containing Howard's complete *Weird Tales* output (including not only stories, but also all of his *WT* poems and letters to the editor), with the pages scanned directly from the pulps in facsimile form, exactly as they appeared in *The Unique Magazine* more than seventy years ago.

And all of that just covers Howard's original stories. The previously mentioned critical anthology, 1984's *The Dark Barbarian*, has been reprinted by Wildside Press in an affordable paperback edition, and in 2004 the same press released a captivating sequel titled *The Barbaric Triumph*. A book of Howard's complete poems—all seven hundred of them!—is in the works, set to be illustrated by famed Hellboy artist Mike Mignola. Several new Howard bibliographies are coming out next year, their gargantuan proportions a testament to the sheer amount of Howardia produced over the last few decades. And scholar Mark Finn just completed the first full-length biography of Howard since 1983's seminal work in the field, *Dark Valley Destiny* by L. Sprague de Camp. Titled *Blood and Thunder: The Life and Art of Robert E. Howard* and weighing in at almost four-hundred pages, Finn's tome will hit bookstores in November. The buzz is that it's good, so watch for it.

Publishers are not the only ones pushing Howard in the modern marketplace. A Swedish media conglomerate, Paradox Entertainment, has spent the last few years buying up multimedia rights to Howard's work, and they are gung-ho about reintroducing Conan and other characters to a whole new generation of fans. On the live-action front, a Bran Mak Morn movie has already been greenlighted, with pictures based on Solomon Kane and Conan also in various stages of pre-production. As for animated films, a full-length feature based on the Conan tale "Red Nails" is nearing completion. Video games, Hyborian pastiches, comics…in all of these areas Howard and Conan is being reseeded into the pop culture sphere almost faster than one can keep up.

And let's not forget the fans. The long-running organization REHupa (The Robert E. Howard United Press Association) has entered its thirty-fourth year of continuous existence, and various editors are producing books, chapbooks, and literary journals at an impressive clip, using modern production techniques to eclipse in both quality and quantity the mountain of material published during the first Howard Boom. To take one example, my own semiprofessional journal, *The Cimmerian*, pays three cents a word, appears bimonthly (*monthly* during this centennial year), and is focused like a laser on Howard's life and work. I say that any author supporting a paying market for literary criticism seventy years after his death has done something right.

So, is this really a second Howard Boom? I think so, yes. Quieter than the halcyon, Frazetta-illustrated '70s for sure, but perhaps in the final analysis a more mature, more permanent phenomenon. It's undeniable that Howard has broken through the glass ceiling of "mere pulp writer" and into the permanent realm of cultural and literary relevance shared by fellow adventure authors such as Arthur Conan Doyle, Robert Louis Stevenson, Dashiell Hammett, and Ian Fleming. There is no doubt in my mind this trend will continue, with Howard creeping further into arenas where he used to be *persona non grata*. For the first time one is seeing REH panels at academic venues such as the yearly PCA/ACA (Popular Culture Association/American Culture Association) conference. He's also starting to be included in critical books released by mainstream academic presses, such as the recent *Conversations with Texas Writers* (University of Texas Press, 2005), a book where Howard had the distinct honor of being the only dead author represented.

Perhaps most tellingly, Howard has gone international in a serious way. Forty volumes of his work, including minor miscellany such as his autobiographical novel *Post Oaks and Sand Roughs*, have been published in France alone. Russia has seen a hundred Conan books, both original Howard and pastiche, while countries as varied as Germany, Italy, Poland, and Japan all have REH available in translation and enough fans to make each new edition a viable publishing proposition. Once the new movies hit Hollywood's ever-more-internationalized marketplace, followed by the previously described onslaught of centennial publishing detritus, who knows how Howard's worldwide popularity and literary reputation will be affected? Will we someday see Robert E. Howard and Conan join fellow pulpsters Dashiell Hammett, Raymond Chandler, and H. P. Lovecraft in prestigious venues such as The Library of America? I wouldn't be the least bit surprised. Nor I daresay would Howard's many fans, scholars, and professional champions, all of whom have known for some time that his best work is eminently worthy of such honors.

Authors who remain read over the decades have a way of aging like fine wine. A hundred years on, Howard has yet to lose his foothold in the minds of appreciative readers, and every year he gains new supporters in academic and critical circles. New generations are primed to rediscover Conan and his brethren all over again. Now that we've reached the end of Howard's first century, it's worth asking what the next hundred years will hold. What do you think—will 2106 pass with REH finally forgotten along with the pulps that spawned him? Fifty years ago, the possibility of Howard's reputation surviving the vast majority of his bestselling contemporaries was a remote one. But that was then. Nowadays, the future is looking pretty bright for lovers of Sword-and-Sorcery, and for the brilliant Texan who conjured the genre out of the darkness for us.

Happy Birthday, Two-Gun.

ROBERT E. HOWARD'S FICTION

by L. Sprague de Camp

Robert E. Howard had over 160 stories published in his lifetime. He left 80 to 100 more unpublished, and fragments of still others. Many of these latter have appeared in recent years, and more will follow.

Howard was one of many mass-production pulp writers of the 1920s and '30s. Nevertheless, his work has shown a staying power and a capacity for arousing enthusiasm far beyond that of most of his contemporaries. It has acquired lasting popularity, despite the fact that (as I wrote in a critical mood), "His barbarian heroes are overgrown juvenile delinquents; his settings are a riot of anachronisms; and his plots overwork the long arm of coincidence."[1]

There must be a reason. Let us look for it.

While still a puny boy, Howard became a voracious reader. He remained so even after he had made himself, by heroic bodybuilding exercises, into a 200-pound mass of muscle. With so avid a reader, one cannot be sure that he was not influenced by any given predecessor.

Jack London was one of Howard's favorite writers. Howard esteemed Sir Richard F. Burton's tales of travel and adventure while doubting Burton's truthfulness. In Howard's writings, one can see the influence of Edgar Rice Burroughs, Robert W. Chambers, Rudyard Kipling, Harold Lamb, H. P. Lovecraft, Talbot Mundy, Sax Rohmer, Robert Louis Stevenson, and Arthur D. Howden Smith.

An alert reader of Howard can pick up echoes of other writings. In his rewritten and posthumously published "The Black Stranger," also called "Swords of the Red Brotherhood" and "The Treasure of Tranicos," I think he got the idea of a little colony on a far savage

---

[1] L. Sprague de Camp: *Science-Fiction Handbook* (Hermitage House, 1953), p. 80.

shore from "The Lady Ursula" in Charles M. Skimmer's *Myths and Legends of Our Own Land* (1896). "The Frost Giant's Daughter" may have come from "The Home of Thunder" in Skinner's book or from a similar incident in William Morris's *The Roots of the Mountains* (1913, p. 76).

In "The Devil in Iron," the death throes of Khostral Khel echo Arthur Machen's "The Great God Pan." The poisoned prong of Zorthus's iron box, in *Conan the Conqueror* (Chapter XII), could be derived from Sax Rohmer's *The Hand of Fu-Manchu* or from A. Conan Doyle's "The Adventure of the Dying Detective." The attack on the king in "By This Axe I Rule!" closely follows the death of Francesco Pizarro as described by William H. Prescott in *The History and Conquest of Peru*. Where Gustave Flaubert, in *Salammbo*, described Hamilcar Barca driving his chariot "up the whole Mappalian Way at full gallop," Howard, in "The God in the Bowl," has Kallian Publico driving his gilded chariot "along the Palian Way."

Many of Robert E. Howard's scenes are based upon movies he saw in the Twenties and Thirties, especially those depicting Roman orgies, Oriental palaces, or medieval castles. He so admired the silent version of *The Hunchback of Notre Dame*, with Lon Chaney, Sr., that he saw it several times, and the Maul in a Zamoran city, in "The Tower of the Elephant," undoubtedly comes from the Parisian thieves' quarter portrayed in this picture. Conan's challenging and killing the pirate captain in "Shadows in the Moonlight" is probably is probably inspired by a similar episode in *The Black Pirate*, with Douglas Fairbanks, Sr.

Still, the man had more than mere imitativeness. A young writer normally imitates admired predecessors. Many have passed through a Hemingway or a Lovecraft period. If the writer is good, he assimilates these influences so that the derivations are no longer obvious. Howard, I think, was just reaching this stage when, in 1936, at thirty, he killed himself.

Three influences on Howard's fiction were, first, romantic primitivism; second, fascination with Celtic history and legend; and third, the racial beliefs of his time.

Romantic primitivism arose in the eighteenth century. In 1672, John Dryden published a verse drama, "The Conquest of Granada." At the beginning, a character declaims:

> "I am free as Nature first made man,
> Ere the base laws of servitude began,
> When wild in woods the noble savage ran."

The phrase "noble savage" was taken over by critics of Jean-Jacques Rousseau, when that weepy Swiss philosopher praised primitive life. So far as I know, Rousseau did not himself use the term. Neither did he ever know any savages, noble or otherwise.

In 1755, Rousseau published *A Discourse on the Origins and the Foundations of Inequality Among Men*. He headed the second chapter: "That Nature has made man happy and good, but that Society depraves him and makes him wretched." "Man," he declared, "is naturally good," but civilization, especially private property, corrupts him and makes him evil.

Rousseau later qualified such statements, as age and experience eroded his youthful idealism. Nonetheless, the romantic illusion of a primitive Golden Age, when all were happy and virtuous, lived on. It effected the many utopian (and usually short-lived) colonies of the nineteenth-century United States, like the communes of the "counterculture" of the 1960s.

Romantic primitivism influenced Kipling, London, and Burroughs, all of whom captivated Howard. Animal characters in Kipling's *Jungle Books* are always sneering at civilized man: "Men are blood-brothers to the Bandar-log (monkeys)." Tarzan is ever denouncing civilization and its representatives: "Always he was comparing their weaknesses, their vices, their hypocrisies, and their little vanities with the open, primitive ways of his ferocious jungle mates...."[2]

The great gap between the fictitious "state of nature" of romantic primitivists and the real thing has often been exposed. For example, Thor Heyerdahl's recent *Fatu-Hiva* tells of the attempt of the young Heyerdahl and his bride to go native in the Marquesas. After a year, they were heartily glad to get back to civilization before primitive life killed them. But the romantic illusion still flourishes, like those pseudo-scientific cults that thrive on exposure and disproof.

Howard swallowed the contentions of romantic primitivism. In his correspondence with Lovecraft, he wished that he had been born a barbarian or on the frontier of the previous century. This caused Lovecraft to castigate him as an "enemy of civilization." Judging from Howard's tales of Texan mayhem and massacre, his trouble was that he did not recognize a barbaric environment when he saw it.

---

[2] Rudyard Kipling: *The Jungle Books* (Dell, 1964), p. 327; Edgar Rice Burroughs: *Tarzan the Untamed* (Ballantine, 1963), p. 72.

Howard was fascinated by the ancient Celts. Lovecraft was an Anglophile. Howard claimed to be of largely Irish ancestry, but a cousin of his said the family was in fact mostly English. In any case, Howard became a Celtophile; but he was more objective towards the Celts than Lovecraft was about the Anglo-Saxons.

This interest appears in Howard's fantasies of Turloch O'Brien, in his historical stories of Cormac Mac Art, and in other historical and contemporary tales with Irish-named heroes: Costigan, Dorgan, Kirowan, O'Brien, O'Donnell, and so on. He wrote many fantasies and historical tales laid in the British Isles, of the struggle of Pict against Briton, of Briton against Roman, and of Irishman against Norseman. He read Donn Byrne's Irish novels but resented Byrne's making heroes of Ulstermen and Anglo-Normans. He studied the eccentric phonology and orthography of the Irish language. He took part in arguments as to which of the two branches of the British Celts, the Goidels, Gaels, or Q-Celts, and the Cymry, Britons, or P-Celts, reached Britain first.

Like Lovecraft, Howard was under the spell of the Aryanist doctrine, which identified Aryans with the tall, blond, blue-eyed Nordic racial type. Hence he wrote of the conquest, in Britain, of small, dark aborigines of the Mediterranean type by "blond, blue-eyed giants"—the supposed Aryan Celts. According to present evidence, the conquering was probably the other way around. The Nordic aborigines were at least twice conquered by swarthy little Southerners, first by the prehistoric Beaker Folk from Spain and secondly by the Romans. Howard himself had black hair and blue eyes—a combination that seems commoner in Ireland than elsewhere. Hence he was less englamorated by mere blondness than Lovecraft.

Many of Howard's views would today be called "racist." In this, Howard followed most popular fiction writers of the time, to whom ethnic stereotypes were stock in trade. If a racist, Howard was, by the standards of his time, a mild one. While he vented conventional Texan views of Negroes and Mexicans, he noted individual Negroes and Mexicans whom he admired.

Howard's primitivism gave his ethnic attitudes a paradoxical twist. He might view Negroes as incorrigibly barbaric; but to him, that was not altogether bad, since he thought that barbarians had virtues lacking in civilized men. In criticizing French novelists, he said: "Dumas has a virility lacking in other French writers—I attribute it to his negroid strain...."[3] While he wrote stories of the Deep South,

---

[3] Howard to Lovecraft, early 1933.

with gallant white men dashing about to foil nigger uprisings, he also, now and then, showed an unexpected flicker of sympathy for the downtrodden blacks.[4] Although a few remarks about Shemites in the Conan stories suggest the hostile Christian stereotype of the Jew, Howard also made Belit, the Shemitish she-pirate, one of his heroines.

At fifteen, in 1921, Howard chose writing as his career. Writing, he thought, would give him more freedom and independence than any other trade. He later maintained that his passion to be his own boss was a larger factor in his choice than any great literary urge. He would, he said, have worked at something else if it promised more money.

One may suspect that a man with Howard's appetite for reading and his storytelling bent would have written, no matter what his main occupation. On the other hand, since he regarded writing mainly as a way of making a living, Howard took a hard-headed commercial view of the craft. This contrasts with H. P. Lovecraft's gentleman amateurish, art-for-art's sake attitude.

In 1921 the adolescent Howard sent a story to *Adventure* magazine, one of the aristocrats of the pulps and a favorite of Howard. The magazine quickly returned the story.

In 1922, Howard's parents sent him to Brownwood to complete his high-school education, since the school in Cross Plains only went to the tenth grade. After graduating, Howard came home in 1923 to try to make a living by writing. After a year of odd jobs and no story sales, his parents sent him to the Howard Payne Commercial School in Brownwood to learn typing and shorthand. After another equally unsuccessful spell at home, he returned to Brownwood for a bookkeeping course in the fall of 1926.

During this time, he also worked a number of jobs: clerking in shops, soda-jerking, secretary in a law office, stenographer, postal clerk, oil-field hand, and surveyor. He also wrote: at first for the Brownwood High School magazine, *The Tattler,* then for a local periodical called *The Yellow Jacket.*

He joined a coterie of eight or ten young people of literary tastes. The group included Harold Preece, later a professional writer. In also contained Howard's lifelong friend Tevis Clyde Smith (with whom he later collaborated on a story) and Truett Vinson. The group issued a round-robin journal, *The Junto,* to which Howard often contributed.

---

[4] *E.g.*, in "Black Canaan," "The Dead Remember," and "The Apparition in the Prize Ring."

In 1923, *Weird Tales* was launched. In the fall of 1924, while at Brownwood, Howard sold his first commercial story. It was a caveman tale, "Spear and Fang." *Weird Tales* had just come under the editorship of Farnsworth Wright, who paid Howard $16.00.

Howard continued writing for *Weird Tales* nearly all his life. "The Lost Race" appeared in the issue of July, 1925. During 1923-25, he also wrote and sold "The Hyena," "In the Forest of Villefere," and "Wolfshead." All four were undistinguished fictions of the standard *Weird Tales* type. "The Lost Race" was a tale of Celt versus Pict in ancient Britain; "The Hyena" and "Wolfshead" about African lycanthropy.

After completing his courses at Howard Payne in 1927, Howard settled down to full-time writing. He later regretted that poverty had kept him from a regular college career. Actually, his parents urged him to go to college, but he refused. The real reason was not poverty but his furious intolerance of any sort of discipline or routine. He wrote ghost, adventure, pirate, and sport stories—even the so-called "true confessions." He submitted them to many magazines, both pulp and slick, but had few sales—usually two to five a year. His earnings were, for 1926: $50.00; 1927: $37.50; 1928: $186.00; 1929: $772.50. Most of the money came from *Weird Tales*. Although his magazine paid low and was often late, it proved Howard's most trustworthy source of income.

Such a time of groping and struggle is usual in a new writer's career. Once he got established, the self-taught Howard did remarkably well, despite an uncongenial environment and isolation from professional contacts. From 1930 on, his earnings (save for 1933, with $962.25) were consistently over $1000 a year. By 1935 they were above $2000. At this time, $1000 was a living wage and $2000 was a fairly affluent one.

****

In 1928 Howard set down a fictional character he had long borne in mind: Solomon Kane, an Elizabethan English Puritan. The story was "Red Shadows," in *Weird Tales* for August 1928. Kane differs from most Howard heroes, who are brawny, brawling, belligerent adventurers. Kane is somber of dress, dour of mien, rigid of principles, and driven by a demonic urge to wander, to court danger, and to right wrongs.

Some of the Kane stories are set in Europe and some in Africa. Kane has gory adventures and overcomes supernatural menaces. In these stories first appears Howard's distinctive intensity—a curious sense of total emotional commitment, which somehow drags the reader along willy-nilly.

Howard's main writing, from 1929 to 1932, was boxing stories. He published twenty tales about a pugilistic sailor named Steve Costigan. Over half of these were sold to *Fight Stories,* and the rest to *Action Stories* and *Jack Dempsey's Fight Magazine.*

Costigan, able-bodied seaman and prizefighter, is an invincible roughneck with fists of iron, a heart of gold, and a head of ivory. These stories are comedies, full of broad, slapstick humor. They deal with prizefights (usually in port cities), with plots, skullduggery, and virtue finally triumphant. The hero is an incorrigible sucker for a hard-luck story, especially from a fair but designing female. Howard explained his preference for heroes of mighty thews and simple minds:

> "They're simpler. You get them in a jam, and no one expects you to rack your brains inventing clever ways for them to extricate themselves. They are too stupid to do anything but cut, shoot, or slug themselves into the clear."[5]

The Costigan tales came so fast that they began to pile up. In 1931, Farnsworth Wright launched *Weird Tales'* shortlived companion, *Oriental Stories* (later *Magic Carpet*). To sell some Costigan stories laid in Oriental places to the new magazine, Howard changed the name of the hero, his dog, and his ship. Sailor Steve Costigan became Sailor Dennis Dorgan. Wright bought four stories and published one before *Magic Carpet* folded. Six remained in manuscript until their recent publication. (*The Incredible Adventures of Dennis Dorgan,* FAX Collector's Editions, 1974.)

These stories would never have been disinterred but for Conan's popularity in the last decade. Still, they have ingenuity, action, and humor. Even at his corniest and pulpiest, Howard is fun to read.

The stories also show Howard's limitations. His knowledge of seafaring was second-hand. The closest he came to going to sea was a motorboat ride in the Gulf of Mexico. Tales of Shanghai, Singapore, and other exotic ports are obviously by one who had never been there. But Howard had neither the time nor the facilities to research the ambiance of these places.

---

[5] E. Hoffmann Price: "A Memory of R.E. Howard," in Robert E. Howard: *Skull-Face and Others* (Arkham House, 1946), p. xxii.

A couple of the Dorgan stories, laid in San Francisco, give a picture of "high society" by one who likewise had never been there. The Societarians flutter limp paws, stare through lorgnettes and monocles, say "my deah" and "rawthath," and swoon at the sight of blood. But then, the class of readers for whom Howard was writing had never been there, either.

After 1932, Howard's production of sport stories dropped off. Only four more in this genre were published in his lifetime.

Ever since he had begun the Solomon Kane stories, Howard had worked off and on at heroic fantasy. In 1926, he started "The Shadow Kingdom," about Kull of Atlantis. Contrary to cultist doctrine, Howard did not assume that Atlantis was the fountainhead of all civilization. Instead, his Atlantis is primitive. Kull, a Stone Age savage, goes to the mainland and becomes king of civilized Valusia (as Conan does later of Aquilonia).

After he finished at Howard Payne in 1927, Howard completed "The Shadow Kingdom." From 1926 to 1930, he followed it by a dozen more Kull stories, three of which he failed to complete. Some Kull tales, like two of the Solomon Kane stories, have no supernatural content.

Howard repeatedly submitted stories to *Adventure* and *Argosy*, but, except for a few sales to the latter, without success. At least one and possibly more of the Kull stories were sent to these magazines and rejected.

Eventually, the Kull stories reached *Weird Tales*. Wright bought "The Shadow Kingdom" and "The Mirrors of Tuzun Thune." He also bought "Kings of the Night," which brings King Kull and Bran Mak Morn, Howard's anti-Roman Pictish hero, together by magical time travel. The other Kull stories, Wright rejected.

Throughout his career, Howard tried to break into the highest-paying pulps such as *Adventure, Argosy, Blue Book,* and *Short Stories,* but with little success. He was competing with such finished writers as Harold Lamb, Talbot Mundy, and Arthur D. Howden Smith. While strongly influenced by these writers, Howard's stories were not up to the standard they set. Had he lived longer and matured, both as a writer and as a human being, while the older writers died off or left pulp writing, Howard might well have achieved his goal.

In 1932, Howard created his most successful character, Conan the Cimmerian. Conan first appeared as the hero of a rewritten Kull story, "By This Axe I Rule!" Howard changed the names and introduced a supernatural element. The result was "The Phoenix on the Sword," in *Weird Tales* for December, 1932.

Conan was a development of King Kull and an idealization of Howard himself. He is a gigantic barbarian adventurer from backward northern Cimmeria. After a lifetime of wading through rivers of gore and overcoming foes both natural and supernatural, Conan becomes King of Aquilonia. Dr. John D. Clark, in an introduction to the Gnome Press edition (1950) of *Conan the Conqueror* (originally a *Weird Tales* serial, "The Hour of the Dragon") said: "Conan, the hero of all of Howard's heroes, is the armored swashbuckler, indestructible and irresistible, that we've all wanted to be at one time or another."[6]

Conan is the barbarian hero to end all barbarian heroes. His later imitations seem pallid by comparison. In "A Witch Shall Be Born," Conan is captured and crucified. As he hangs on the cross, a vulture flies down with the intention of pecking his eyes out. Conan bites the vulture's head off. You can't have a tougher hero than that. (The scene may have been inspired by a similar incident in Burroughs's *Tarzan the Untamed,* Chapter VIII. Lost in the desert, Tarzan saves himself by luring a vulture within reach, seizing it, and devouring it.)

Actually Kull has more in common with Robert Howard than does Conan. Kull is given to mystical broodings on the meaning of it all. Conan is more the pure extrovert, more interested in wine, women, and battle than in abstractions. Another of Howard's characters says of Conan:

> "The Cimmerian might have spent years among the great cities of the world; he might have walked with the rulers of civilization; he might even achieve his wild whim some day and rule as king of a civilized nation; stranger things have happened. But he was no less a barbarian. He was concerned only with the naked fundamentals of life. The warm intimacies of small, kindly things, the sentiments and delicious trivialities that make up so much of civilized men's lives were meaningless to him.... Bloodshed and violence and savagery were the natural elements of the life Conan knew; he could not, and would not, understand the little things that are so dear to civilized men and women."[7]

---

[6] Robert E. Howard: *Conan the Conqueror* (Gnome Press, 1950), p. 12.
[7] Robert E. Howard: "Beyond the Black River," in *Conan the Warrior* (Lancer Books, 1967), p. 200.

This is, of course, a romantic primitivist's view of barbarism. In conceiving Conan, Howard invented a whole world to go with him. He assumed that 12,000 years ago, after the sinking of Atlantis and before recorded history, there was a Hyborian Age, when:

> "...shining kingdoms lay spread across the world like blue mantles beneath the stars—Nemedia, Ophir, Brythunia, Hyperborea, Zamora with its dark-haired women and towers of spider-haunted mystery, Zingara with its chivalry, Koth that bordered on the pastoral lands of Shem, Stygia with its shadow-guarded tombs, Hyrkania whose riders wore steel and silk and gold. But the proudest kingdom of the world was Aquilonia, reigning supreme in the dreaming west."[8]

Howard sold seventeen Conan stories, from shorts to a book-length novel, to *Weird Tales*. Five more were either rejected or never submitted. Four were left unfinished. One of those rejected, "The Frost Giant's Daughter," Howard rewrote as "Gods of the North." He changed the hero's name to "Amra of Akbatana" but otherwise made only trivial alterations and gave the story to a non-paying fan magazine.

From 1932 to 1934, Conan stories were Howard's main preoccupation. Then he began to taper off, as Western stories took more and more of his time. His last published Conan story was the 29,000-word "Red Nails." This was completed in July, 1935, although not published (as a three-part serial) until a year after. The final installments appeared after Howard's death.

* * * * * * *

All through Howard's fantasy period, when he was writing tales of Kull and Conan, he kept pushing out into other areas of fiction. He wrote many tales of weird and fantasy along conventional *Weird Tales* lines. In a couple of these, such as "The Thing on the Roof," he used elements from Lovecraft's Cthulhu Mythos. To the Mythos, Howard contributed the sinister volume, *Nameless Cults*, by "Friedrich Von Junzt."

---

[8] Robert E. Howard: *Conan* (Lancer Books, 1967), p. 34.

Howard sold several detective stories. All have fantastic elements, like sinister Oriental cults and African leopard-men. They were no great success, for Howard disliked meticulous, intricate plotting. Moreover, never having lived in a big city, he found the urban atmosphere hard to present convincingly.

He wrote his only interplanetary novel, *Almuric*. This was the nearest he came to science fiction proper, although he sometimes introduced super-scientific elements into Conan stories. *Almuric* is an obvious imitation of Burroughs. Esau Cairn is transported by super-scientific gadgetry to a planet of a distant star. There he finds himself among brawny barbarians, fighting a race of winged beings. Howard exaggerates the hero's brawn to the point of burlesque; Esau can drive a knife blade into solid rock.

Howard also wrote some tales of ancient, medieval, and modern adventure. Some brought in fantastic elements—magic, racial memory, monsters, lost cities, or prehistoric races—while others did not. He sold over two dozen of these tales, but others he failed to place.

Howard wrote about twenty series of stories built around one character. One such series has a Texan hero, Francis X. Gordon, adventuring in modern Afghanistan. Rifles crack, scimitars swish, and everybody kills everybody with gusto.

These tales are derived from those that Lamb and Mundy had been publishing in *Adventure*. Gordon is an avatar of Bran Mak Morn and Turlogh O'Brien: dark, of medium size but preternatural strength, speed, and agility. Another series, also laid in Afghanistan, features a double of Gordon called Kirby O'Donnell.

In a letter to Lovecraft, Howard scorned Broadway cowboys who wrote Wild West stories without having been west of Hoboken. Howard, though, wrote many stories laid in places thousands of miles from where he had ever been. He admitted his sketchy, second-hand knowledge of the Orient, confessing that his Turks, Mongols, and Afghans were merely "Irishmen and Englishmen in turbans and sandals." Even his Breckenridge Elkins Westerns are laid in western Nevada, over a thousand miles from Cross Plains.

Still, Howard had to make a living. A writer does not live long enough to learn to write well and also to visit all the places he may wish to write about. So Howard did what others do. He read up on the places and filled in the gaps with his imagination. But here he was hopelessly handicapped by lack of access to big-city and university libraries.

In another series, Howard wrote of a crippled man, James Allison. By "racial memory," Allison recalls his incarnations as various heroic barbarians: Hunwulf in "The Garden of Fear," Niord in "The Valley of the Worm," and Hialmar in "Marchers of Valhalla."

Howard sold two stories of Turlogh O'Brien, an eleventh-century Irishman, and failed to finish two others. Four stories of an earlier Gael, Cormac Mac Art, he failed to place. Four stories of the Crusades and the first Turkish siege of Vienna, Howard published in *Oriental Stories/Magic Carpet.*

After the demise of that magazine, however, he wrote but few tales in the straight historical vein. Although he said he would like to spend his life writing such fiction, he had tried it often, but with meager success. The short-lived magazine of historical fiction, *Golden Fleece* (1938-39), would have been a natural for him; two of his stories were in fact posthumously published therein.

The market for short stories of this type has always been very limited, and Howard never tried a book-length historical novel. It is too bad that he was not alive in the 1950s, when the swashbuckling historical novel, for which he had a natural bent, reached its peak of popularity. Then, books by such authors as Costain, Duggan, and Renault made the best-seller lists as a matter of course.

Howard sold several stories to *Spicy Adventures,* a magazine of a kind then called "the hots." They were deemed pornographic, although by present standards they are as mild as milktoast. In 1935, writing to Lovecraft, Howard said he had used one of his own sexual adventures in the plot. He urged Lovecraft (of all people) to do likewise. We may take his talk of "sexual adventures" with salt. Howard only began to show a normal male interest in women in his late twenties, and it is unlikely that his "adventures" went further than a bit of necking.

****

Although self-taught, Howard achieved a sound, unobtrusive prose style. He wrote in sentences of short to medium length, as became general after the Hemingway revolution of the 1930s. He could give the impression of a highly colorful scene with only sparing use of action-slowing modifiers. Consider the beginning of *Conan the Conqueror:*

> The long tapers flickered, sending black shadows wavering across the walls, and the velvet tapestries rippled. Yet there was no wind in the chamber. Four men stood about the ebony table on which lay the green sarcophagus that gleamed like carven jade. In

the upraised right hand of each man a curious black candle burned with a weird greenish light. Outside was night and a lost wind moaning among the black trees.[9]

The mood is set and the scene depicted with broad strokes of color, in straightforward, economical prose. He also used rhythm, alliteration, and personification.

An editor has little occasion to correct Howard's English, even though Howard had some idiosyncracies like "surprize" and making two words out of "cannot." Present-day editors might quibble about some of his punctuation, but conventions have changed since Howard's time.

Howard was a devotee of the "well-wrought tale," as opposed to the "slice-of-life" technique of fiction. Stories of either kind have their place. For pure, escapist entertainment like Howard's stories, the well-wrought tale is usually better.

Howard's faults arose mainly from haste. Like his pulpwriting colleagues, he had to turn out a large volume to make a living. He rarely wrote more than two drafts of a story and sometimes only one. Hence his stories have many inconsistencies, anachronisms, and other bits of careless craftsmanship. In Chapter XII of *Conan the Conqueror* (in its earlier editions), in the space of a few pages, Conan's helmet is variously called a morion, a basinet, and a burgonet.

Howard was often inconsistent in spelling foreign words and exotic names, *e.g.*, kaffia and kafieh, "Kush" and "Cush." He tended to repeat certain elements over and over, such as the combat with a gigantic serpent or ape, the stone city built on the lines of the Pentagon, and the menace in the form of a winged ape or demon.

Critics have blamed Howard for his violence and his immaturity in human relations, especially in his heroes' attitudes toward women. Howard must have been as uncomfortable with love as a small boy who, viewing a Western, is loudly disgusted when the hero kisses the heroine rather than his horse. One critic was so staggered by the splashing of gore that he said Howard's stories "project the immature fantasy of a split mind and logically pave the way to schizophrenia."[10]

---

[9] Robert E. Howard: *Conan the Conqueror* (Gnome Press, 1950), p. 15.
[10] H.R. Hays, in *The New York Times Book Review*, 29 September 1946, p. 34.

Bloodshed and emotional immaturity, however, were normal in the pulp fiction of Howard's time. Writers did not deem it their duty to endow their heroes with social consciousness, to sympathize with disadvantage ethnics, and to show their devotion to peace, equality, and social justice. A story that displayed these now-esteemed qualities would not have gotten far in the pulps.

****

Howard early essayed to write Westerns, since he knew this milieu at first hand. He found the going hard. Knowing a setting too well, he said, would be a handicap.

In 1933, Howard engaged Otis A. Kline as his literary agent. At Kline's urging, he gave more attention to the western genre. Soon his Western production all but crowded out his other work. About thirty Western stories were sold in his last three years. He said that he thought his natural bent lay in that direction and that he might give up fantasy entirely for Western writing.

Many of Howard's Westerns are filled with broad frontier humor, close to burlesque, such as he had used in his Costigan and Dorgan stories, *e.g.*: "I don't know nothing that makes me madder'n getting shot in the ear."[11] These stories are really funny: one who had read only Howard's serious tales would never have expected them of him. His humorous Western heroes are as big as Conan, even less bright, and genial in a homicidal way.

Howard also wrote many non-humorous Westerns, grim and somber like most of his stories. These are only competent hack work. They are harmless amusement, with adequate dialogue and fair suspense. They are conventional shoot-'em-up yarns, wherein steely-eyed Texans, ruthless and unscrupulous but chivalrous towards women, perforate even wickeder Westerners.

In his last years, Howard hinted of writing a "Southwestern epic." He may have had in mind something like the later "realistic" Westerns by such authors as A. B. Guthrie. Such an epic, however, would have needed a deeper grasp of human relationships, and of the politico-economic factors in human affairs, than appears in stories like "The Vultures of Whapeton."

The view of the Wild West in Howard's existing Westerns is superficial, as if gotten mainly from the library. He might have developed this insight, for his letters show an awareness of such fac-

---

[11] Robert E. Howard: "Guns of the Mountains," in *A Gent From Bear Creek* (Grant, 1965), p. 72.

tors. In the Western pulps of the thirties, however, such vision would have been a handicap. The stories in these magazines were the world's most conventional, cliché-filled, formula-ridden fictions, and Howard merely wrote what he knew would sell.

When Howard's virtues and faults as a writer have been set forth, however, there remains to be explained that curious grip that his narrative has on many readers. Apart from the headlong narrative pace and verse and zest of Howard's storytelling, as Lovecraft put it, "the real secret is that he himself is in every one of them."[12]

The "himself" that Howard wrote into his stories with such burning intensity and hypnotic effect was a very flawed human being. He suffered from an abnormal devotion to his mother, delusions of persecution, and a fascination with suicide. This somber self, with its nightmarish view of a hostile, menacing universe, its irrational fears and hatreds, and its love affair with death, comes across in his fiction. It grips the reader whether he will or no, somewhat as do Lovecraft's fictional versions of his nightmares and neuroses. Thus the very traits that gave Howard's stories lasting interest are those that in the end destroyed him.

In any case, Howard's stories, despite their patent faults, but fair to be enjoyed for their action, color, and furious narrative drive for many years to come.

---

[12] H. P. Lovecraft: "Robert Ervin Howard: A Memoriam," in *Skull-Face and Others*, p. xv.

THE ART OF ROBERT E. HOWARD

by Poul Anderson

When a subject has been discussed by intelligent men for any length of time, it becomes virtually impossible to say anything new about it. This is even more true of literature than of politics, philosophy, or the other arts. Science, including the highly developed science of textual criticism, is exempt, because the dialogue is less between man and man than between man and the quasi-infinite universe. Thus there can be no more original praises of the immortal Sherlock, but his Canon remains an inexhaustible field for scholarly research. Friends of Conan should therefore, I think, devote more effort to close examination of the chronicles than to simple adulation of the hero. But being caught short on time and materials, I must now deny my own precept and go for one of those rambles known as a familiar essay—over ground long ago covered by such people as John D. Clark and P. Schuyler Miller.

It might first be asked if I am entitled to call myself a friend of Conan. I did treat him rather roughly in a little burlesque called "The Barbarian." But, I submit, *imprimis,* that friends may be forgiven for a bit of horseplay; *secundus,* that Conan is far too powerful to be hurt by such blows of the quill; *tertius,* that to the extent I have been at odds with him, I only supply that often overlooked necessity of the hero, a villain.

You will recall that the great Demon lords in *The Worm Ouroboros* came to recognize this need, and to turn time itself back so that their enemies of Witchland might again contest their existence. It is heresy, but I have always felt this to be a flaw in an otherwise magnificent book. Hotheaded youth may deliberately seek risk and hardship; men responsible for broad lands have neither the right nor, if they are sane, the wish to do wild deeds for the deeds' own sake. I can far more readily believe in Odysseus, who wrought so mightily to get back to some home cooking. Tennyson's reconstruction of the aftermath is pure sentimentalism. The Fellowship of the Ring were likewise forced to high emprise, and wished throughout for nothing more than peace and security for whose restoration they strove against Sauron himself. Gunnar of Lithend and Grettir the Strong were driven to the wall by malicious circumstance: only then did they show what manhood can be when it must.

Here, then, is a point at which Conan rings true. He grows. He starts as a larcenous young soldier of fortune; he learns, almost by accident, what it is to lead men and how much duty is implied by the concept of "chief"; finally, as King of Aquilonia, he puts dwn the banditry by which he once made his own living, fights less for himself than for his country, and even settles down with a lawful wife. Naturally he still gets restless—we all do—but I think that if the powers of darkness had only left him alone, his sword would not again have troubled the earth. He would have gotten nostalgic about the old days; he never would have developed into a Grand Old Man, but rather would have shocked his decorous offspring with oaths and ale hoisting; but he would have been wise enough to compromise with reality.

However, let us admit that Conan does not have the human stature of the greatest adventurers. He lacks complexity. I do not mean that a hero should be neurotic. On the contrary, the protagonist of the typical modern novel is a sniveling little wretch, a hundred of whom would not make one Conan, even with respect to the interesting virtues. But Conan is too singleminded, shall we say. Compare the tenth-century Icelander, Egil Skallagrimsson: a rover and warrior from Greenland to Russia, confidant of one king and mortal foe of another—but also a poet of the first rank, a shrewd trader, a still more shrewd observer, a man of sardonic humor (often directed at himself) as well as undying hatreds: finally, aged and blind, he kills a man for some half-senile reason, but about the same time, when his son is drowned, he composes the unforgettable *Sonnotorrek*. To be sure, Egil is a historical figure, but whoever wrote his saga (the best guess is Snorri Sturlason) was one of the best biographical novelists of all time.

Conan is much less of an individual. His characteristics are few and obvious. Fearless in battle, through prone to superstitious terrors, he is a moody soul, his mirth rare and crude. He is unflinchingly loyal to his friends, unrelentingly fierce to enemies. He picks up some knowledge of tactics, but seems innocent of all strategic concepts, and is handicapped (I should think) by such peculiar prejudices as his belief that the bow is an unmanly weapon. Until rather late in his life, he looks on women immaturely, as mere toys, and shows no particular interest in starting a family. This is atypical of people in general and barbarians in particular; possibly Conan's rather traumatic childhood caused it. However, it should certainly have occurred to him earlier than it did, that the King of Aquilonia had an obligation to beget a legitimate heir. Conan possesses a rough chivalry, and it is not at all sadistic; but neither does he ever seem to think that the men he cuts down in such wholesale lots are human too. This, with much else, betrays his limited intelligence. I suspect Aquilonia was well governed under him simply because, like Genghis Khan, he had wit enough to pick good bureaucrats.

But when we have thus delimited Conan, what remains is still good. He *is* brave, honest in his own fashion, steadfast, vaguely conscious of *noblesse oblige.* Once his juvenile-delinquent phase has been outgrown, he does his dogged best. You can like him, even if you wouldn't invite him to dinner.

And, of course, the things that happen to him! In this, I think, the art of Robert E. Howard was hard to surpass: vigor, speed, vividness. He had not the command granted an Eddison or a Tolkien, but nonetheless he fulfilled the story teller's prime obligation, to make scenes and events come real. Howard was a highly visual writer; I imagine what he treated of stood clearly before him as he wrote. And not all that he saw was dark, evil, or violent. There are scattered passages of considerable beauty—for example, in *Conan the Conqueror,* a description of the southern Aquilonian landscape, seen from a hill top near sunset. And always there is that furious, galloping narrative pace. If Conan is not the greatest of warriors, neither is he the least.

HOWARD'S STYLE

by Fritz Leiber

John Poscik's well-rounded article about Solomon Kane in *Amra* Vol. 2, #14 led me to read "The Moon of Skulls" and "Red Shadows" for the first time. I'm once more impressed with Howard's simple, youthful, melodramatic power.

He painted in about the broadest strokes imaginable. A mass of glimmering black for the menace, an ice-blue cascade for the hero, between them a swathe of crimson for battle, passion, and blood—and that was the picture, or story, rather, except when a vivid detail might chance to spring to life, or a swift thought-arabesque be added.

He knew the words and phrases of power and sought to use them as often as possible, the words and phrases that the writer with literary aspirations usually avoids (sometimes quite mechanically) because they're clichés or near-clichés, words and phrases like (I select from "The Moon of Skulls") black, dark, death, volcanic, ghost, great black shadow, symbol of death and horror, menace brooding and terrible, shrubs which crouched like short dark ghosts, outposts of the kingdom of fear, black spires of wizards' castles, ju-ju city, grim black crags of the fetish hills, henchmen of death, the Tower of Death, the Black Altar....

These aren't bad words and phrases really. In fact they are the same general sort that still make some Americans embarrassed about Edgar Allan Poe and his European reputation and influence. And Howard didn't use them like a hackwriter; he used them like a poet. (Who but Howard could work into a good poem and make effective a pulpish bit like, "Jets of agony lance my brain"?) Yet his boyish, sincere, poetic use of words of power will always make it difficult for us to demonstrate to literary people unsympathetic to the swordplay-and-sorcery field what we see in Howard.

The landscape, plan, diagram, or microcosm of each of Howard's earlier stories is as simple, limited, and complete as that of a boy's daydream, a hewn-out stage setting that can be held in the mind as the story progresses. It has no more parts than a good diagram. There is no worry at all how it intersects the real world. It is an inner world for a boy's solemn adventuring. In most fantasy there are only traces of this boyish stage of the development of the dream world (Eddison naming his rival nations in *The Worm Ouroboros* Demons, Witches, Pixies, Goblins, Imps, and Ghouls), but in Howard (especially, to my mind, in the King Kull and Solomon Kane stories) it is dominant.

Most of us, I imagine, create in childhood starkly simple landscapes for adventuring. I spent a lot of time on a rope bridge over a dark chasm; often there was a tiger at one end and a lion at the other. But it took Howard's unique talent and intensity to make powerful, genuine stories directly out of these materials with no disguise at all.

Broad strokes, stark landscapes, near-clichés of power—like I said.

I am not belittling Howard when I denominate his writing boyish. I'm thinking of his freshness, sincerity, and exuberance as much as anything else, and there is an undeniably boyish element to all sword-and-sorcery fiction, even the most sophisticated or wickedly decadent. When the author of *Vathek* came of age, or into his great inheritance, his comment was something like "Now my friends will expect me to behave like a man. How much they are deceived, for I intend to remain a child always!" This was the same Beckford who when a great tower he was having built on his estate collapsed, instantly reacted, "Ah, if only I'd been there to see it fall!" (This anecdote rings true. At least, I am vastly more inclined to believe it than, say, the story of Keats reacting to one of his last deadly hemorrhages with, "I know it's my life's blood, but Christ, what a color!")

Nor am I saying that Howard used clichés of the order of stony silence, iron will, morbid curiosity seekers, and rapier-like wit—but rather the near-clichés of the horror story, such as words like strange, weird, and eerie. (If something is strange, a good writer ought to be able to spot wherein the strangeness lies, and surely his description will be more effective if he can.) Howard didn't generally over-use those particular words, but he leaned heavily on such cousin-words as grim, black, dark, ghostly.

The landscape of the Conan stories shows a definite growth from the Kull and Kane tales. (Interesting, those three K-sounds, Kull, Kane, and Conan.) No longer to we find so many hosts of killers inhabiting giant rooms, ancient cyclopean ruins, and impenetrable forests—hosts whose means of sustenance is hard to comprehend and whose day-to-day life down the centuries hardly picturable. In the Conan stories there are usually hewers-of-wood, drawers-of-water, merchants, sailors, farmers, scholars, priests, along with the fighters and magicians—even if the wolves do seem at times to outnumber the sheep.

The girl-whipping-girl references in "The Moon of Skulls"—which became girl-whipping-girl scenes in several of the Conan stories—reminds me that Howard must have discovered what a potent sexual stimulus this particular image is, along with the more-or-less veiled lesbianism that is frequently linked with it. *Weird Tales* probably attracted a few readers in this harmless way, especially when the cover showed a tasty, rather tasteful girl-whipping-girl tableau by Mrs. Brundage or another. Such references and scenes were really daring then, in contrast to today's "anything goes" paperbacks and magazines. Well, *almost* anything...except for perverted—which includes married—sex in *Playboy* and its several imitators; stories and pictures of girls with small breasts (one of my theories is that the favoritism shown mammothly mammalian milk-cow maidens in photo and illo is an elaborate gesture of contempt on the part of male homosexual editors for women in general and the simple-minded men who go for them); stories that attempt to present and fully understand human beings as they are today (especially if the stories involve problems arising from the death-grapple of technology and individuality or if they involve a deep analysis of individuals—especially in the entertainment field—who specialize in catering to an manipulating the masses); and of course swordplay-and-sorcery stories!

The means by which whipping scenes are purveyed to the reading and viewing public change constantly, in accord with available materials and the vagaries of censorship. Currently there is a flurry of whipping and torture scenes in the texts but especially on the covers of (Demons defend us!) male adventure magazines; judging from these the prime current sexual stimulus is the stalwart Nazi maiden in befrogged military tunic open to the navel and wielding a blacksnake whip or preparing to inflict or supervise some other torment—her antics are apparently even more popular than those of the apelike, green-jacketed Japanese and his fair victims. (Mrs. Brundage is high art compared to these garish depictions!) But the flagellation involved is chiefly confined to mixed whipping scenes. Apparently the editors doubt or have never discovered what Howard seems to have known from the start: that mixed whipping is a less potent stimulus than girl-whipping-girl. There seem to be reasons for this that go quite deep (for instance, rituals in which women whipped women were part of the women's mystery cult in ancient Rome) but I am not prepared to analyse them in scholarly fashion or any other—beyond the thought that the girl-whipping-girl may appeal to the male voyeur because the scene involves no male actor of whom he might be jealous (to him it is pure sex—I mean completely useless, like pure mathematics—art for art's sake).

Once again, I am not criticizing Howard for harping on this matter. Spicy scenes fit as naturally into the swordplay-and-sorcery story as they do into the related, larger category of the picaresque—they they are by no means a necessary part of it: several of the best Conan stories have no sex scenes at all—notably my own favorite, "Beyond the Black River."

Although it was one of his first long stories, "Red Shadows" is a wonderful compendium of Howard. Kane and Le Loup, developed withan almost equal fullness, present twin good and evil sides of one man's adventurous nature; there is a magnificent hymn to the jungle running through the prose; the African witchcraft is superb; and even the Giant Ape (which appears so often as a stock menace in Howard's subsequent tales) is handled with sympathy as well as power.

I imagine that Jack London was one of the chief influences shaping Howard's writing. There is the same preoccupation with feats of physical prowess, with the strong man of fixed purpose whom nothing daunts, with a savagely Darwinian view of life (battle for survival, Nature bloody in tooth and claw, civilization a false fleeting dream in the reality of barbarism). And there is much of the same boyishness. London's *The Star Rover* is not quite swordplay-and-sorcery—sorcery is lacking. But like Jensen's *The Long Journey* it is the closest thing to it.

WHAT HE WROTE AND HOW THEY SAID IT

by Robert Weinberg

When I first started reading Robert E. Howard approximately fifty years ago, I was immediately struck by the fact that this was writing unlike anything I had ever encountered before. I realized that Howard had a way of describing a scene, a battle, an event, that made it come alive that no other writer could match. More than that, he had a method of telling a story that seized the reader from the first line or two of print and held on tight until the story was done.

As I grew older and wiser and learned the lingo of the field, I discovered that Howard was what other writers called "a natural born storyteller." Or, as others put it, "a teller of tales," or "a pulp writer of astonishing talent." Lots of interesting words, but none of them made any sense to me. Exactly what was meant by "a teller of tales?" Howard was a writer, no question about that. He told tales, as did every writer. He was natural-born? As opposed to what, unnatural-born? I was confused and wanted to know more.

Only gradually, as I started writing myself, did I realize what those phrases meant. Howard was a writer whose work flowed. He wrote stories that read as if they could be told around a campfire by rugged men after a long day spent on the range. His tales of Conan and Kull and Kane were filled with passion, with danger, with love, and most of all, with death. Most men wrote stories that were songs; Howard wrote stories that were operas.

Howard was one of the three great writers for *Weird Tales*; a trio that consisted of H. P. Lovecraft, Clark Ashton Smith, and Robert E. Howard. Of those three, try reading a Lovecraft story aloud. Read it to a crowd, or read it to yourself. See how long it takes before you start stumbling over the dry prose, the long, dull, blurred descriptions? Or try reading Smith to some friends, and watch as they scramble for dictionaries or ask if such words even belong to the English language.

Afterwards, and only afterwards, read Howard. Read "The Shadow Kingdom," or "The Phoenix on the Sword," or "Red Shadows." No yawns, no sidelong glances wondering how long it will be before you finish. Howard is different. He reads right. His words ring true. His stories are equally outlandish as anything penned by Lovecraft or Smith, but he told them with a dedication, a drive, a fierceness that makes the words jump off the printed page. Howard wrote melodrama, as did his fellow *Weird Tales* contributors. That's what readers wanted. Noble heroes, beautiful maidens, hideous monsters, all part of the game. But while Lovecraft and Smith and Leiber and Whitehead and Moore and Kuttner and so many others read wonderfully well in print, only Howard reads truly well aloud.

Now, that's not Howard's only secret, not the only thing that made him a natural-born storyteller. There's another talent, one that it took me years and years of reading and rereading his work to fully comprehend. He was master of a skill so rare that it's almost non-existent in popular, genre fiction. A skill that others would kill to possess but that came instinctively to a natural-born storyteller.

Quick, a pop quiz. Recite a line of dialogue from any swords-and-sorcery story written by L. Sprague de Camp, John Jakes, Robert Jordan, Fritz Leiber, or any other scribbler of heroic fantasy. What's your favorite remark made by Elak of Atlantis, Brak the Barbarian, Fahfrd and Gray Mouser, etc. etc. etc.? Can you remember one? Or two? Or, miracle of miracles, three? Anything? Anything at all?

Now, do the same for Robert E. Howard. How about when Solomon Kane finds a dying girl and says, "Men shall die for this." Or when Kull is backed into the corner of his bedroom and takes a line from Pizarro, "Who dies first?" Or, a favorite of most, the words said by the forester at the end of "Beyond the Black River":

> "Barbarism is the natural state of mankind," the borderer said, still staring somberly at the Cimmerian. "Civilization is unnatural. It is a whim of circumstance. And barbarism must always ultimately triumph."

Howard had an ear for dialogue that has never been matched by another writer of swords-and-sorcery (by this, I am purposefully excluding high fantasy, such as *The Lord of the Rings*, as I am not going to be dragged into a meaningless fight about the relative worth of Howard and Tolkien). Overdone, over-dramatic, over-the-top, call it what you will. But, Howard wrote words that were unforgettable. He wrote words that might have been out of place or out of context, and surely out of time, but they were never boring. His characters reacted to great peril with unbelievable courage and unbelievable but incredibly striking dialogue.

Need convincing? Read the final pages of "By This Axe I Rule!" the King Kull story that Howard reworked into the first Conan story, "The Phoenix on the Sword." Specifically, read out loud, the moment when Kull, dragged down by the rules and regulations of his ancient kingdom, finally snaps and makes it clear who runs his kingdom:

> "Here stand the two who have saved my life. Henceforward they are free to marry, to do as they like."
>
> "But the law!" screamed Tu.
>
> "I am the law!" roared Kull, swinging up his axe; it flashed downward and the stone tablet flew into a hundred pieces. The people clenched their hands in horror, waiting dumbly for the sky to fall.
>
> Kull reeled back, eyes blazing. The room whirled before his dizzy gaze.
>
> "I am king, state, and law!" he roared and seizing the wand-like sceptre which lay near, he broke it in two and flung it from him. "This shall be my sceptre!" The red axe was brandished aloft...
>
> "By this axe I rule! This is my sceptre! I have struggled and sweated to be the puppet king you wished me to be—to rule your way. Now I use mine own way. If you will not fight, you shall obey. Laws that are just shall stand, laws that have outlived their times I shall shatter as I shattered that one. *I am king!*"

Find an actor who can recite those lines convincingly, while bleeding from a dozen wounds, looking only half-alive, but still holding the greatest war axe in the kingdom aloft, and you will have found a star truly worthy of playing Conan.

The fights are great, the monsters are deadly, the villains are evil, but what matters most is that Conan says the right words—not the proper words, not the city slang of that period, not the garbled language of ancient tongues, but the melodramatic lines that give life to operas and great plays and great movies.

Think a fight is too emotional a place to judge Conan's speeches? Then listen when he speaks of his gods on a trip with Belit up a demon haunted river. Belit asks:

> "Conan, do you fear the gods?"
> "I would tread on their shadow."
> "...What do you believe?"
> He shrugged his shoulders. "I know not, nor do I care. Let me live deep while I live, let me know the rich juices of red meat and stinging wine on my palate, the hot embrace of white arms, the mad exultation of battle when the blue blades flame and crimson, and I am content. Let teachers and priests and philosophers brood over questions of reality and illusion. I know this; if life is illusion, then I am no less an illusion, and being thus, the illusion is real to me. I live, I burn with life, I love, I slay, and am content."

The perfect philosophy for a barbarian who is presented as a true man of the wild, a natural man, a noble man. Still, it's easy to have barbarians talking about the meaning of life. Was Howard able to write dialogue for his monsters, for his menaces with the same vigor and imagination? Could he give them words that made their monstrous deeds sing? Any Howard fan knows that oftentimes the villains in the story had the very best dialogue. Or at least the most dramatic. Take for example, the encounter between Conan and one of the children of Jhebbal Sag:

> "Why have the gods of darkness doomed me to death?" growled Conan.
> "You dared make the sign which only a priest of Jhebbal Sag dare make. Thunder rumbled through the black Mountain of the Dead and the altar-hut of Guliah was thrown down by a wind from the Gulf of Ghosts. The loon which is messenger to the Four Brothers of the Night flew swiftly and whispered your name in my ear. Your race is run. You are a dead man already. Your head will be eaten by the black-winged sharp-beaked Children of Jhil."

The monster talks a good talk, but when it comes to fighting a good fight, Conan manages to defeat it. Anything material enough to talk is material enough to be killed, and in the Conan stories, there are no immortals.

I've offered just a few examples of Howard's outstanding use of melodramatic dialogue to move and improve his swords-and-sorcery fiction. I don't claim that it's only his dialogue that makes the stories great, but I do think that anyone reading Howard's work needs to appreciate the importance of what is said by the characters in those stories, heroes and villains both. We remember the adventures of Conan and Kull and Kane as featuring great battles and triumphs over the forces of darkness and decay. Yet, when we analyze exactly why these warriors appeal to us on such a basic, primitive level, we remember their words, their dialogue—"Who dies first?" and "By this axe I rule!" Those lines are the essence of Robert E. Howard's fiction and give his work the vitality and passion most other tales of swords-and-sorcery lack.

BARBARISM VS. CIVILIZATION

Robert E. Howard and H. P. Lovecraft in Their Correspondence

by S. T. Joshi

Robert E. Howard and H. P. Lovecraft, two of the towering figures of weird literature of their time, engaged in a six-year correspondence that currently constitutes more than 400,000 words—a treasure-trove of immense value to students and scholars of both writers. We have seen large fragments of it in the last two volumes of Loveraft's *Selected Letters* and in the two volumes of Howard's *Selected Letters*; but only recently, in *A Means to Freedom: The Letters of H. P. Lovecraft and Robert E. Howard* (2009), has the joint publication of their correspondence finally appeared after years of delay. We are now at last able to gauge the intense intellectual arguments in which the two engaged, ranging from ancient history to contemporary politics.

The very survival of the extant correspondence could be considered almost an accident. Lovecraft scupulously preserved all of Howard's letters (the great majority of them typewritten), sending them down to Howard Payne University in Brownwood, Texas, following Howard's death. The fate of the Lovecraft side is less happy. Whether Howard himself preserved Lovecraft's letters entirely intact is not certain; in any event, after the death of both Howard and Lovecraft, Howard's father, Dr. I. M. Howard, allowed August Derleth to have the letters transcribed for ultimate publication in Lovecraft's *Selected Letters*. Derleth put the letters into the hands of his secretary, Alice Conger, having indicated which portions of the letters were to be transcribed. While Derleth did have substantial portions transcribed, he decided (as he did with almost every other body of letters that came into his hands for this purpose) that some of the more ephemeral sections could be omitted. This would not be a problem if the original letters had not, through an apparent accident, been destroyed in the early 1940s. As a result, all we are left with, for Lovecraft's side of the correspondence, are the so-called Arkham House Transcripts—an amount totalling more than 150,000 words, but nonetheless not absolutely complete. Some entire letters appear to be missing—whether through Howard's own oversight, or through their loss before they reached Derleth, or through Derleth's decision not to transcribe them, cannot now be ascertained.

The rather peculiar initiation of the correspondence is well known. Lovecraft's "The Rats in the Walls" (first published in *Weird Tales,* March 1924) had been reprinted in *Weird Tales* in June 1930. When Howard read the story, he was struck by what he believed to be Lovecraft's advocacy of a minority view regarding the invasion of Britain by successive waves of Gaelic and Cymric peoples from mainland Europe, and wrote a letter to Farnsworth Wright, editor of *Weird Tales,* to this effect (see *REH* 1.48–49). Wright forwarded the letter to Lovecraft, who admitted sheepishly to Howard that he knew very little about the Gaelic or Cymric peoples and had merely borrowed some Gaelic phrases from Fiona Macleod's "The Sin Eater" (1895) for his story. In this way, in the summer of 1930, an intense and voluminous correspondence, lasting till Howard's death, began—a correspondence of which a slight majority was written by Howard (although that may be in part a result, as just indicated, of the loss of some of Lovecraft's letters after Howard's death). The correspondence is unusual in being very largely philosophical, as each writer emphasises—perhaps to excessive and repetitive length—his understanding of the nature of the universe and, more particularly, his preferences in regard to social and political matters. In the broadest terms, the fundamental divergence of views between the two writers can be encapsulated by Howard's preference for the barbarian life and Lovecraft's preference for civilisation; but within this simple formulation lie masses of complexity and fine shades of meaning and emphasis that in some senses render these views not quite as antipodal as they may appear.

For much of the first year of their correspondence, Howard and Lovecraft were studiously respectful of each other: each expressed unbounded admiration for the other's writings, Howard declaring flamboyantly that "no writer, past or modern, has equalled you in the realm of bizarre fiction" ([c. 1 July 1930]; *M* 17), while Lovecraft praised the "suggestion of unholy antiquity" (20 July 1930; *M* 24) found in "The Moon of Skulls" (*Weird Tales,* June and July 1930). Howard also acknowledged his inferiority in book learning:

in their early discussion of prehistoric Britain, Howard admitted that "I am not scholar enough to present any logical argument" ([9 August 1930]; *M* 32), but this did not prevent him from quoting at substantial length a number of published books on the subject. Howard let himself in for another disillusionment when he innocently asked Lovecraft about the sources in folklore or myth of Cthulhu, Yog-Sothoth, and the like, especially in light of a letter to *Weird Tales* by N. J. O'Neail (published in the March 1930 issue) linking Cthulhu to Howard's Kathulos (in "Skull-Face" [*Weird Tales*, October, November, and December 1929]). Lovecraft wryly replied (14 August 1930) that the whole mythology was his own invention. Howard's reaction to this can be gauged by his letter to Tevis Clyde Smith ([c. September 1930]): "I got a letter from Lovecraft wherein he tells me, much to my chagrin, that Cthulhu, R'lyeh, Yuggoth, Yog Sothoth, and so on are figments of his own imagination" (*REH* 1.57).

To be frank, both writers were united in their racism: Lovecraft, in relating the history of Rhode Island and of New England, found occasion to note that the "foreign overrunning of America...[is] the most tragic event in the continent's history" (4 October 1930; *M* 76), while Howard, although engagingly relating the oral ghost stories he heard from the local Negroes ([c. January 1931]), could not help lamenting, "I'm afraid that in a few generations Texas will be overrun with mongrels" (*M* 120). He goes on:

> On the Border there is a large Latin element, and on the coasts swarms of foreigners. The inevitable Jew infests the state in great numbers. You can hardly find a town of three thousand or more inhabitants that does not contain at least one Jew in business. And the Jew almost invariably has the country trade. It is a stock saying among rural Texans that if the Jew cannot sell his stuff at his price, he will sell it at yours. What they cannot seem to realize is that at whatever price he sells his shoddy junk, he is making a bigger profit than the legitimate merchant can make. No Aryan ever outwitted a Jew in business.... Houston, the largest city, has a vast alien population—Jews, Slavs, and Italians, the last drifting up from New Orleans. Dallas fairly swarms with Jews, in ever increasing numbers. (*M* 120)

This allowed Lovecraft to wax eloquent on his customary theme of the Semitisation of New York City:

> Yes—New York is pretty well lost to the Aryan race, and the tragic and dramatic thing is the *speed* with which the change occurred. People hardly past middle age can still recall the pleasant, free and easy New York which really formed an American metropolis, and in which there was nothing more foreign than the wholesome, cheerful immigrants from Ireland and Germany. As late as 1900 this old New York was still the visible state of things on Manhattan Island—but then the packed East Side, which had been silently filling up with Russian and Polish Jews since 1885 or 1890, began to disgorge its newly-prosperous foreign-born and first active generation. In 1905 certain troubles in Russia sent over countless hordes of cringing Jews; and by 1910 people began to notice the overwhelmingly Semitic tinge of the crowds on all the New York streets. (30 January 1931; *M* 133)

How exactly the correspondence veered to the matter of civilisation vs. barbarism is not entirely clear, but it may have something to do with Howard's invention of the character of Conan, as he tells in a letter to Lovecraft of c. April 1932: "I've been working on a new character, providing him with a new epoch—the Hyborian Age, which men have forgotten, but which remains in classical names, and distorted myths. [Farnsworth] Wright rejected most of the series, but I did sell him one—'The Phoenix on the Sword' which deals with the adventures of King Conan the Cimmerian, in the kingdom of Aquilonia" (*M* 279). This thread was not picked up immediately in the correspondence, but it eventually led Howard (who had already mentioned to Lovecraft [c. December 1930] his hatred of ancient Rome, especially the Romans in Britain) to confess that his interest in the ancient Greeks and Romans was quite limited:

> I can not understand their viewpoints. The Achaeans of the Heroic Age interest me, and to a lesser extent, the Romans of the early republic, when they were a struggling tribal-state, if they could be called that. But soon that interest dwindles. I attribute this, not to any real lack of interest those times contain, but to a

defect in my own make-up. I am unable to rouse much interest in any highly civilized race, country or epoch, including this one. ([9 August 1932]; *M* 338)

This was a passage that—in spite of Howard's admission that his lack of interest was a result of "a defect in my own make-up"—caused Lovecraft to see red. After Howard's death, he would admit that "When I run up against a person with a strong anti-Roman bias—like the late Robert E. Howard, who championed the northern barbarians—I feel an almost personal affront" (*SL* 5.352). And so Lovecraft launched the first salvo of his defense of civilisation, in the course of a general defense of classical antiquity:

> To me Greece and Rome are prime realities because they had the same general problems and attitudes which the settled nations of modernity have. They had measurably conquered the salient natural phenomena around them, and had won sufficient material security to expand other parts of their mental and emotional endowment than those directly connected with self-defense and ego-assertion. Important brain areas—such as those connected with pure intellectual curiosity and with the finer nuances of rhythm and coördination—which had been necessarily underdeveloped in the peril-beset barbarian, began to expand and enrich life among the people who had reached a stage of relatively stable adjustment to nature and to the problem of group-defense. Where the barbarian had only a few simple motives and pleasures, and used only a small fraction of his heritage as a highly evolved primate, the civilised man had the infinitely vaster variety of stimuli and rewards which accrued from a more all-around development of his capacities. What he lost in the process was more than balanced by what he gained—so that not until his later decadence did he need to mourn any of the simple ruggednesses he had left behind. (16 August 1932; *M* 359)

All the tens of thousands of words of Lovecraft's subsequent debates with Howard on this issue amount to little more than elaborations and refinements of this basic utterance.

Lovecraft had also, perhaps unwittingly, made a passing remark that caused Howard to see red: "The ideology of the frontier could not work in a thickly settled community where everything depends upon the preservation of order" (*M* 369). This remark had been made in the course of a discussion of police methods, and in a broader debate over the precise balance of personal liberty and government control—an issue to which I shall return later. Howard's response makes it abundantly clear that he considered his defense of barbarism part and parcel of his defense of the frontier, specifically the frontier of his own native Texas, from which he could legitimately consider himself scarcely a generation removed. But the precise nature of his initial defense (made in a letter that Lovecraft received around 22 September 1932) is of interest. Howard acknowledges that "if I should be suddenly confronted with the prospect of being transported back through the centuries into a former age, with the option of living where I wished, I would naturally select the most civilized country possible. That would be necessary, for I have always led a peaceful, sheltered life, and would be unable to cope with conditions of barbarism" (*M* 377). (Lovecraft wryly remarked to another correspondent: "When [Howard] says his life is 'tame & uneventful', he is thinking only of Western standards. Actually, he sees a vast amount of violence" [*SL* 5.108].) But Howard went on to say, "if I were to be reborn in some earlier age and grow up nothing no other life or environment than that, I would choose to be born in a hut among the hills of western Ireland, the forests or Germany or the steppes of Southern Russia; to grow up hard and lean and wolfish, worshipping barbarian gods and living the hard barren life of a barbarian—which is, to the barbarian who has never tasted anything else—neither hard nor barren" (*M* 377).

There would not seem, up to now, to be much room for debate, for Howard clearly appears to be expressing a mere *preference* rather than asserting some kind of quasi-objective superiority of barbarism over civilisation. It was Lovecraft, in his reply of 3 October 1932, who continued to harp on the issue. While admitting that "Both barbarism and civilisation have their advantages, and it is probable that some individuals naturally prefer one type to the other," he goes on to say: "I still think that the odds *may* be in favour of civilisation for those who utilise its advantages to the full" (*M* 401). Later in the same letter Lovecraft accuses Howard of vaunting physical combat to such a degree that he cannot see the virtues of civilised life: "I certainly regard the intellect and aesthetic sense as the highest development of human personality, and believe that the goal of civilisation must necessarily be a state in which they can have the maximum opportunity for unhampered operation. At the same time I am not blind to the need of preserving a certain amount of the old physical stamina as a supplement to the newer qualities" (*M* 421).

Howard's reply ([c. 2 November 1932]) is curious. He begins with an elaborate apology:

> I am afraid my last letter may have appeared rather churlish in spots, though rudeness was not my intention. The fact is, I wrote while in the grip of one of the black moods which occasionally—though fortunately rarely—descend upon me. With one of these moods riding me, I can see neither good nor hope in anything, and my main sensation is a blind, brooding rage directed at anything that may cross my path—a perfectly impersonal feeling, of course. At such times I am neither a fit companion nor a gentlemanly correspondent. (*M* 432)

Now there was nothing in Howard's previous letter that could be interpreted as particularly "churlish"—certainly it was less so than several of the letters Howard would write in the next several years. Possibly Howard was frustrated by Lovecraft's apparent inability to understand the points he was trying to make ("When I get out of my depth—which is easy—the Devil himself couldn't get what I'm trying to say" [*M* 433]), specifically on the all-important point that Howard was merely expressing a *preference* in regard to barbarism, physical activity over mental activity ("I would rather watch a football game than to see a scientist work out a really important problem in economics or mathematics" [*M* 433]). In any case, Howard is emphatic that "when I voice a preference for anything I am not depreciating its opposite" (*M* 434). And later in the same letter:

> I didn't say that barbarism was superior to civilization. For the world as a whole, civilization even in decaying form, is undoubtedly better for people as a whole. I have no idyllic view of barbarism—as near as I can learn it's a grim, bloody, ferocious and loveless condition. I have no patience with the depiction of the barbarian of any race as a stately, god-like child of Nature, endowed with strange wisdom and speaking in measured and sonorous phrases. Bah! my

> conception of a barbarian is very different. He had neither stability nor undue dignity. He was ferocious, vengeful, brutal and frequently squalid. He was haunted by dim and shadowy fears; he committed horrible crimes for strange monstrous reasons. As a race he hardly ever exhibited the steadfast courage often shown by civilized men. He was childish and terrible in his wrath, bloody and treacherous....He had no mental freedom, as civilized man understands it, and very little personal freedom, being bound to his clan, his tribe, his chief. (*M* 439)

Nevertheless, Howard concludes: "But I do say that if I had the choice of another existence, to be born into it and raised in it, knowing no other, I'd choose such an existence as I've just sought to depict. There's no question of the relative merits of barbarism and civilization here involved. It's just my own personal opinion and choice" (*M* 440).

In his reply (7 November 1932) Lovecraft professes to understand Howard's attitude ("I can see your point of view completely, and do not believe that any real controversy is involved" [*M* 459]), but then proceeds to argue as if Howard had really said something altogether different. (As early as August 1930, Howard had remarked to Tevis Clyde Smith on Lovecraft's method of debate: "He starts out by saying that most of my arguments seem logical enough and that he is about on the point of accepting my views—and then follows with about three or four closely written pages with which he rips practically all my theories to shreds" [*REH* 1.53].) Lovecraft himself puts forward his own views as merely a set of preferences ("To me, the few possible advantages of barbarism seem infinitely overshadowed by the overwhelming mass of hopeless lacks and disadvantages—so that I feel sure I would never have found enough to live for in primitive times, except perhaps as a history-chanting bard or mystery-making shaman" [*M* 478]), and there he seems to leave the matter. Howard's reply ([December 1932]) picks up on the shaman comment:

> As for being a shaman or minstrel among barbarians—those are the very last things I should wish to be, were my lot cast among the uncivilized. It is evident that a shaman, however fantastic and barbarous his thoughts and methods, represents the nearest approach to civilized man, in his tribe and age.

> Therefore, he is able to glimpse, in a dim way, some of the vistas that lie above (I say "above" for the sake of argument; I am by no means sure that "progress" is necessarily a step upward.) and to feel the lack of intellectual attainment—oh, very, very dimly, without doubt. (*M* 507)

That parenthetical comment may or may not conflict with Howard's previous attestation that he was not disparaging civilisation when vaunting his own preference to barbarism, but Howard's continued emphasis on the physical over the mental ("We live, after all, in a physical world. Few of us are fortunate enough to be able to move in a mainly mental sphere. This is especially true of this part of the country" [*M* 490]) clearly set Lovecraft off, and in his reply (21 January 1933) he once again attempted to establish that there might indeed be a pseudo-objective standard or criterion whereby civilisation could be considered "above" barbarism in an absolute sense:

> If anything is close to an axiom, it is that *superiority* in the organic field means *degree of evolutionary removal from* the unicellular stage....the one real criterion of cosmic value is *degree of evolution*—advance from the gorilla, the Piltdown skull, the Neanderthaloid, the Australian blackfellow, or the nigger. *This advance of evolutionary degree, marking absolute superiority, is not in any way measured by physical strength, but is directly measured by the development of the intellect, the imagination, and the more complex and delicate emotions.* To me, at least, that argument seems unanswerable; and I cannot see how you can fail to concur in its essence. It does not mean that physical strength is contemptible or other than desirable, but is simply a reminder *to put first things first.* (*M* 522)

Lovecraft is also keen to establish that, in regard to the relative happiness of barbarians over civilised people, the palm must be awarded to the latter:

> The happiness of primitively organised or undeveloped forms of life is to some extent—or in certain directions—more like the painlessness of oblivion,

non-existence, or inorganic existence than like the active, varied, and poignant pleasure of a fully utilised consciousness, for even its most violent physical and crudely emotional forms are strongly localised in an extremely small part of the potential experience-field of the human species. The barbarian is really only a quarter or a sixteenth alive, since the most human and finely organised parts of his fabric are left inactive or dormant. For him the complex rhythms of energy-transformation which give consciousness its most intense vitality and pleasure-reactions do not exist. (*M* 527)

Lovecraft even thinks he can quantify the relative happiness—or what he calls "the amount of pleasurable energy-conversion"—of various entities: "In the stick it will be 0; in the starfish it will be (let us say) 5; in the dog, 100; in the savage, 1000; and in the civilised man, 100,000" (*M* 527). It is not clear on what basis Lovecraft has devised these figures, but it is evident that he is seeking an objective means of validating his preference for civilisation over barbarism. He concludes by saying: "Only the sheerest academic quibbling can dispute the absolute and intrinsic improvement in the transition to civilisation" (*M* 529).

Howard's reply ([6 March 1933]) begins by asserting that the physical-mental debate is "unnecessary," because "My position on the matter is much the same as yours, modified on my part only by a greater interest in physical things than you possess" (*M* 535). Well, perhaps not exactly. He misinterprets Lovecraft's position as follows: "Simmered down, the real difference between our opinions is: you are interested wholly in the fruits of the mind, and I divide my interest between the fruits of the mind, and the exertions of the body" (*M* 537). (Lovecraft had in fact stated that "no rational anti-physicalist objects to the continued athletic training of those whose actual occupation demands physical strength" [*M* 520].) While Lovecraft had acknowledged that anti-physicalists did on occasion exhibit a certain contempt for physical strength because "under the existing social-economic order, only inferior individuals need to use physical strength in the struggle for survival" (*M* 520), Howard replies that he is not about to endure the contempt of these anti-physicalists, because "I can not afford to neglect my physical side" (*M* 538). Howard does not in fact address Lovecraft's regarding an entity's "degree of evolutionary removal from the unicellular stage," perhaps because he did not understand it or see its relevance to the discussion; but he then unloads a bombshell that Lovecraft would later seize upon:

> Leaving my own feelings and experiences aside, I see no reason why a fine athlete shouldn't feel a real pride in his athletic ability, when it brings him wealth, fame, and happiness that would not have been his had he depended on his mind. If Jack Dempsey's muscles pulled him up out of the gutter and the hobo-jungle into the ranks of the millionaires, while many a man infinitely his mental superior is still drudging away at a one-horse job, why shouldn't Jack be proud of his tigerish thews? I'd rather be an athlete with my pockets full of gold, than a university professor or a scientist with patches in the seat of my breeches. (*M* 538)

How this constitutes a valid response to Lovecraft's argument is difficult to see. Even though Howard, later in the letter, declares that "What I'm trying to show is that the physical side of man—*admittedly inferior to the mental side*—is nevertheless a living vital factor in the development of society" (*M* 541), Lovecraft was quite right in suspecting that Howard was really expressing a scorn for brain-work, especially since his example of Jack Dempsey emphasised the artificial criterion of money as the arbiter of value, something Lovecraft would vigorously reject.

In regard to the specific civilisation-vs.-barbarism debate, Howard now declares that "if I could choose my age and place, there is no country and no time I would choose except the American frontier, between 1795 and 1895" (*M* 546)—another indication of how intimately the notion of the frontier was fused with Howard's conception of barbarism, even though he would later admit that the people who colonized the frontier could in no precise sense be considered barbarians. He goes on to remark:

> Because I have read a few more books than my grandfathers read, and can scribble things on paper they couldn't, I am not such a conceited jackass as to fancy that my life is fuller and richer than theirs, who helped to fight a war, open a frontier and build up a new nation. Of all snobberies, the assumption that intellectual endeavors, attainments and accomplish-

ments are the only worth-while and important things in life, is the least justifiable. (*M* 546)

But Lovecraft had never said that intellectual accomplishments were the "only" worthwhile things in life; only that they constituted a further degree of removal from the unicellular stage.

Lovecraft's reply (25-28 March 1933) begins by stating: "Your tendency to judge things merely in relation to the fulfillment of certain immediate material needs seemed to me (whether erroneously or not) to be blinding you emotionally (though perhaps not intellectually) to the actual relative values concerned in the problem at issue" (*M* 554). This remark is clearly directed at Howard's comment on Jack Dempsey, as is a later and more exhaustive passage:

> You appeared to deny the supreme emotional value of intellectual and aesthetic experience for their own sakes—to regard as mythical or feigned the fact that for people of the highest type *the intrinsic acts of intellectual expansion or artistic creation are primary and satisfying ends in themselves,* forming the main and indispensable objects of life, and conducted without ulterior motives or hope of material gain....Perhaps you did not specifically and consciously form this denial and repudiation, but you tended to show a certain ironic contempt in alluding to highly evolved experience—as in your recent letter, when you belittle rather bitterly the 'artists who smudge their canvas and scientists who pry into the secrets of the cosmos'; ignore the titanically increased opportunities for a full mental-aesthetic life which civilisation has brought; prefer gold-betting pugilists to idea-enjoying college professors; and (in asserting that you write for money alone) deny by implication the superlatively keen joy of literary creation—or any aesthetic craftsmanship for its own sake...a joy which for many forms the sole reason for remaining alive. (*M* 558-59)

That remark about "artists who smudge their canvas" is worth examining: it actually occurred in Howard's letter in a very different context—that of the relative level of freedom possible in contemporary civilised society. Howard, asserting rather histrionically that the object of government today "is to emasculate all men, and make good little rabbits and guinea pigs out of them that will fit into the nooks designed for them," went on to say:

> Oh, no doubt we will have freedom of thought; a man sitting in a dungeon with his legs in iron stocks can think as he wishes. And no doubt our artists will be allowed to smudge their canvas and scribble their sheets just about as they desire. And our scientists will be allowed to pry into the secrets of the cosmos, no doubt. But what about the people who are neither artists, intellectuals, or scientists? They do exist, in large numbers. (*M* 543)

Howard would later remark that "I was not aware that the expression 'smudge their canvas' reflected any particular bitterness" ([c. May/June 1933]; *M* 591), and later in the same letter: "it seems to me that my unfortunate use of the word 'smudge' is still rankling a little bit" (*M* 595). Whether this is the case or not, Lovecraft now resumed the civilisation-vs.-barbarism debate by concluding that "My sole reason for debate is what seems to be an underlying assumption on your part that the barbaric state is *intrinsically superior*—in a serious sense—to civilisation" (*M* 564); but no such remark can be found in Howard's letters, and he is always careful to emphasize that he is merely expressing a preference. Whether there is an "underlying assumption" of intrinsic superiority is difficult to establish, since we have no way of ascertaining it—and Lovecraft had no way, either, aside from inferences from Howard's correspondence.

Howard, in his letter of c. May/June 1933, defended himself on various fronts. First, he denied that he was using financial success as a criterion of value: "I was merely trying to point out that a successful man need not be denied a real pride in his occupation just because it didn't happen to be of an intellectual nature" (*M* 590). Howard goes on to say: "You criticize me for saying that I 'prefer a rich athlete to a poor professor'; as a matter of fact, I didn't say that, though perhaps I might have expressed myself more clearly. What I said was that *I would rather be the rich athlete*. This implies no belittling of the professor" (*M* 590). I fear that this strikes me as both false (Howard is in fact expressing a preference for being a rich athlete than a poor professor) and disingenuous, since the remark about the professor's "patches in the seat of [his] breeches" certainly suggests a certain amount of contempt. Howard also denies that he is "anti-intellectual": "I have no hostility whatever toward either an intellectual or an artist." But "I refuse to place art on a pedestal above and beyond everything else; I refuse to believe that a million generations of human beings have lived, suffered, toiled and died in order that certain men may make marks on paper or canvas. In a word, I do not believe that artistic expression is the sole and only reason for evolution" (*M* 591). Howard goes on to say: "The average artist is no more important in the scheme of things than is the average lawyer, physician, engineer, farmer or politician. A painting is of no more importance to a painter, or a story to an author, than a bridge is to the engineer, a well-pleaded case to the lawyer, or a fine crop to the farmer. It seems to me that artists as a whole are prone to exalt themselves and their work beyond all natural proportions" (*M* 593).

To this, Lovecraft responded sharply in his letter of 24 July 1933:

> As for the status of art—by which I mean not only the process of creation but the whole development of personality which includes appreciation and general tasteful living—I don't know that I called it the 'only reason for evolution'; for indeed, evolution is a matter of chance which has no reason or object. Rather did I suggest that it is simply something which is *characteristic* of those types which are most evolved. (*M* 620)

And later:

> No one has ever claimed that the artist is more important in the maintenance of some sort of civilisation than is the farmer, mechanic, engineer, or statesman....It is not that we regard art as "sacred", but that we recognise the importance of something which naturally forms the chief life-interest of the most highly evolved types. Art certainly *is* more intrinsically removed from the unevolved protoplasmic stage of organic reaction than any other human manifestation except pure reason—hence our grouping of it as one of the "highest" things in life. By "highest" we do not mean "most important to survival", but simply "most advanced in intrinsic development." (*M* 622)

Howard replied with a seemingly clever counter-argument—that the ability to appreciate both "high" and "low" aesthetic products is a sign of breadth of taste and outlook:

> It seems to me that a capacity for enjoying certain simple thing [*sic*], when combined with an ability to appreciate the "higher" things as well, is, if anything, the indication of a broader, rather than a narrower personality. If I can enjoy (for instance) both [Robert W.] Service and Baudelaire, I see no reason why I should feel inferior to the man who can enjoy only Baudelaire, any more than to the man who can enjoy only Service. You must admit the scope of enjoyment is broader, whatever is to be said about the esthetic value. (*M* 635)

It is that last remark that is the key; for there are clear limits to this kind of breadth of taste: if one enjoys both Baudelaire and, say, Nictzin Dyalhis, then this indicates not a commendable breadth but a deficiency in aesthetic sensibility, for *no* genuinely cultured person could derive aesthetic enjoyment out of the latter. Howard goes on to say, "It's really a matter of indifference to me whether or not my preferences, pursuits and desires are 'superior' according to some arbitrary standard" (*M* 635)—but the standard is not "arbitrary," but based upon widely acknowledged aesthetic principles that have been recognized as sound for centuries. Howard predictably adds the typical anti-intellectual argument, "I know what I like, and what I want, and that's enough for me" (*M* 635).

Lovecraft's response of 2 November 1933 emphasizes these points, noting that there is a difference between genuine aesthetic appreciation and appreciation based on the arousal of "agreeable *associations* either consciously or subconsciously" (*M* 662). He offers an example:

> It does not argue defective taste to be tickled by a jingle of Eddie Guest because it reminds us of something pleasing, although it does argue defective taste to accept such junk as serious emotional expression. In the latter case, serious acceptance requires a defective receiving equipment because the material is so vapid, stale, ill-formed, and unrelated to anything in life or human feeling as intelligently understood, that it could not produce any response at all from a

sensitive or well-developed receiving equipment. (*M* 662)

Howard made another blunder: in arguing that "art is no more characteristically human than some other things" (an argument Lovecraft had never made), such as "treachery, and chicanery, and sex perversions" (*M* 635), he claimed to adduce evidence from the animal world:

> ...honesty and decency are not exclusively human characteristics. Most animals have them in larger abundance than man. It is just as impossible for an amoeba to crack the stock market and beggar thousands, plot and start a war in order to acquire valuable concessions, and having exhausted himself with debauchery, turn to perverse pleasures, as it is for him to paint a picture or write a book.... We call our enemies swine, dogs, skunks, etc. I never saw a dog, hog or pole-cat commit any of the crimes and vices that human beings perpetrate day after day. (*M* 636)

Lovecraft replied that the very existence of such reprehensible traits as treachery and chicanery argued a superiority in human beings:

> Lower animals have the same natural greed and ferocity that man has; and if they get less through unscrupulous means, it is merely because they don't know enough. Man cheats more for two reasons—because he is more capable, and because some of his number erect standards higher than those of the other animals, to which the inferior specimens can't conform. If man as a whole did not strive to be better than the beasts, his narrower-visioned members wouldn't be (in some ways, if your allegation is true) worse than the beasts. (*M* 668)

Howard did not give up on the point, however, writing in his next letter ([c. January 1934]):

> I have, it is true, noticed shadows of almost human depravity in animals—treachery, greed, cowardice, perversions—but I never saw an animal whose

> whole life was devoted to these things. And I never saw any bestial trait that was not possessed in greater volume by humanity. You say I say that animals are "superior" because "in my opinion" they are more "honest." I didn't say, or mean to say, that. I merely said that animals possess all the characteristics of courage, kindliness, and honesty that we are taught are the exclusive possessions of the human race....I've spent all my life in the country and in small towns, among horses, cattle, hogs, dogs, cats and less domesticated beasts. And it is my judgment, borne upon me by experience and observation, that the average animal is a cleanly, decent, respectable and altogether worthy citizen compared to the average man, when judged by moral standards. (*M* 696)

Lovecraft responded (3 April 1934) with what he should have said previously—that the traits Howard is attributing to animals cannot be so attributed because animals in all likelihood are not self-conscious to the degree that they can recognize "honesty" or "treachery" as virtues or vices:

> What the bulk of organic creation does is simply to react to external stimuli in a fixed way—conditioned by the nature of each organism as determined by fortuitous evolution. There is no such thing as conscious choice of conduct. Each species is merely a machine which behaves in a certain way when certain buttons are pushed. Reflexes can be conditioned, but they are just as automatic for all that. Whether we like or dislike the typical reflexes of a certain species is wholly irrelevant. There is no more reason to call a lower animal (or a primitive man) "good" or "bad", "decent" or "evil" than there is to apply these terms to a volcano or wind or river or sandstorm. (*M* 736-37)

By this time, the debate was becoming somewhat more acrimonious—at least on Howard's side. In his letter of January 1934 he felt that Lovecraft was accusing Howard of "refus[ing] to accept the basic standards of human development" (*M* 693) because Howard was questioning the superiority of art or artists in human affairs. Howard countered by saying that many other human activities can indicate "superiority"; but in making this assertion Howard again put forward an implausible argument: "You have said that it is impossible for an inferior man to be a poet, a great novelist or a great painter. It is equally impossible for an inferior man to be a great physician, engineer, general, statesman, agriculturist or football coach" (*M* 694). That last example of "greatness" (coming from one who had regaled Lovecraft with long accounts of some of the exciting college football games he had watched) was one Lovecraft could not pass up unrefuted, and his letter of 3 April makes pungent note of it:

> We call [certain] goals and pursuits "important" if they embody and provide for man's "higher" qualities (taste, intellectual curiosity, sense of order, intelligent civic and economic projects, art, drama, museums, literature, public works, etc. etc.), and "trivial" if they embody and provide only for the "lower" human qualities (physical sense-gratification, play of primitive instinct and immature, undeveloped emotion, etc.—as embodied in overemphasised sports, low-grade writing, acting, or iconography aimed at childish and undeveloped personalities, etc.) which do not involve man's greatest differentiation from other organisms in the direction of complexity. It may seem strange and unacceptable to you, at present, to have a distinction drawn between the human effort which seeks to measure the universe, or crystallise a phase of beauty, or evolve a more harmonious social order, and that which seeks to apply science to the mutual slugging of two sullen giants—but that is something which must be left to time and to your instinctive *sense of proportion.* (*M* 734)

Howard, in his reply of c. July 1934, professed amazement at the resurrection of the mental-vs.-physical argument; but it was Howard himself who had brought up the example of the football coach as an example of "greatness," and in that same letter he had also made an unwise comparison of the boxer Jim Corbett and Michelangelo: "That prize fighting is not to be compared with Angelo's [*sic*] artistic triumphs goes without saying. Nevertheless, Corbett can not be called an inferior man; certainly his accomplishments can not be compared with Angelo's. Nevertheless, Corbett was as supreme in his line as Angelo was in his" (*M* 713-14). And yet, Howard now professes outrage at Lovecraft, and compounds the error by going on to assert that "it was not Corbett's physical development at all that caused my remark, but his mental equipment" (*M* 771).

This letter of Howard's is particularly bitter and curt because he had taken umbrage at one particular passage in Lovecraft's April letter. Lovecraft had asserted that Howard's admiration for both barbarism and the frontier was essentially "moralistic" because

> You praise the frontier because it emphasises certain *moral qualities*—qualities of *character* like courage, resourcefulness, honesty, fairness, and so on—*at the same time ignoring its unfavourable effect on other phases of human development*...its absence of good educational facilities, etc. That would seem to argue *that you value moral qualities more than you value a general development of the personality.* (*M* 744)

At this point Lovecraft seemed to get a bit carried away, producing a passage that was quite unfair to Howard and not a sound inference from his previous letters:

> You think a crude, narrow, ignorant man of few vistas and sensitivenesses, but of great physical strength, native keenness of judgment, acquisitive ability, courage, and honesty, represents just as perfect and worthy a development of the human raw material as does a man of balanced vision, trained sense of proportion, enlightened information, developed taste, and awakened sensitivenesses, possessing in addition many of the courageous and honourable qualities of the other type.... You would prefer that nothing be known of the world and universe beyond the savage's or barbarian's narrow ken; that no rhythmic eloquence ever fall from human lips, nor any painting, sculpture, music, and architecture ever flow from the human imagination.... You would rather see three-fourths of man's personality—the ¾ involving those instincts highest in the scale of evolution—forever drugged to sleep and uselessness by ignorance, violence, and the material struggle. (*M* 745-46)

And in conclusion Lovecraft made the breathtaking remark, "You sneer at human development—and as Dean Milman said (or rather, *quoted* from Paley) in his preface to Gibbon, 'Who can refute a sneer?'" (*M* 746).

Well, Howard was not about to take this lying down. In the first place, he misunderstood Lovecraft's "moralistic" comment by thinking that Lovecraft was accusing him of being a Puritan bluenose, when in fact Lovecraft was merely saying that Howard was overemphasising the importance of morals in human affairs. While Howard did leave himself open to accusations of adhering to false values in vaunting Jim Corbett and a football coach as "great," he curtly enumerated the fundamentals of his views on these subjects:

> 1. I do not exalt physical strength above everything else.
> 2. I do not exalt ethics beyond the point that any normal, intelligent man does.
> 3. I do not repudiate, or fail to recognize, the standards of basic development. (*M* 771)

But Howard continues to insist that all these matters are mere personal preferences, and that Lovecraft is merely trying to change Howard's preferences so that they match his own. But Lovecraft was putting forward what he believed to be objective, if relative, standards to measure human development, and Howard never once addressed these standards.

Lovecraft tried to make this point in his reply of 27-28 July 1934:

> ...I have tried to found my likes and dislikes on actual cosmic evidence and not on mere caprice. I know how hard it is to talk of external standards in dealing with human preferences, and would scarcely care to call my criteria infallible ones. On the other hand, I think the long biological, psychological, and philosophical explanations of these *proximate* or *pseudo-absolute* standards which I have made in former letters will convince you that they are not superficial, capriciously-adopted pieces of guesswork and prejudice. You may consider them *wrong,* but you can hardly consider them as *lightly or arbitrarily held....*Thus when I say that civilisation is superior to barbarism, I am doing more than uttering a personal

preference for civilised as distinguished from barbaric life. I am maintaining that civilisation utilises vast reservoirs of human capacity which barbarism leaves undeveloped; and that the effect of this utilisation is to make mankind an infinitely higher and more important being, as measured in distance from the condition of primitive slime, than he would otherwise be. (*M* 798-99)

But Lovecraft went on to add a potentially (and, in the event, actually) inflammatory utterance:

I believe that there are *certain real and specific reasons* for considering civilisation as different from barbarism in a direction intrinsically favourable to man's degree of importance, enjoyment, symmetry, and completeness in the cosmic flux; a direction to which we may logically apply the term "upward" (as based on the only scale of progressive organisation in the cosmos), and which we cannot help endorsing if we are friends rather than enemies of mankind. (*M* 799)

That last comment—even if, as Lovecraft would argue, not explicitly directed at Howard—sent Howard off the deep end. Clearly taking the remark personally, he exploded (in a letter of c. December 1934):

Throughout our debate you have attributed to me the worst possible motives for my beliefs and tastes. Every time, when I have expressed an opinion that differed from yours, or even a personal taste, you have condemned it as sentimentalistic, romantic, a result of prejudice or distorted thinking; and denounced me as an enemy of development and enlightenment! Just as in this case, when you call me an enemy to humanity, and therefore imply that I am a villian [*sic*] of the deepest dye.... (*M* 809)

Now this itself is an overreaction to Lovecraft's "enemy of mankind" remark—and, in general, to Lovecraft's vigorous method of argumentation—but nevertheless it is undeniable that Lovecraft had opened the door for it. But once again Howard continues to insist that the debate is merely a matter of differing tastes ("there was never any real use in most of these arguments, anyway" [*M* 807]), failing even to address the "pseudo-absolute" standards Lovecraft was putting forth. Howard also unjustly accused Lovecraft of vaunting his own New England region as the ideal to which the rest of the country (particularly Howard's Texas) failed to measure up—something that cannot be plausibly adduced from any of Lovecraft's remarks.

This phase of the debate now begins to peter out. Several of Lovecraft's responses of this period do not survive, so it is difficult to gauge the exact course of the discussion. In his letter of c. January-February 1935 Howard apologizes "if I have misunderstood any of your statements, or attitudes, or seemed to be doing you an injustice" (*M* 810); but since Howard continues to throw the "enemy of mankind" remark back in Lovecraft's teeth, it does not appear as if Lovecraft had withdrawn that remark just yet. Indeed, in an indication that Howard's resentment had not yet cooled, he accuses Lovecraft (in a letter of c. July 1935) of making a succession of charges against Howard as a person:

> Recalling off-hand the charges you have made against me, I remember that at various times you have accused me of being: Exalter-of-the-Physical-Above-the-Mental; Enemy of Humanity; Foe of Mankind; Apostle of Prejudice; Distorter of Fact; Repudiator of Evolutionary Standards; Over-Emphasizer of Ethics; Sympathizer of Criminals (that one broke all altitude records); Egotist; Poseur; Emotionalist; Defender of Ignorance; Sentimentalist; Romanticist. (*M* 863)

It need hardly be said that Lovecraft had not specifically directed many, or perhaps any, of these epithets at Howard; and it must also be said that in several regards Howard does lay himself open to these charges. He is outraged at the "Sympathizer of Criminals" accusation, but it was he who filled his letters with long, loving accounts of the bravery and courage of such outlaws as Billy the Kid and John Wesley Harden. Lovecraft, in any case (in his letter of 7 August 1935), denied any "bitter resentment" at Howard's interpretation of his attitudes, and went on to say:

> As for what you appear to interpret as accusing or vituperative words on my part—let me repeat that

the things I define adversely are *not persons but attitudes*. I may, for example, say that 'anyone who believes or wishes a certain thing' is an enemy of mankind or defender of ignorance—but that does not prove that any specific person really believes or wishes that thing in the light of all its implications. If I think, from his own utterances, that anyone in particular believes or wishes such a thing, I may be mistaken. I may fail to comprehend, through lack of a system of reference-associations in common, just what it is that he does believe and wish. Therefore there is nothing personal in anything I may say about a certain sort of attitude or method. (*M* 885)

Howard's reply ([5 December 1935]) noted: "As for the charge of 'enemy of humanity,' the distinction you draw between attitudes and individuals seems a bit fine to me. I see no difference between telling a man he is an enemy of humanity and telling him that his attitude constitutes an enmity to humanity" (*M* 900). Lovecraft's reply to this is not extant, but in his reply ([11 February 1936]) Howard observed dryly:

I'm glad you've decided that I'm not an "enemy of humanity" after all. You say you use the term only to designate such people who "would voluntarily destroy the kind of life prevailing in Scandinavia or Britain or pre-war Germany in favour of the kind of life prevailing in Borneo or ancient Gaul or the Djuka country." Well, that must let everybody out for I can't imagine any sane person having such an ambition as this. (*M* 915)

But to this Lovecraft responded (in a letter of 7 May 1936—the last letter he wrote to Howard):

As for the term "enemy of humanity" as I used it—I think there is always present in society a small minority to whom that term can be applied in the given sense. While not all of this minority would care to lower the prevailing life-level to the wholly savage state, it is undeniable that they would like to see it pulled down to an intolerable degree of mediocrity. This actual hostility to the best human achievements is found in many proletarian groups and peasantries, and was markedly manifest in the earlier stage of both French and Russian revolutions. (*M* 924)

The debate over personal freedom, specifically in an industrialized society, is an interesting offshoot of the whole debate regarding barbarism (or the frontier) and civilisation, as Howard—who, in today's political jargon, would be regarded as a libertarian—was lamenting what he believed to be the decreasing amount of liberty in modern society, while Lovecraft—who was moving toward his distinctive final position of "fascistic socialism," whereby economic wealth would be equitably distributed to the many but political power (specifically the right to vote) be restricted to the few—argued that the necessity for law and order in heavily populated areas necessitated some minimal restrictions of freedom from earlier eras. As in the other debates, much of this dispute was based upon mutual misunderstanding and a failure to clarify the exact terms and parameters of the discussion.

Howard raised the issue first by casually remarking: "Personal liberty, it would seem, is to be a thing of the past" (*M* 274). This occurs in his letter of [2 March 1932], in the course of a discussion of the current international scene and the possibility of tyranny in the United States: "It seems we must choose between a strong soviet government, and a strong dictatorship on the fascist style" (*M* 274). Lovecraft did not pick up on this immediately—in spite of his unfortunate devotion to the word "fascism" as a characterization of his political philosophy—and Howard himself returned to the issue in his letter of [9 August 1932], speaking of impending tyranny in America both because of the violent suppression of the "bonus army"—the impoverished World War I veterans who had come from all parts of the country to Washington, D.C., and demanded the early payment of a bonus that was not to be paid to them for a decade or more—and because of what he regarded as "the detestable police practise of grilling prisoners" (*M* 349). This theme of police brutality would become a dominant one in Howard's letters. In his reply of 16 August, Lovecraft put in some words on the other side, remarking that sometimes a certain harshness by the police is necessary to extract information out of "known members of the toughest criminal class" (*M* 368). His letter of 7 November 1932 outlines the essentials of his "fascistic socialism," which includes such features as "the government's control of industry in a manner designed to spread work and reward it adequately, and to eliminate the profit motive as much as possible in favour of the demand-supplying motive" (*M* 469), as well as "adequate public education both for industry and for the increased leisure of a mechanised era" (*M* 470). In regard to the current situation, Lovecraft is pungent: "Democracy—as distinguished from universal opportunity and good treatment—is today a fallacy and impossibility so great that any serious attempt to apply it cannot be considered as other than a mockery and a jest" (*M* 469).

Howard, in his reply ([December 1932]), actually expressed agreement with Lovecraft in regard to the limitation of the suffrage, and did not see it as conflicting with his professed yearning for freedom: "Individual liberty doesn't necessarily entail blind dabbling in governmental affairs" (*M* 502). Howard did express skepticism as to whether the tidy political scheme Lovecraft had outlined could ever be put into effect, or, even if it were put into effect, whether it would remain stable and not descend into actual tyranny. He concluded:

> I do not expect a permanent state of slavery, but I do look for a period of more or less length, in which class and individual liberty will be practically unknown—oh, it won't be called slavery or serfdom. They'll have another name for it—Communism, or Fascism, or Nationalism, or some other -ism; but under the surface it will be the same old tyranny, modified, no doubt, to fit modern conditions. (*M* 500)

It seems that Howard is not expressing some sound opinion on modern political conditions but rather an emotional reaction to the necessary restrictions of contemporary social existence. In any case, Lovecraft's reply of 21 January 1933 rejected the notion of an imminent tyranny: "I can't agree that anything resembling wholesale slavery is likely to result from the present confusion, since (as I said before) such a course would demand a greater concentration of obedient man-power than the controlling elements are ever likely to command again during the life of this civilisation" (*M* 516). Lovecraft went on to remark that "Untrammelled individual freedom of action is nothing sacred or necessarily inviolate," but added: "To my mind, the irreducible minimum of personal independence worth fighting for till the last is *freedom of thought, opinion, research and art*. These are the things which really constitute human personality in its finest sense, and without them all the boasted physical freedom of the savage means nothing. Grant them, and slavery cannot exist" (*M* 518).

Howard, in his reply of [6 March 1933], somewhat recklessly remarked, "Slavery? If three-quarters of the world isn't enslaved now I'm much mistaken," and went on to say: "I don't know as I said it was anybody's fault that there's no such thing as individual freedom any more. Unless I'm much mistaken I said it is a dream which is outworn.... I realize that such a state is impossible in a highly developed civilization; which is one thing I have against such civilizations" (*M* 542). Exactly what Howard's ideal of freedom actually constituted is by no means clear. It was, let us recall, in this letter that he made the remark that "a man sitting in a dungeon with his legs in iron stocks can think as he wishes," and he also noted somewhat hysterically that the purpose of modern government "is to emasculate all men, and make good little rabbits and guinea pigs out of them that will fit into the nooks designed for them, and stay there contentedly nibbling their fodder until they die of inanition" (*M* 543)—a remark whose precise application to American or European society is dfficult to specify.

Lovecraft's response, in his letter of 25-28 March 1933, was frank:

> Just *what is* the wild and untrammeled "freedom" that our modern radicals are so vociferously clamouring for? What is it that they *want* to do that they *can't* do? I am curious to know, for they never seem to convey a clear idea. I don't see many honest and well-disposed people 'sitting in dungeons with their legs in iron stocks', nor do I see in the varied and active life of the modern average man anything resembling emasculation or reduction to the guinea-pig or rabbit stage. Just what do our "free souls" *want* to do? Ride bicycles on the sidewalks, disregard traffic signals and collide with other people's cars, play the radio at 3 a.m., shoot and carve people for fun, or what? (*M* 562)

Howard's response (in his letter of [23 April 1933]) was perhaps not what Lovecraft was expecting:

> Well, in Cross Plains I can ride a bicycle on the sidewalk; there are no traffic signals; I can—and do—play the radio at all hours of the day and night, and I'd like to see anybody try to stop me; I have never yet shot or carved anybody for fun, but so far I

have never been arrested for emptying my pistol into the air or using trash cans for targets in moments of alcoholic exuberance, and if we step outside the corporation lines, a friend and I can pummel each other unmolested by police interference. I don't suppose I would be allowed to pitch a tent, as you suggest, in the middle of the main street, but so far I have never experienced any overpowering desire to pitch such a tent. (*M* 595-96)

It does not appear that Howard has given sufficient thought as to whether such actions—representing "liberty" for him—might in fact constitute a diminution or infringement of "liberty" to others, specifically the liberty to be left alone and not be unnecessarily bothered by others. More seriously, Howard does acknowledge that his ideal of freedom is impossible, and also that it is intimately tied to his thirst for frontier life:

What I want is impossible, as I've told you before; I want, in a word, the frontier—which is compassed in the phrase, new land, open land, free land—land rich and unbroken and virgin, swarming with game and laden with fresh forests and sweet cold streams, where a man could live by the sweat of his hands unharried by taxes, crowds, noise, unemployment, bank-failures, gang-extortions, laws, and all the other wearisome things of civilization. Failing in that, I want as much personal freedom as is possible under this system, and if I can't have at least as much as I have now, I don't want to live at all. (*M* 594-95)

Lovecraft's reply (24 July 1933) argued that "It was impossible for an industrialised nation to return to the agrarian-handicraft stage typified by the frontier and its transient conditions" (*M* 624) (something Howard had not at all suggested), and went on to say, more sensibly, "nor is it logical to assume that frontier conditions were necessarily superior, as a whole, to those of a more settled order. Advantages have vanished, but other compensating advantages have appeared in their place—so that the net result is at least highly debatable" (*M* 624).

At this point the discussion shifted to current political and economic conditions, and Howard (in his letter of c. September 1933) could not resist poking a finger in the eye of modern civilisation by pointing out the catastrophic effects of the Depression: "You can't dismiss twelve and a half million men and women without work and on the point of starvation as theories. It would be well for the capitalists, perhaps, if they could be so dismissed. As for the 'alleged horrors' of civilization—if you would inquire into the condition of some of these people, and if you had ever seen what modern machinery can do to the human frame, you'd realize that all the horrors are not 'alleged'" (*M* 640). Lovecraft had a pungent response (2 November 1933), in which he again put forth the virtues of his socialistic scheme:

> The present year, just before the beginning of the new administration's remedial programme, marks the low point of the workman's fortunes in America. The tendencies crushing him under a "free" or laissez-faire economic system were steadily growing, yet the "free" system of Hoover individualism was unchecked. Now, under the "slavery" of a governmentally regulated economy, there will be a steady but slow trend toward relief.... "Freedom" means concentrated power for the strong and servitude and starvation for the weak. *Government*—which he calls "slavery"—is *the only possible avenue of rescue he has*. (*M* 672)

It was at this point, as noted earlier, that Howard, believing Lovecraft to have accused him of "hating human development," became quite hostile and even a bit irrational, stating ([c. July 1934]): "If we were living under your ideal intellectual-ruled government, you could doubtless have me burned at the stake as a heretic. But since we haven't reached that enviable stage of civilization, it looks like you'll just have to classify me as another of the imperfections and crudities allowed to exist under a democratic form of government, and let it go at that" (*M* 771-72). There was no justification for Howard to make this kind of snide comment, and Lovecraft responded vehemently but tactfully (27-28 July 1934):

> You say you do not hate human development, and yet you sneer at my ideal of a government restricted to men who are properly trained for the job and who know what they are doing! Moreover, you say that if my ideal of government were in force, I

would—or could—have you burned at the stake because of your tastes and interests. Now that is *precisely the opposite* of anything which my kind of government would ever do, want to do, or permit to be done! The *absolute first* requisite of any mature or genuine civilisation is *complete intellectual and artistic freedom;* so that no restriction whatever would be placed upon any sort of individual thought or tastes. (*M* 792)

Lovecraft, however, did not help his cause by adding lamely, "Do not judge the sort of fascism I advocate by any form now existing" (*M* 792). What Lovecraft was really advocating was not fascism in any meaningful sense of the term, but democracy—only a democracy circumscribed by limitation of the suffrage.

Howard replied forcefully ([c. December 1934]): "I do not condemn the reforms you say would be possible under Fascism. I simply do not believe they would exist under a Fascist government. Of course you can draw glowing pictures of a Fascist Utopia. But you can not prove that Fascism is anything but a sordid, retrogressive despotism, which crushes the individual liberty and strangles the intellectual life of every country it inflicts with its slimy presence" (*M* 808). Lovecraft's next several responses are missing, so it is difficult to gauge the course of the debate. The crux of the matter, of course, is Lovecraft's putting forth an idealized scheme that sounds good on paper, and Howard noting keenly that the actual instances of oligarchical government then in existence are very far from the tidy formulations of Lovecraft's political theory.

* * * * * * *

In the end, what can we say about the overall progression of the Lovecraft-Howard correspondence? In large measure, it appears that on nearly every issue there was considerable misunderstanding on both sides, as each writer struggled to convey to the other the precise shades of meaning in the issues in question. Howard, in his letter of [December 1932], admitted that temperamental differences between the two often caused difficulties ("Your impartial viewpoint is admirable. For myself, I must admit that I am motivated more often by emotion and sentiment than by cold logic" [*M* 501]), and toward the end of their correspondence Howard made a keen analysis of their differing psychologies and upbringings:

> My life has been almost antipodal, in its associations, to yours. I've had little acquaintance with scholars, artists and literary people, whereas these types obviously have formed the bulk of your companions. Not being familiar with these types, it's easy for me to misunderstand their ideas and opinions. I'm also but little fitted to deal with abstract ideas which do not, apparently, have any connection with everyday reality as I know it. I've never had much time to devote to theories and philosophies....On the other hand it seems obvious from your own arguments that you've had little if any first-hand contact with the rough sides and the raw edges of existence; if you had, you couldn't possibly have some of the ideas you have, and so many of my views and statements wouldn't seem so inexplicable and outrageous to you. It is inevitable that we should constantly misunderstand each other. ([5 December 1935]; *M* 896)

Both writers were also aware that their differing methods of argumentation—Lovecraft's at times excessively involved rationalizations and use of highly abstract philosophical conceptions that Howard had difficulty applying to any reality within his sphere of knowledge, and Howard's at times blunt and clumsy debating style that frequently resulted in a lack of clarity as to his true ideas and feelings (this in spite of the fact that, as Rusty Burke has told me, actual rough drafts of Howard's letters to Lovecraft have been unearthed, indicating his painstaking care in holding up his end of the debate)—resulted in considerable misconstrual of even the essence of the discussion, let alone its finer points. In the last two or three years, as we have seen, Howard also exhibited a considerable hostility and resentment (precisely as many of his recent devotees do) at what he fancies to be Lovecraft's insulting treatment of him. Some Howard fans, perhaps adopting the inferiority complex Howard himself occasionally did when confronting a man of substantially greater education, have asserted somewhat truculently that Howard definitively "won" the various debates in which he engaged with Lovecraft—as if their correspondence was some kind of sporting event. But at this point there is no need to act as some kind of referee in determining who "won" or "lost" their multifaceted discussion. Both writers scored some key rhetorical points, and both suffered rhetorical defeats. But the real value of their correspondence—as they frequently acknowledged both to each other and to other associates—was the broadening of outlook that both experienced as a result of the clash of two such opposing viewpoints on central questions of life, society, freedom, civilisation, and moral values.

WORKS CITED

Howard, Robert E. *Selected Letters.* Ed. Glenn Lord *et al.* West Warwick, RI: Necronomicon Press, 1989–91. 2 vols. [Abbreviated in the text as *REH.*]

Lovecraft, H. P. *Selected Letters.* Ed. August Derleth, Donald Wandrei, and James Turner. Sauk City, WI: Arkham House, 1965–76. 5 vols. [Abbreviated in the text as *SL.*]

Lovecraft, H. P., and Robert E. Howard. *A Means to Freedom: The Letters of H. P. Lovecraft and Robert E. Howard.* Ed. S. T. Joshi, David E. Schultz, and Rusty Burke. New York: Hippocampus Press, 2009. 2 vols. (numbered consecutively). [Abbreviated in the text as *M.*]

CRASH GO THE CIVILIZATIONS

Some Notes on Robert E. Howard's Use of History and Anthropology

by Mark Hall

INTRODUCTION

"The Hyborian Age" is Robert E. Howard's essay outlining the fictional history, anthropology and geography of his Hyborian world. This is the world inhabited by Conan, Howard's most popular and well-known character. As to why Howard wrote this essay, he noted in the introduction of "The Hyborian Age":

> When I began writing the Conan stories a few years ago, I prepared this "history" of his age and the peoples of that age, in order to lend him and his sagas a greater aspect of realness. And I found that by adhering to the "facts" and spirit of that history, in writing the stories, it was easier to visualize (and therefore to present) him as a real flesh-and-blood character rather than a ready-made product. In writing about him and his adventures in the various kingdoms of his Age, I have never violated the "facts" or spirit of the "history" here set down, but have followed the lines of that history as closely as the writer of actual historical-fiction follows the lines of actual history. (381)

While Howard's quest for historical realism may seem odd to some, it must be kept in mind that he had a strong personal interest in anthropology and history. His personal library contained several books in these subject areas, by such authors as Sydney Herbert, Stanley Lane-Poole, Patrick Weston Joyce, and H. G. Wells.[13] This interest is expressed at length in comments from many of his letters to Tevis Clyde Smith and Howard Phillips Lovecraft. Furthermore, for those unfamiliar with Howard and his works, it should be noted that he wrote several historical adventure stories before starting on the Conan saga. While historians may flinch when the adjective "historical" is used to describe some of Howard's adventure stories,[14] the Crusader stories are highly considered by critics (Dickson ix-xi, Louinet "Hyborian Genesis" 434, Louinet "Introduction" vii) and considered to form part of his best work.[15]

The purpose of this paper is twofold. The first is to examine "The Hyborian Age" as a historical narrative. While Frye (52-66) and White ("The Historical Text as Literary Artifact," 15-33) have argued that non-fiction historical narratives can be analyzed like fic-

---

[13] An early version of the list of books in Robert E. Howard's library can be found in Eng (1982). A lengthier, online version has been compiled by Rusty Burke.

[14] "Historical" has been used to describe Howard's Crusader stories by both Blosser (10) and Louinet (vii-xii).

[15] While Howard did do some research into the historical periods he was writing about, he often relied on secondary works of varying quality. As demonstrated by Irwin, particularly for the works on the Third Crusade and Saladin, the secondary works often depend on clichés and stereotypes that are inaccurate. Add to this, the anachronisms appearing in some of the stories—such as firearms in "Lord of Samarcand," and Irish crusaders in the Cormac FitzGeoffrey tales—and one can understand why historians would object to using the adjective "historical."

While not unanimous in their attitudes, historians over the decades have written on what constitutes good historical fiction. Contemporary to Howard, the historians Butterfield and Sheppard both stressed that good historical fiction must maintain the historicity of events and the unique mindset of the past age must be faithfully conveyed. A little more than a generation later, Nye stressed "[...] the artist tries to find in his treatment of the past, as Proust did, is the relation of the individual to his present experience, in the context of his relation to the past experience of others" (147). More recently, Munz has downplayed anachronisms and stressed the importance of using generalizations from the period being covered in the novel (865-866). Irwin, in the same volume, though takes a more traditional stance by arguing against anachronisms, and stressing fidelity to the mindset of the time in question. He also is against artistic license in both secondary works and historical fiction—for example he is critical of both non-fiction and fiction writers who present a physical description of Saladin since there is no contemporary account describing Saladin's appearance.

tional ones, I would suggest that pseudo-histories and imaginary world creation stories, like Howard's "Hyborian Age," or some of Tolkien's *Lost Tales*, can be beneficially examined as historical narratives. The advantage of this approach is that it allows us to see how well each imaginary world was created, and gain insights into possible intellectual models the author used for the imaginary world.

A second goal is to examine some of the historical and anthropological ideas and themes present in "The Hyborian Age." While this is a work of fiction, it was nonetheless shaped by Howard's reading, his personal ideas and beliefs, and the social milieu of the 1920s and early 1930s. This examination is to see whether Howard incorporated mainstream ideas, or took a subversive approach and utilized more unorthodox ideas.[16]

As we look at the anthropological and historical ideas present in "The Hyborian Age" though, we need to be careful to avoid presentism. The 1920s and 1930s were a time when anthropology, archaeology and history were still developing theories and methodologies that we take for granted today. Furthermore, the mindset of the American public and scholars was different than ours today—the Civil Rights movement had yet to occur; women had only recently been allowed to vote; and not everyone lived with electricity or the telephone.[17]

"The Hyborian Age" as Historical Narrative

"The Hyborian Age" is a fictional narrative describing the creation, rise and fall of the Hyborian continent and its cultures. The narrative opens in the Pre-Cataclysmic Age, in a world inhabited by Atlanteans, Lemurians, Picts and others.[18] The Hyborian world rises from the continents and cultures left after a cataclysm. While How-

---

[16] Stowe (646-663) has suggested that popular fiction is one arena where authors, consciously or unconsciously, can expose readers to critiques of cultural norms and values.

[17] While not relevant to Howard *per se*, Menand's *The Metaphysical Club* is an engrossing read looking at individuals, ideas, politics, technology and social change in the United States from the 1860s to 1920. A wonderful, introductory overview of life in the 1920s in the United States is Downe and Huber's *The 1920s*.

[18] By including this section on Atlantis, Howard tied together the Kull and Conan stories.

ard does not go into detail as to its nature or cause, one can surmise he envisioned a single, massive event since he capitalized the catastrophe throughout "The Hyborian Age."

The bulk of the narrative focuses on the achievements, battles, evolution, and migrations of the various "races" inhabiting the Hyborian world. Not only is the rise of Hyborian civilizations chronicled, so is their decline and destruction. The scope and scale of this pseudo-history spans thousands of years, and at times is reminiscent of Lovecraft's cosmicism in such stories as "At the Mountains of Madness" and "The Shadow out of Time." "The Hyborian Age" does miss the cosmic sweep of Lovecraft's works since it stays focused on humanity's struggles with itself and against nature.[19] The focus on humanity should not be considered as a shortcoming, but should be seen as adding a realistic touch.

Compared to the Conan stories, some readers and critics may feel that "The Hyborian Age" lacks adventure and dynamism. It must be kept in mind, though, that Howard was not writing a fictional story, but was attempting to write a history as a historian would. As such, "The Hyborian Age" needs to be critically examined less as a fictional story, and more as a historical narrative.

Frye (52-66) provides one way of looking at historical narratives.[20] As he notes, once historians have finished their research, their writing can be guided by a *mythos* or plot. Frye sees four myths that are incorporated by historians into their narratives. Romantic historical myths are those based on a quest or pilgrimage to a classless society; comic historical myths are based on the idea of progress via evolution or revolution; tragic historical myths look at the decline and fall of civilizations and cultures; and ironic historical myths are based on re-occurring or casual catastrophe.[21] Historical

---

[19] Herron (161-3) notes that Howard was far too interested in humanity and individuals to make a concerted effort at emulating the cosmicism of Lovecraft and Smith.

[20] This approach has also been espoused by the historian Hayden White in "The Historical Text as Literary Artifact."

[21] Frye provides little explanation of his schema in *Fables of Identity*. Other than stating that Gibbon and Spengler are historians employing the tragic historical myth (54), Frye gives no examples. Hayden White, while also employing this schema, also provides minimal examples. For myself, I would see works detailing the search for such legendary lands as El Dorado or Shangri-La as exemplifying the romantic myth; E. H. Carr's or George Kennan's work on the Russian Revolution would exemplify the comic historical myth; and works

works exemplifying these myths are considered to be meta-histories (Frye 54). Historical writing, as seen by Frye (54), is an inductive process, while the writing of meta-history and poetics is deductive.

While meta-histories are usually large tomes, the brief "The Hyborian Age" can be classed as a meta-history also. "The Hyborian Age" exemplifies the tragic historical myth due to its focus on the rise and fall of the Hyborian kingdoms.[22] Despite the two cataclysms, "The Hyborian Age" does not exemplify the ironic historical myth since these two cataclysms are used only as framing devices to begin and end the story. Furthermore, human agency is the primary cause for the destruction of most of the Hyborian kingdoms.

This stress on human agency adds further realism to Howard's narrative. Despite being set in an imaginary world, the magic and sorcery that is present in the Conan and Kull stories is noticeably absent here. Humans are the ones who create the action and then respond to it.

When looking at human agency in meta-histories, one must distinguish between individual and group actions. Romanticist historical thought sees the individual as being the sole casual agent in the historical process (White, *Metahistory* 80). Works by Parkman, Prescott and Wells all stressed individuals who created the conditions of change. In contrast to this, the "New History" which emerged at the turn of the century, tried to make the discipline more scientific by focusing on evolutionary development, and social movements, with the downplaying of the Romantic view of individual actions (Kelley 285-303, 310-317).

Howard takes a fairly scientific, impersonal view in his account of the Hyborian Age. His essay focuses on the tribes and cultural groups in the Hyborian continent, and for the most part neglects individuals. Change is primarily provoked through migrations and warfare between the various population groups.[23] While Howard is

---

looking at economic "boom and bust" cycles as exemplifying the ironic historical myth.

[22] The tragic historical myth is one that goes back to the Greek authors and is a very pervasive one in the writing of history (Herman 15-20). Polybius noted the decay of political systems, while Plato theorized a developmental cycle for the rise and fall of the city-states. For the modern reader though, Spengler's and Toynbee's works come to mind.

[23] Trigger (96-108) notes that the diffusionist and migrationist schools of thought developed in the 1880s as a reaction to the evolutionary approaches. Essentially these two intellectual schools espoused that cultures were static and conservative, with change occurring only when encountering new cultural groups.

silent in most cases on why people migrated or went to war with one another, this silence is typical of the archaeological and culture historical works, and meta-histories of its day.

One example, particularly relevant to Howard, is Wells' *Outline of History* (167-182). This secondary history was part of Howard's personal library (see Burke). Wells provides a short account of the Indo-European migrations but neglects to explain why the Indo-Europeans began migrating in the first instance.[24] Other accounts of migration and diffusion in Wells (136-149) are used to account for the distribution of "races" throughout the world.

Another example, though we have no evidence that Howard ever read it, is V. Gordon Childe's *The Aryans: A Study of Indo-European Origins.* This academic monograph by a leading prehistorian of the 1920s and 1930s, details the Indo-European migrations throughout Europe and Western Asia. Throughout this volume, Childe gives no substantive reason on why the migrations occurred in the first place.

Despite the heavy emphasis on tribes and cultural groups, "The Hyborian Age" is not totally devoid of individuals. Howard's barbarian heroes Conan and Kull do not appear; instead it is the Pictish chieftain Gorm and the Nemedian priest Arus. Arus' religious mission, instead of converting the Picts, only inspires their greed. The result is that the Picts, led by their ambitious chief Gorm, ride westwards against the Hyborian nations. In this particular episode, Howard does provide us with causation as to the origins of a war and migration.[25]

This idea of barbarians destroying a decadent civilization is an old and popular idea in anthropology and historiography (Trigger 104). The source of it is rooted in the Germanic and Hunnic invasions of the Roman Empire in the fourth and fifth centuries AD, and has been used by such historians as Gibbon, Spengler, Toynbee, and

---

The leading proponents of these schools were Franz Boas at Columbia, Fritz Graebner at the Vienna School, W. H. R. Rivers and Grafton Elliot Smith in Britain. With time, each intellectual tradition borrowed freely from the other and ultimately incorporated elements of evolutionary thinking. The later works of the archaeologist V. Gordon Childe exemplify this fusion of ideas (Trigger 110-113).

[24] This is also a case where Wells does not attribute the migration being due to an individual's actions. Individuals take a more prominent role in Wells' history when he is dealing with states or proto-states.

[25] This is also done for the later Æsir migrations southwards (Howard 395).

Wells. Unlike historians though, Howard championed the barbarians.[26] While they too have their cultural zenith and collapse, Howard did not see them as falling into decadence or loosing their "virility" (Howard 395-397).

Some Notes on Race and Ethnicity in "The Hyborian Age"

Before making a few brief notes on Howard's use of race and ethnic identity in "The Hyborian Age,"[27] a few words need to be said on race and ethnicity in the USA during the early twentieth century. The word "race" was used in similar fashion then, as "ethnic group" is colloquially used today.[28] For example, Coon in *The Races of Europe* (241-665) made a case for eighteen different "races" in early twentieth-century Europe.[29]

Also prevalent in the 1920s and 1930s, though in decline, was an essentialist view of race, religion and nation which often resulted in equating the three together (Gerstle 14-139; Guterl 307-352; Slotkin 472-476; Smedley 264-265). For example, Bolshevism was equated with Judaism and the Slavic ethnic groups (Gerstle 101).

---

[26] In a letter to Lovecraft, received on November 2nd, 1932, Howard explains he champions the barbarians due to their freedom and physical ability (Howard *Selected Letters: 1931-1936* 35). He also makes it clear that he in no way sees their life as an idyllic one. Herron (151), in reference to all of Howard's barbarian heroes, notes that none of them exemplify Rousseau's Noble Savage.

[27] Howard's use of race and ethnicity in his stories is a topic that deserves a detailed examination. Ditommaso in "Robert E. Howard's Hyborian Tales and the Question of Race in Fantastic Literature" has tried to address whether Howard was a racist or not by looking at the Conan stories. In addition to only being limited to the Conan series, the article suffers from a lack of defining what constitutes racist versus racialist ideas, does not incorporate Howard's letters, and does not discuss the socio-political climate of Texas in the late 1920s and 1930s.

[28] It also bears noting, that most anthropologists today would define an ethnic group as a sub-group in a culture that possesses a common identity and name, a common origin (fictive or actual), and is recognized as such by both insiders and outsiders. Most anthropologists see them as fluid entities and individuals can belong to multiple ethnic groups. In colloquial American usage, ethnic groups are denoted usually on the basis of physical features.

[29] While some may consider Coon extreme, A. C. Haddon, who noted race was a social and mental construct (1), proposed a classification system with eleven racial groups living in Europe (25-31).

Eugenics was also popular in both the United States and Britain at this time (Black 16-85; Cuddy and Roche 9-59; Gerstle 105-7; Jones 717-728; Smedley 285-287). Eugenicists essentially saw human personality traits being inherited; thus, given the racial essentialism that existed at the time, deleterious traits were seen as arising from breeding with other racial groups. Degeneracy and criminality were two commonly cited deleterious traits arising from miscegenation. While we may view these ideas as laughable today, eugenics was a major intellectual trend in the United States and Britain, with hundreds of universities offering courses in it, and tens of thousands of students enrolled in course work (Black 75).

The results of this racialist and racist thinking were a variety of federal and state laws limiting immigration from Europe, Africa, and Asia, codifying segregation between whites and African-Americans, and barring miscegenation. Racialist thinking permeated the works of many authors, including Mary Austin (Richards 148-163), Erskine Caldwell (Holmes 240-258), and Jack London (Hopkins 89-101).

The racial schema presented in "The Hyborian Age" echoes some of the ideas and attitudes prevalent in the United States at that time. Racial groups are distinguished by a variety of physical traits, and occasionally cultural features. For example:

> [...] the Cimmerians are tall and powerful, with dark hair and blue or grey eyes. The people of Nordheim are of similar build, but with white skins, blue eyes and golden or red hair. The Picts are of the same type as they always were—short, very dark, with black eyes and hair (Howard 387).

And later in the text:

> The Bossonians are of medium height and complection [sic], their eyes brown or grey, and they are mesocephalic. They live mainly by agriculture, in large walled villages, and are part of the Aquilonian kingdom (Howard 387).

These are just two examples of Howard employing the racialist thinking of his time in "The Hyborian Age."

Despite the popularity of eugenics and anti-miscegenation laws during the 1930s, many of the races inhabiting the Hyborian world are of "mixed blood." The Bossonians (Howard 387), Hyperboreans

(Howard 386), and Zhemri (Howard 384) are but a few examples. And while some of the mixed race groups like the Bossonians fell short in their accomplishments, others, like the Aquilonians, are not weakened by mixing (Howard 386). Miscegenation is not seen as being responsible for the decline of the Hyborian kingdoms since Howard writes:

> Five hundred years later the Hyborian civilization was swept away. Its fall was unique in that it was not brought about by internal decay, but by the growing power of the barbarian nations, and the Hykranians. The Hyborian people were overthrown while their vigorous culture was in its prime (Howard 387).

CONCLUSIONS

While it is a fictional account, "The Hyborian Age" is written like a meta-history employing the tragic historical myth. Even though it is a fantasy world, it is practically devoid of the supernatural or fantastic. The reader does not encounter any sorcerers, wizards or fantastic beasts in this account, despite their appearance in the Conan and Kull stories. This absence of the fantastic lends the "The Hyborian Age" a sense of realism.

Human agency is the primary source of causation for events in "The Hyborian Age." For the bulk of the narrative, Howard focused on group action. He does present two individuals though, Gorm and Arus, when he details the how and why of the Pictish campaigns which led to the downfall of the Hyborian kingdoms. While Howard expressed his belief in "great men" as a driving force in history in a letter to Clark Ashton Smith in 1934 (Howard, *Selected Letters: 1931-1936*: 61), this belief is only weakly evidenced in "The Hyborian Age."

While Howard's handling of race and ethnicity reflects both the public and scientific views prevalent in the 1920s and 1930s, "The Hyborian Age" possibly contains a critique of eugenics and anti-miscegenation laws. As noted above, many of the Hyborian kingdoms are of mixed ancestry and yet, they are not lacking in vitality or vigor, nor are they degenerate. Whether this was conscious or unconscious on the part of Howard requires further examination.

ACKNOWLEDGMENTS

Thanks are in order to Rusty Burke, Charles Gramlich, and Steve Tompkins for their comments on earlier versions of this manuscript. The reviewer's comments have also helped strengthen this paper. Other useful ideas and comments were provided by the audience at the Robert E. Howard sessions at the 34th Annual Popular Culture Association meeting in San Antonio, Texas.

WORKS CITED

Black, Edwin. *War Against the Weak: Eugenics and America's Campaign to Create a Master Race.* New York: Four Walls Eight Windows, 2003.
Burke, Rusty. *The Robert E. Howard Bookshelf.* <http://www.rehupa.com/bookshelf.htm>.
Butterfield, Herbert. *The Historical Novel.* Cambridge: Cambridge University Press, 1924.
Childe, V. Gordon. *The Aryans: A Study of Indo-European Origins.* 1926. Port Washington, NY: Kennikat Press, 1970.
Coon, Carleton Stevens. *The Races of Europe.* New York: The Macmillan Company, 1939.
Cuddy, Lois A., and Claire M. Roche. "Introduction: Ideological Background and Literary Implications." *Evolution and Eugenics in American Literature and Culture, 1880-1940: Essays on Ideological Conflict and Complicity.* Ed. Lois A Cuddy and Claire M. Roche. Lewisburg: Bucknell University Press, 2003. 9-58.
Dickson, Gordon R. Introduction. *The Road of Azrael.* By Robert E. Howard. New York: Bantam Books, 1979. ix-xiii.
Ditommaso, Lorenzo. "Robert E. Howard's Hyborian Tales and the Question of Race in Fantastic Literature." *Extrapolation* 37:2 (1996): 150-170.
Downe, Kathleen and Patrick Huber. *The 1920s.* Westport: Greenwood Press, 2004.
Eng, Steve. "Appendix A: Robert E. Howard's Library." *The Dark Barbarian.* 1984. Ed. Don Herron. Wildside Press edition. Gillette, NJ: Wildside Press, 2000. 183-200.
Fredrickson, George M. *Racism: A Short History.* Princeton: Princeton University Press, 2002.
Frye, Northrop. *Fables of Identity: Studies in Poetic Mythology.* New York: Harcourt, Brace and World, Inc., 1963.

Gerstle, Gary. *American Crucible: Race and Nation in the Twentieth Century*. Princeton, N. J.: Princeton University Press, 2001.

Guterl, Matthew Pratt. "The New Race Consciousness: Race, Nation, and Empire in American Culture, 1910-1925." *Journal of World History* 10 (1999): 307-352.

Haddon, A. C. *The Races of Man and Their Distribution*. New York: Macmillan Company, 1925.

Herron, Don. "The Dark Barbarian." *The Dark Barbarian*. Ed. Don Herron. 1984. Wildside Press edition. Gillette, NJ: Wildside Press, 2000. 149-181.

Holmes, Sarah C. "Re-examining the Political Left: Erskine Caldwell and the Doctrine of Eugenics. *Evolution and Eugenics in American Literature and Culture, 1880-1940*. Eds. Louis A. Cuddy and Claire M. Roche. Lewisburg: Bucknell University Press, 2003. 240-258.

Hopkins, Lisa. "Jack London's Evolutionary Hierarchies: Dogs, Wolves, and Men." *Evolution and Eugenics in American Literature and Culture, 1880-1940*. Eds. Louis A. Cuddy and Claire M. Roche. Lewisburg: Bucknell University Press, 2003. 89-101.

Howard, Robert E. "The Hyborian Age." *The Coming of Conan the Cimmerian*. Ed. Patrice Louinet. New York: Ballantine Books, 2003. 379-400.

___. *Selected Letters: 1931-1936*. Ed. Glenn Lord with Rusty Burke, S. T. Joshi, and Steve Behrends. West Warwick, R. I.: Necronomicon Press, 1991.

Irwin, Robert. "Saladin and the Third Crusade: A Case Study in Historiography and the Historical Novel." *Companion to Historiography*. Ed. Michael Bentley. London: Routledge, 1997. 139-152.

Jones, Greta. "Eugenics and Social Policy between the Wars." *The Historical Journal* 25 (1982): 717-728.

Kelley, Donald R. *Fortunes of History: Historical Inquiry from Herder to Huizinga*. New Haven: Yale University Press, 2003.

Louinet, Patrice. "Hyborian Genesis." *The Coming of Conan the Cimmerian*. By Robert E. Howard. Ed. Patrice Louinet. New York: Ballantine Books, 2003. 429-52.

___. "Introduction." *Lord of Samarcand and Other Adventure Tales of the Old Orient*. By Robert E. Howard. Ed. Rusty Burke. Lincoln: University of Nebraska Press. vii-xii.

Menand, Louis. *The Metaphysical Club*. New York: Farrar, Strauss and Giroux, 2001.

Munz, Peter. "The Historical Narrative." *Companion to Historiography*. Ed. Michael Bentley. London: Routledge, 1997. 851-872.

Murji, Karim and John Solomos, eds. *Racialization: Studies in Theory and Practice*. New York: Oxford University Press, 2005.

Nye, Russell B. "History and Literature: Branches of the Same Tree." *Essays on History and Literature*. Ed. Robert H. Bremner. Columbus: Ohio State University Press, 1966. 123-159.

Richards, Penny L. "Bad Blood and Lost Borders: Eugenic Ambivalence in Mary Austin's Short Fiction." *Evolution and Eugenics in American Literature and Culture, 1880-1940*. Eds. Louis A. Cuddy and Claire M. Roche. Lewisburg: Bucknell University Press, 2003. 148-163.

Sheppard, Alfred Tresidder. *The Art and Practice of Historical Fiction*. London: Humphrey Toulmin, 1930.

Slotkin, Richard. "Unit Pride: Ethnic Platoons and the Myths of American Nationality." *American Literary History* (2001): 470-498.

Smedley, Audrey. *Race in North America: Origin and Evolution of a Worldview*. 2nd ed. Boulder: Westview Press, 1999.

Stowe, William W. "Popular Fiction as Liberal Art." *College English* 48 (1986): 646-663.

Trigger, Bruce. *Sociocultural Evolution*. Oxford: Blackwell Publishers, Ltd., 1998.

Wells, Herbert George. *The Outline of History*. 2 vols. New York: The Macmillan Company, 1921.

White, Hayden. *Metahistory: The Historical Imagination in Nineteenth-Century Europe*. Baltimore: John Hopkins University Press, 1973.

___."The Historical Text as Literary Artifact." *History and Theory: Contemporary Readings*. Eds. Brian Fay, Philip Pomper, Richard T. Vann. Malden, Mass.: Blackwell Publishers, 1998. 15-33.

RETURN TO XUTHAL

Howard's Original Sin City Revisited

by Charles Hoffman

A TALE OF TWO LOST CITIES

The first Robert E. Howard story I ever read was "Xuthal of the Dusk." I discovered it in that great old Lancer paperback, *Conan the Adventurer*. "Xuthal of the Dusk," appearing under the title "The Slithering Shadow," was actually the second story in the collection. Preceding it was the novella "The People of the Black Circle," one of the most popular and acclaimed of Howard's works. "Black Circle" was an excellent choice to open the book, the first in a series of Conan paperbacks, and introduce the character to a new generation of readers. Many years later, I do not clearly recall why I postponed reading it when I first purchased *Adventurer*. Possibly because it ran to nearly a hundred pages and I wanted to sample the book's contents with a story I could complete in one sitting. "Meet Conan, the gigantic adventurer from Cimmeria—and discover one of the greatest thrills in modern fiction!" the book's cover copy had promised. As it happened, I first met Robert E. Howard's giant Cimmerian in the lost city of Xuthal.

Lost cities have been featured in many works of adventure fiction, most famously those of H. Rider Haggard and Edgar Rice Burroughs. At the turn of the twentieth century, Africa was still very much the Dark Continent, and both Haggard and Burroughs imagined its unexplored vastness to be honeycombed with the last surviving outposts of vanished civilizations. Robert E. Howard followed closely in their footsteps in the lengthiest of his Solomon Kane stories, "The Moon of Skulls." Kane, in the course of his wanderings through sixteenth-century Africa, discovers the lost city of Negari.

Like Burroughs' Opar, Negari is a lost colony of Atlantis, and its alluring queen Nakari recalls both La of Opar and Ayesha, Haggard's "She-who-must-be-obeyed."

It was while writing the Conan stories a few years later that Howard placed his own distinctive stamp on the lost civilization genre. Conan's Hyborian world, itself a lost age remembered only in legend, is littered with remnants of even more remote antiquities. Haunted ruins are encountered from time to time in the course of Conan's adventures, and the Cimmerian twice discovers an entire inhabited lost city while venturing into unexplored regions. The lost cities of Xuthal and Xuchotl are found in "Xuthal of the Dusk" and "Red Nails" respectively. In both stories, the societies within the cities are in decline. Howard frequently expressed the thesis that civilizations carry the seeds of their own destruction. Xuthal and Xuchotl are both microcosms that enable the author to portray a civilization in its death throes. Their cultural decadence is emphasized by being shown from the perspective of the wilderness-bred Conan.

The importance of this theme to Howard, as well as his belief that he did not quite do justice to it in "Xuthal of the Dusk," are both demonstrated by the fact that he felt moved to return to it at greater length in "Red Nails." The novella "Red Nails" was Howard's final Conan story and the last fantasy he wrote before pressing financial concerns forced him to abandon fantasy altogether in favor of more commercial fiction. For his final allegorical statement, Howard returned to the themes of "Xuthal of the Dusk."

"Red Nails," to be sure, is the superior treatment of the themes. In fact, "Red Nails" has come to be regarded as not only one of the best Conan stories, but also as one of the finest of all Howard's works. "Xuthal of the Dusk," on the other hand, tends to be slighted as a mid-level Conan yarn at best. In his essay "Howard's Fantasy," Fritz Leiber singled it out as "a good (or bad!) example of a run-of-the mill Conan story."[30] Patrice Louinet, in "Hyborian Genesis Part III," asserts that "*Xuthal of the Dusk* is a rather inferior Conan tale…. The heroine was insipid and the story was clearly exploitative."[31]

I cannot help but to regard this out-of-hand dismissal of "Xuthal of the Dusk" as unfortunate. I have already acknowledged

---

[30] Fritz Leiber, "Howard's Fantasy," in *The Dark Man* (Westport, CT: Greenwood Press, 1984) p. 9.
[31] Patrice Louinet, "Hyborian Genesis III," in *The Conquering Sword of Conan* (New York: Del Rey Books, 2005) p. 383.

my personal sentimental reasons for liking the story. Also, I don't think it's too outrageous to suggest that it would be somewhat more highly regarded were it not overshadowed by "Red Nails." More significantly, however, I believe that "Xuthal of the Dusk" has points of interest apart from the ingredients it shares with "Red Nails." Facets of the tale serve to illuminate aspects of the character Conan and Howard's writing, as well as foreshadowing trends in latter day popular culture. These attributes make "Xuthal of the Dusk" an intriguing story in its own right.

FEAR AND LOATHING IN XUTHAL

The first noteworthy element of the story is its very title. The lost city of Xuthal is "of the Dusk." It has reached the end of its day. Before the story even begins, Howard employs dusk as an unambiguous metaphor for the city's impending doom. Unfortunately, the story did not originally appear under Howard's title. For its initial publication in the September 1933 issue of *Weird Tales,* editor Farnsworth Wright changed the title to "The Slithering Shadow." This title, lurid where Howard's was subtle, was retained when the Conan stories were collected in the Gnome Press hardback editions of the 1950s, and in the subsequent Lancer and Ace paperback editions of the '60s and '70s. Surely this proved a liability that further hindered appreciation of the story over the years. Consider the awkwardness of any discerning reader attempting to cite a story called "The Slithering Shadow" as a favorite.

The next point of interest is a mere line drop away. The story opens:

> The desert shimmered in the heat waves. Conan the Cimmerian stared out over the aching desolation and involuntarily drew the back of his powerful hand over his blackened lips. He stood like a bronze giant in the sand, apparently impervious to the murderous sun, though his only garment was a silk loin-cloth, girdled by a wide gold-buckled belt from which hung a saber and a broad-bladed poniard. On his clean-cut limbs were evidences of scarcely healed wounds.
> At his feet rested a girl, one white arm clasping his knee, against which her blond head drooped. Her white skin contrasted with his hard bronzed limbs; her short silken tunic, low-necked and sleeveless,

girdled at the waist, emphasized rather than concealed her lithe figure.[32]

If this description sounds familiar, it is because it was the basis of Frank Frazetta's portrait of Conan that first graced the cover of *Conan the Adventurer*. Starting with this image of a battle-scarred titan in a loincloth, Frazetta fine-tuned some details, such as substituting a more characteristic broadsword for the saber, and so created both his own most famous painting and the depiction of Conan that influenced every subsequent illustration of the character. It is Frazetta's masterpiece, an iconic image, and the definitive visual portrayal of Robert E. Howard's Conan. And it didn't come from "The People of the Black Circle."

In addition to offering this key image to Frank Frazetta, "Xuthal of the Dusk" was essential in defining the character of Conan to Howard's original audience, the readers who saw the saga unfold in the pages of *Weird Tales*. "Xuthal of the Dusk" was the fifth Conan story to appear in *Weird Tales*. The first two tales featured Conan as the middle-aged king of Aquilonia, an adventurer who seized the throne from a tyrant. The third story, "The Tower of the Elephant," presented Conan as a teenage thief green to civilization, indicating that subsequent installments would fill in the backstory of this remarkable individual. The fourth Conan adventure, "Black Colossus," had Conan assume the role of mercenary warrior. "Xuthal of the Dusk" followed, again featuring Conan as a wandering soldier of fortune and thus suggesting that this was the Cimmerian's usual occupation. The Conan series was off and running.

In the story, Conan and his female companion, Natala, are survivors of a defeated army whose flight leads them to the lost city of Xuthal. Xuthal is located in a vast desert south of the proto-Egyptian realm of Stygia and the black kingdom of Kush. It is my opinion that in the Hyborian Age maps featured in various Conan volumes, the southern lands, Stygia and the black countries, are not to scale. This is not unlike the Eurocentric Mercator projection maps of our own world that diminish Africa's true immensity. In his own sketches of Conan's world, Howard allotted more space to Stygia. It follows that Xuthal is located in the vast "African" portion of the Hyborian supercontinent, making it in a sense an African lost city in the Haggard-Burroughs tradition.

---

[32] Robert E. Howard, "Xuthal of the Dusk" in *The Coming of Conan the Cimmerian* (New York: Del Rey Books, 2003) p. 219.

Conan and Natala explore the eerie walled city, finding it seemingly deserted and haunted by some strange menace. The mysteries of Xuthal are explained when they meet a stunningly beautiful woman called Thalis. Thalis is not a native of Xuthal, but a Stygian who arrived there as a young girl. She informs the wanderers that the people of Xuthal spend most of their time in death-like slumber, dreaming hallucinogenic visions induced by their consumption of the "black lotus."[33] The city dwellers' science is sufficiently advanced to provide for all their basic material needs without much effort on their part. Their lives have become "vague, erratic, and without plan."[34] Thalis also tells of a shadowy horror called Thog that stalks the city and occasionally devours an inhabitant. The Xuthalians simply accept this gruesome state of affairs with a complacent fatalism. Thalis opines that this is not so different from the human sacrifices practiced in her native Stygia.

Hearing this, Conan is moved to declare, "I'd like to see a priest try to drag a Cimmerian to the altar! There'd be blood spilt, but not as the priest intended."[35] This sort of dry action-hero wit was not characteristic of such pulp magazine do-gooders as The Shadow and Doc Savage. Wry comments such as this are much more typical of latter day heroes such as James Bond or Dirty Harry.

"Xuthal of the Dusk" is one of the tales in which Robert E. Howard delineated a new type of hero—cool, supremely confident, with more than a hint of ruthlessness and sinister menace. Let us call this sort of hero "the badass" for lack of a better name. Tough and lethal, ever ready for a brawl, the badass has more in common with the hard, dangerous enemies he fights than any candy-ass types he might end up protecting. The latter regard him not with fawning admiration, but with nervous relief that he's on their side. Though popular enough in Howard's day, the Conan character was destined to strike a chord with the reading public in the later, raucous decades of the 1960s and '70s.

It comes as no surprise that Thalis, having tired of her city-bred lovers, is attracted to Conan. She therefore attempts to get rid of Natala —but not before tying her up and whipping her. Thalis is one of the more beguiling evil women to appear in Howard's fiction. In his essay, Fritz Leiber describes her as "sophisticated, hard as nails, sadistic, catlike, and schooled in every vice."[36] Her name appears to

---

[33] *Ibid.* p. 230.
[34] *Ibid.*
[35] *Ibid.*, p. 231
[36] Leiber, *op cit.*, pp. 9-10.

have been derived from Thais, a courtesan who became the mistress of Alexander the Great, and also the name of the title character of a novel by Anatole France and an opera based on it by Jules Massenet. In "The Garden of Fear," Howard mentions Thais in company with Cleopatra and Helen of Troy.

To the readers of *Weird Tales*, Thalis the Stygian was the first *femme fatale* to appear in a Conan story. Howard had previously introduced the golden-haired siren Atali in "The Frost-Giant's Daughter," but the story did not see print in the author's lifetime.[37] In any event, Atali has little in common with the other *femmes fatale* encountered by Conan. She is not a poisonous seductress, but a kind of ultimate cock-tease able to get away with her adolescent cruelty thanks to the protection of her menacing big brothers and her daddy's power and authority. Thalis, on the other hand, is a jaded sophisticate, and the *femmes fatale* who subsequently appear in the series—Akivasha, Salome, and Tascela—are brunette sybarites who resemble her so closely that they could all be members of the same clique.

In fact, the next of these übervixens Howard wrote of, Akivasha, so nearly mirrors Thalis that she, too, is a Stygian princess. It is interesting to compare Conan's first sight of each. Howard's initial description of Thalis reads:

> ...A figure framed itself in the doorway.... It was a woman who stood there staring at them in wonder. She was tall, lithe, shaped like a goddess; clad in a narrow girdle crusted with jewels. A burnished mass of night-black hair set off the whiteness of her ivory body.... The Cimmerian had never seen such a woman; her facial outline was Stygian, but she was not dusky-skinned like the Stygian women he had known; her limbs were like alabaster.[38]

And here is Howard's introduction of Akivasha in *The Hour of the Dragon*, written nearly a year and a half later:

---

[37] Although Howard did donate a variant version of the tale, with the hero's name changed to Amra of Akbitana, to a fan publication. This version has appeared under the titles, "The Frost-King's Daughter" and "Gods of the North."
[38] Howard, "Xuthal", *op cit.*, p. 228.

> ...A girl stood at the mouth of a smaller tunnel, staring fixedly at him. Her ivory skin showed her to be Stygian of some ancient noble family, and like all such women she was tall, lithe, voluptuously figured, her hair a great pile of black foam, among which gleamed a sparkling ruby. But for her velvet sandals and broad jewel-crusted girdle about her supple waist she was quite nude....[39]

In much of his writing, Howard seems blessed with a pipeline to his reader's unconscious. The provocative dream-like image of an alluring woman framed in a doorway or passageway, as though poised on some mysterious threshold, seems uncannily resonant. Clearly the image of Thalis lingered long in Howard's imagination, and undoubtedly in Conan's as well.

The blonde Natala is the dark-haired Thalis' victim, and a character generally deemed worthy of little attention. Some commentators on Howard's work, in an effort to proactively appease feminist critics, cite the author's ability to create "strong female characters." Bêlit, Valeria of the Red Brotherhood, and the Devi Yasmina are dutifully trotted out. Of course a woman like Thalis is also a "strong female character," but the *femme fatale* tends to be narrowly regarded as another demeaning stereotype, rather than seen as a powerful archetype. "Insipid" heroines like Natala, who merely spice up the story in their capacities as damsel-in-distress and/or sex kitten, are scornfully noted and quickly glossed over.

Natala, however, merits scrutiny precisely *because* there is so little of the "strong female character" in her makeup; she is almost astonishingly weak and passive. Compared to Natala, heroines like Octavia and Sancha are like Amazons. Wandering through Xuthal with Conan, Natala is at all times timid and easily spooked. When they discover food and drink, Natala worries that they may anger someone by helping themselves, even though she and Conan are dying of hunger and thirst. A sex kitten character like Yasmela may not be much help to Conan, but Natala is explicitly shown to be a downright hindrance. She literally steps on Conan's heels and endangers them both by clutching at his sword-arm.

Early in the story, when they are stranded in the desert, Conan actually considers putting Natala to death as an act of kindness:

---

[39] Robert E. Howard, "The Hour of the Dragon," in *The Bloody Crown of Conan* (New York: Del Rey Books, 2004) p. 214.

> [Conan] had not come to the limits of his endurance, but he knew that another day under the merciless sun in those waterless wastes would bring him down. As for the girl, she had suffered enough. Better a quick painless sword-stroke than the agony that faced him.[40]

The point is made that Natala is not Conan's equal when it comes to facing the perils of the wilderness. Interestingly, Thalis, like Conan, also regards Natala as less than an equal in terms of her fitness to survive. Rather than the wilderness, however, it is the urban perils of Xuthal that Thalis declares Natala unfit to face. Still, Thalis comes to the same conclusion as Conan when she suggests that Natala should be put to the sword because of it:

> "...[I]t would be better for you to cut that girl's throat with your saber, before the men of Xuthal waken and catch her. They will put her through paces she never dreamed of! She is too soft to endure what I have thrived on...."[41]

Natala is thus deemed inferior in some sense to both Conan and Thalis. This point is emphatically reinforced. Crossing the desert to reach Xuthal, Conan carries Natala not only figuratively, but also literally: "Stooping, he lifted Natala in his mighty arms as though she had been an infant. She resisted weakly."[42] Later, Thalis carries Natala with similar ease: "With a lithe strength [Natala] would not have believed possible in a woman, Thalis picked her up and carried her down the black corridor as if she had been a child...."[43]

Natala and Thalis contrast startlingly with one another, no less than De Sade's virtuous Justine and her depraved sister Juliette. Natala, the fair, is meek but good-hearted. Thalis, the dark, is haughty and cruel. "I am the daughter of a king, no common woman," boasts Thalis.[44] Concerning Natala's background, we are told:

> The girl was a Brythunian, whom Conan had found in the slave-market of a stormed Shemite city

---

[40] Howard, "Xuthal", *op. cit.*, p. 220.
[41] *Ibid.*, p. 232.
[42] *Ibid.*, p. 220.
[43] *Ibid.*, p. 236.
[44] *Ibid.*, p. 232.

and appropriated. She had had nothing to say in the matter, but her new position was so far superior to the lot of any Hyborian woman in a Shemitish seraglio, that she accepted it thankfully....[45]

Among the secondary Conan women we find a "buccaneer's plaything,"[46] a "dancing girl" or two, and even several designated "captive." But it is Natala who is explicitly relegated to the role of slave. The "slave girl" is, of course, a common erotic fantasy figure, her popularity attested to by John Norman's *Gor* series.

To the extent that she conforms to the "slave girl" fantasy, Natala compliments Thalis as well as contrasting with her. In the whipping scene, they represent different sides of the same coin: top and bottom, dominant and submissive. It is revealing that both women arrived in Xuthal under similar circumstances:

> [Conan and Natala] were, so far as he knew, the sole survivors of Prince Almuric's army, that mad, motley horde which, following the defeated rebel prince of Koth, swept through the Lands of Shem like a devastating sandstorm and drenched the outlands of Stygia with blood. With a Stygian host on its heels, it had cut its way through the black kingdom of Kush only to be annihilated on the edge of the southern desert....
>
> From that final slaughter...Conan had cut his way clear and fled on a camel with the girl. Behind them the land swarmed with enemies; the only way open to them was the desert to the south....
>
> For days they had fled into the desert, pursued so far by Stygian horsemen that when they shook off their pursuit, they dared not turn back. They pushed on, seeking water, until the camel died....[47]

Natala's backstory is recounted in the third person, while Thalis boldly narrates her own tale:

---

[45] *Ibid.*, p. 221.
[46] Robert E. Howard, "The Pool of the Black One" in *The Coming of Conan the Cimmerian* (New York: Del Rey Books, 2003) p. 255.
[47] Howard, "Xuthal", *op cit.*, pp. 220-21.

> "...I was abducted by a rebel prince, who, with an army of Kushite bowmen, pushed southward into the wilderness, searching for a land he could make his own. He and all his warriors perished in the desert, but one, before he died, placed me on a camel and walked beside it until he dropped and died in his tracks. The beast wandered on, and I finally passed into delirium from thirst and hunger, and awakened in this city. They told me I had been seen from the walls early in the dawn, lying senseless beside a dead camel...."[48]

Thus, both Thalis and Natala owe their presence in Xuthal to the thwarted ambition of a "rebel prince" and a subsequent flight on camelback in the company of the sole surviving warrior. In Xuthal, Thalis and Natala become rivals for Conan's attention, possibly due in part to Thalis's memory of her own one-time protector. There the similarities between the two women end.

While Thalis is contemptuous of Conan's "little blond,"[49] we are told that "[Natala] felt small and dust-stained and insignificant before this glamorous beauty."[50] It comes as little surprise when Thalis and Natala are joined in a scene of girl-on-girl sadomasochism. Howard has done everything to depict Natala as a meek submissive short of spelling her name with a lower case "N."

The whipping scene itself is erotically charged:

> ...As in a nightmare Natala felt her tunic being stripped from her, and the next instant Thalis had jerked up her wrists and bound them to the ring, where she hung, naked as the day she was born, her feet barely touching the floor. Twisting her head, Natala saw Thalis unhook a jewel-handled whip from where it hung on the wall, near the ring. The lashes consisted of seven round silk cords, harder yet more pliant than leather thongs.
>
> With a hiss of vindictive gratification, Thalis drew back her arm, and Natala shrieked as the cords curled across her loins. The tortured girl writhed,

---

[48] *Ibid.*, p. 232.
[49] *Ibid.*
[50] *Ibid.*, p. 229.

> twisted and tore agonizedly at the thongs which imprisoned her wrists.... Every stroke evoked screams of anguish. The whippings Natala had received in the Shemite slave-markets paled to insignificance before this....[51]

This may seem strong stuff for a magazine sold over the counter in 1933. Nevertheless, this very scene was depicted in full color on the September *Weird Tales* cover. One of Margaret Brundage's exquisite pastel compositions illustrates the whipping of a demure Natala by a stern Thalis. In a 1973 interview, Mrs. Brundage revealed that the entire print run of that month's issue sold out, and remarked that they could have used a couple thousand extra copies. Although this was the first Brundage *Weird Tales* cover to depict a whipping scene, it was not the last.

It has been suggested that *Weird Tales* began to feature whipping scenes on its covers in a bid to remain competitive with the "weird menace" magazines or "shudder pulps" that began to appear in the mid-thirties. Lurid pulps like *Terror Tales* and *Thrilling Mystery* featured covers and stories that depicted grotesque acts of sadism in the tradition of the Grand Guignol Theater of Paris. However, the first shudder pulp was *Dime Mystery Magazine*, which adopted the weird menace format in October 1933, one month *after* Howard's "Xuthal of the Dusk" appeared in *Weird Tales* as "The Slithering Shadow." *Terror Tales* did not begin publication until September 1934, nearly a year later, and its companion magazine, *Horror Stories*, debuted in January 1935. *Weird Tales* did eventually feel the heat from this competition and attempted to get in the game by inaugurating the "Doctor Satan" series, concerning a costumed sadist, in the August 1935 issue.

Howard himself dabbled in the weird menace genre, later contributing "Graveyard Rats" and "Black Wind Blowing" to *Thrilling Mystery*. It has therefore been suggested that the instances of flagellation and bondage that occur in the Conan stories are examples of the author "pandering" to his readers. However, a look at the contents of Howard's library reveals a more than passing interest in sadomasochism. "I...have in my possession a very good book on sadism and masochism by a noted German scholar,"[52] he wrote to H. P. Lovecraft. His collection also included small press publications

---

[51] *Ibid.*, p. 237.
[52] Robert E. Howard to H. P. Lovecraft, 5 December 1935, in *Selected Letters 1931-1936* (West Warwick, RI: Necronomicon Press, 1991) p. 68.

that could be considered soft-core erotica, such as *An Amateur Flagellant: Experiences of Flagellation* and *A History of the Rod*. A listing of additional titles for sale such as *Painful Pleasures* and *Presented in Leather* was found among his papers. Glenn Lord believed that Howard was interested in acquiring such volumes for "research" purposes. The amount of "research" essential for writing for the shudder pulps notwithstanding, mild sadomasochism, such as the spanking of adult women, occurs in some of Howard's erotic poetry as well. This does seem to indicate something more than academic interest. Considering that REH was a physically vigorous young male with no regular sexual outlet and possessed of one of the most vivid imaginations on the planet, it would actually be surprising if he possessed no kinks whatsoever.

Returning to the perils of Natala, we find things going from bad to worse. Natala's screams attract the blob-like monster Thog, which engulfs Thalis and carries her off. Before long Thog returns for Natala:

> ...A dark tentacle-like member slid about her body, and she screamed at the touch of it on her naked flesh. It was neither warm nor cold, rough nor smooth; it was like nothing that had ever touched her before, and at its caress she knew such fear and shame as she had never dreamed of. All the obscenity and salacious infamy spawned in the muck of the abysmal pits of Life seemed to drown her in seas of cosmic filth. And in that instant she knew that whatever form of life this thing represented it was not a beast.[53]

In his essay, Fritz Leiber notes that, "The lost city is terrorized by the beast-god Thog, who dwells in a deep well which strikes me as a symbol (unconscious?—probably) of female sexuality, and who is an amorphous and ravening Lovecraftian monster with the addition of an unlikely sexual hunger...Thog kills Thalis and at least attempts the rape of Natala."[54]

Thog is some sort of gelatinous invertebrate, solid but shapeless, and Leiber regards the notion of such a creature lusting after a human female as outlandish. To Howard, however, this sequence

---

[53] Howard, "Xuthal", *op cit..*, p. 238.
[54] Leiber, *op cit.,* p. 10.

represents a kind of ultimate perversity. Boneless, Thog is a creature composed entirely of hungry flesh, essentially a monstrous roaming appetite. We are told that the Xuthalians themselves "'live only for sensual joys. Dreaming or waking, their lives are filled with exotic ecstasies, beyond the ken of ordinary men.'"[55] Lustful and voracious, Thog is the embodiment of the city-dwellers' unwholesome appetites. However, Thog is also a step above the Xuthalians on the food chain, devouring and defiling them in the manner of a natural predator.

We have already seen that Howard was ahead of the curve when it came to introducing sadomasochistic elements into pulp fiction. In depicting Natala being violated by Thog, he was a good half-century ahead of his time. Today there is an entire pornographic sub-genre of Japanese *anime* commonly referred to as "tits and tentacles." These adults-only animated cartoons portray the plight of young women, usually teenage schoolgirls, who are sexually abused by monsters very much like Thog.

The only thing even remotely resembling this in the pulps was to be found in the science fiction magazines. There covers depicted attractive female astronauts clad in skintight spacesuits and fishbowl space helmets being menaced by "bug-eyed monsters." No sexual context was explicit or implied; it was simply a way to pair a cute damsel-in-distress with a scary monster. And again, this could not have influenced Howard. Mort Weisinger introduced the bug-eyed monster format when he became editor of *Wonder Stories* (which then became *Thrilling Wonder Stories*) with the August 1936 issue. Howard was dead by the time it appeared.

All things considered, Natala was perfectly justified regarding her many forebodings of dread concerning Xuthal. Conan has his work cut out for him in dealing with the city's menaces. And here too we see how Howard was ahead of his time as a purveyor of popular entertainment.

When Conan and Natala first enter the city, they find the gatekeeper lying motionless in the courtyard. Cold and lifeless upon examination, the supposedly dead man rises and attacks moments later. The presumed dead or defeated menace that abruptly launches a new attack has become a horror movie cliché in recent decades. This episode is the first of several plot elements of "Xuthal of the Dusk" that exemplify motifs which became commonplace in later works of popular culture.

---

[55] Howard, "Xuthal", *op cit.,* p. 233.

Later, Conan finds himself under attack by twenty swordsmen of Xuthal. Unskilled and inexperienced, they are no match for Conan as he slices through them and escapes. In Fritz Leiber's words, "Conan cuts up a besworded bunch of the 'ridiculously slow and clumsy' drug addicts in a battle described with butcher-shop thoroughness."[56] Fred Blosser has observed that Leiber's remarks about "butcher-shop thoroughness" seem quaint in light of today's ultra-violent entertainment.

Taking this observation further, it is worth noting that the battle of a lone protagonist against numerous multiple attackers is the chief scenario of modern video games. Frequently censured for their violence, such games often feature the hero (the game-player's surrogate) slaughtering whole herds of enemies in bloody combat. Though seemingly hopelessly outnumbered, the hero is possessed of great prowess while his opponents are comparatively lousy. The latter are like the walking dead in George Romero-type zombie movies—another modern violent entertainment—in that they are not all that dangerous one-on-one, but potentially lethal *en masse*.

In the end, of course, Conan prevails and rescues Natala. Natala believes that Conan's flirtation with Thalis led to their troubles, and Fritz Leiber admits that "Conan's humorous and matter-of-fact, happy acceptance of the two girls' rivalry for him is refreshing."[57] In her last thoughts concerning Thalis herself, Natala admits, "'She tortured me—yet I pity her.'"[58]

Submissive to the last.

XUCHOTL OF THE DUSK (OR, RED NAILS IN THE SUNSET)

Long after the sun set on Xuthal, Conan would tread the gloomy corridors of another lost city with a similar name, Xuchotl, in his final adventure, "Red Nails." Like Xuthal, Xuchotl is home to a decaying civilization; only here the inhabitants are addicted to homicidal mayhem rather than sex and drugs.

This was not the first instance of Howard's reworking elements of early Conan stories into later installments of the series. Fred Blosser described how Howard recycled plot elements from "Black Colossus" and "The Scarlet Citadel" to create the novel *The Hour of the Dragon*, an example of what Raymond Chandler called "canni-

---

[56] Leiber, *op cit.*, p. 10.
[57] *Ibid.*
[58] Howard, "Xuthal", *op cit.*, p. 247.

balizing." In this case, Howard was revamping and improving some of his best material to make his only book-length Conan adventure as hard-hitting as possible.

In other instances, however, Howard may have felt that he had failed to do justice to ideas with greater potential. "Xuthal" and "Red Nails" together comprise the most notable example of this principle, but not the only example.

"Iron Shadows in the Moon," written in November 1932, and "The Devil in Iron," written in October 1933, both feature Conan in the Eastern lands of Hyrkania. In both stories, he is a member of the *kozaks,* marauders of the wastelands who prey on civilized outposts. However, in the former story, the power of the *kozaks* has been broken and Conan is first seen as a hunted fugitive hiding in swamps. In the latter tale, Conan is the chieftain of all the *kozaks* and a thorn in the side of the king himself. Both stories feature similar supernatural menaces found in an island's haunted ruins. Yet the earlier story's menace consists of mere "Iron Shadows," statues that mysteriously come to life and kill some people offstage. The later story raises the stakes with a veritable "Devil in Iron"—a demon walking the earth in a body of iron because flesh is too fragile to contain it. Here we see Howard reworking the story to give it more of a punch.

Howard could also revamp the concept of a previous story to create a purer subtext. Case in point: "The God in the Bowl" and "Rogues in the House." "The God in the Bowl," written in March 1932, was Howard's third Conan story. It was rejected by *Weird Tales*, and he subsequently reconfigured elements of it in the composition of "Rogues in the House," believed to have been written in January 1933. In both stories Conan is a youthful thief at odds with civilized society. The action of each story takes place mostly indoors, within some sort of bizarre edifice where a strange creature is on the loose.

Each story was also written as an exposé of the hypocrisy and corruption of civilized authority. Characters in "The God in the Bowl" include a wealthy merchant who plans to steal a treasure and set up an employee as the fall guy, and a foppish young nobleman after the same treasure who hires and then betrays Conan. Then there are police officials who routinely torture confessions from suspects. However, the cast also includes honest men just trying to do their jobs.

In "Rogues in the House," on the other hand, *no one* is pure. The "rogues" of the title are Conan, thief and hired assassin; Murilo, another unscrupulous, foppish young nobleman; the Red Priest Nabonidus, who exploits his power in the kingdom for his own gain; and arguably the ape-man Thak, a missing link who endeavors to become more human through murder and theft. But, as though that were not enough, there is also an assortment of unsavory minor characters as well. These include Conan's partner in crime, who deserted from the army; a priest who plays both ends against the middle as both a fence for stolen goods and a police informer; the girl who sells out Conan to the police; the girl's new lover, yet another thief; and a jailer who accepts bribes and has underworld ties. There is also an honest jailer, but he is portrayed as petty and drunk with his own authority. A group of assassins attempt to kill the Red Priest for the good of the kingdom, but they are assassins nonetheless. Everyone is guilty of something or has something to hide.

Returning to "Red Nails" and "Xuthal of the Dusk," we find that "Red Nails" owes much more to its predecessor than those other examples of reworked stories. The lost cities of Xuthal and Xuchotl have nearly identical names, sharing the same first syllable and beginning with the letter "X"—a similarity that invites comparison. They are both located somewhere south of the black kingdoms of Kush and Darfar. Hyborian Age maps show them in roughly the same vicinity. The twin "X" cities are the Sodom and Gomorrah of Conan's world.

Conan is amazed to discover that the city of Xuchotl is constructed almost entirely of jade. In his earlier adventure, he observed that Xuthal was constructed of "a smooth greenish substance that shown almost like glass."[59] Green or "greenish" building materials are used from time to time in the Conan series to impart a hint of eldritch menace to mysterious ruins or alien structures. The "shadowy ruins"[60] discovered in "Iron Shadows in the Moon" were built of "greenish stone."[61] The ruins on Xapur in "The Devil in Iron" that were inexplicably rebuilt overnight, a thing "monstrously out of joint,"[62] were also erected with the "iron-like green stone found only on the islands of Vilayet."[63] The citadel of the inhuman giants in "The Pool of the Black One" is composed of some "green semi-translucent substance"[64] that heightens the effect of architecture

---

[59] *Ibid.,* p. 221.
[60] Robert E. Howard, "Iron Shadows in the Moon" in *The Coming of Conan the Cimmerian* (New York: Del Rey Books, 2003) p. 198.
[61] *Ibid.,* p. 194.
[62] Robert E. Howard, "The Devil in Iron" in *The Coming of Conan the Cimmerian* (New York: Del Rey Books, 2003) p. 330.
[63] *Ibid.,* p. 322.
[64] Howard, "Pool", *op cit.,* p. 260.

"alien to human sanity."[65] Outside of the Conan canon, the winged man's tower in "The Garden of Fear" is also built "of a curious green stone, highly polished, and of a substance that created the illusion of semi-translucency."[66] One wonders if REH would have described the Emerald City of Oz as "monstrously out of joint" or "alien to human sanity."

In addition to being composed of similar building materials, Xuthal and Xuchotl are constructed along similar lines. Each city actually consists of a single massive self-contained structure. In "Red Nails," this is obvious to Conan as he enters Xuchotl. In "Xuthal of the Dusk," however, he is unaware that the buildings of Xuthal are all interconnected until Thalis so informs him. Her revelation comes when the story is well underway, suggesting that this detail occurred to Howard as he was writing it. An embryonic concept in "Xuthal of the Dusk," the enclosed city is one of the most striking elements of "Red Nails."

Other similarities between the two cities include the fact that the inhabitants of both have abandoned agriculture and livestock raising. Instead, all food is produced indoors. The inhabitants of Xuchotl cultivate fruit that "obtains its nourishment out of the air."[67] In Xuthal, food is manufactured out of the "primal elements."[68] Each city is illuminated by gems or fossils with luminescent properties. And more interestingly, each city is home to a dark-haired *femme fatale* whose name begins with the letter "T"—Thalis of Xuthal and Tascela of Xuchotl.

Of course there are differences as well as similarities between the two stories, and the most striking departure from the earlier tale is undoubtedly the depiction of Conan's romantic interest. In "Red Nails" the demure Natala is replaced by the bold warrior-woman, Valeria of the Red Brotherhood. Natala and Valeria are both blondes, but there the similarities end. Valeria fights at Conan's side and more than holds her own.

"Red Nails" is not without its "exploitative" elements. As in "Xuthal," sadomasochistic elements enter the story. Unlike the winsome Natala, however, Valeria assumes the dominant role. When a young woman of Xuchotl attempts to drug her, Valeria strips her

---

[65] *Ibid.*
[66] Robert E. Howard, "The Garden of Fear" in *Eons of the Night* (Riverdale, NY: Baen Books, 1996) p. 45.
[67] Robert E. Howard, "Red Nails" in *The Conquering Sword of Conan* (New York: Del Rey Books, 2005) p. 246.
[68] Howard, "Xuthal", *op cit.,* p. 230.

naked, ties her up, and whips her, as Thalis whipped Natala, with "hard-woven silken cords."[69] Nevertheless, Valeria meets her match in Xuchotl's resident *femme fatale,* Tascela. Their encounter ends with Valeria herself in bondage and finally nude. Readers are treated to the spectacle of a dominant woman being dominated herself.

Throughout "Red Nails," Valeria of the Red Brotherhood is presented as a fitting companion for Conan, nearly his equal —yet not quite. Mention is made of the fact that, due to spending so much of her life aboard pirate ships, Valeria cannot run very fast or very far. Therefore, when they are pursued by a carnivorous dinosaur en route to the city, Conan must pick her up and carry her along. Not unlike the meek Natala, Valeria has to be carried by Conan...for a little while at least.

CONCLUSIONS

In evaluating "Xuthal of the Dusk" in his essay, "Hyborian Genesis," Patrice Louinet remarks, "The basic plot of the tale— Conan and a woman finding an isolated city peopled by decadent inhabitants and a wicked woman—would indeed be considerably enriched and developed in the future *Red Nails* (1935). The theme had profound psychological resonance in Howard's psyche. In late 1932, however, Howard was not ready to give it the treatment it deserved, and *Xuthal of the Dusk* pales in comparison with the future Conan tale."[70]

Perhaps so. Yet it bears repeating that if "Red Nails" had not been written, "Xuthal of the Dusk" would almost certainly be held in higher esteem. Apart from that, "Xuthal" deserves to be seen as more than just a kind of blueprint or rough draft for "Red Nails."

If Robert E. Howard is remembered for nothing else, he merits recognition as an important figure in twentieth century art for his key role as a pioneer of sexy, violent entertainment. Howard understood clearly that consumers of narrative art have an innate hunger to identify with protagonists placed in extreme circumstances. After all, Romanticism and its Gothic subgenre were all about unusual situations, intense moods and heightened emotional states. Sex and violence in entertainment are routinely condemned by politicians, teachers, and other authority figures that have an interest in keeping the masses docile. On the other hand, every storyteller, good or bad,

---

[69] Howard, "Red Nails", p. 254.
[70] Patrice Louinet, "Hyborian Genesis" in *The Coming of Conan the Cimmerian* (New York: Del Rey Books, 2003) p. 449.

knows instinctively that no situation is more dramatic than physical conflict, and that no concept is more compelling than the prospect of total sexual fulfillment. Sex and violence are like the primary colors of the artist's palette, regardless of how they may subsequently be blended, softened and refined. Howard was adept in employing the "primal elements" of sex and violence in his prose. He made use of them in ways that were decades ahead of his time, and did so in a sure, knowing fashion. Conan eventually superseded Tarzan in the popular imagination owing in part to Howard's awareness that the typical male's macho fantasies don't consist of monogamy and beating up animals.

Howard was without question an accomplished purveyor of electrifying entertainment, but of course that wasn't *all* he was. Many readers *come to* REH for the high adventure, the action and horror, the sex and violence; but they *stay for* the darker, more compelling aspects of his artistic vision. Howard regarded writing as a profession—he worked at it; he didn't play at it. He believed in giving his readers their money's worth, yet as H. P. Lovecraft noted in his obituary of Howard, he was adept at embodying his worldview within even his most outwardly commercial fiction. Martin Scorcese acknowledged a similar practice among filmmakers when he referred to "the director as smuggler."

Concerning "Xuthal of the Dusk," Howard wrote to Clark Ashton Smith that, "It really isn't as exclusively devoted to swordslashing as the announcement [in *Weird Tales*] might seem to imply."[71] Even so, he later admitted to Lovecraft that he wrote "Red Nails" because "I have been dissatisfied with my handling of decaying races in stories...."[72] "Xuthal of the Dusk" may not rank among the best of the Conan stories, but as we have seen, it is a virtual showcase for the innovative manner in which Howard crafted sexy, violent entertainment. For that reason alone, it merits some attention in its own right.

"Red Nails" casts a deep shadow, but "Xuthal of the Dusk" has been obscured by that slithering shadow for far too long.

WORKS CITED

Herron, Don (ed.). *The Dark Barbarian*. Westport, CT: Greenwood Press, 1984.

---

[71] Robert E. Howard to Clark Ashton Smith, quoted by Patrice Louinet in "Hyborian Genesis", *op cit.,* p. 449.
[72] Howard to Lovecraft, *op cit.,* p. 72.

Howard, Robert E. *The Bloody Crown of Conan*. New York: Del Rey Books, 2004.
___. *The Coming of Conan the Cimmerian*. New York: Del Rey Books, 2003.
___. *The Conquering Sword of Conan*. New York: Del Rey Books, 2005.
___. *Eons of the Night*. New York: Baen Books, 1996.
___. *Selected Letters, 1931-1936*. West Warwick, RI: Necronomicon Press, 1991.

HOWARD'S ORIENTAL STORIES

by Don D'Ammassa

Robert E. Howard is, of course, best known for his heroic fantasy fiction, but the body of his work is surprisingly diverse, making use of contemporary as well as historical and fantastic settings, and his heroes include professional boxers, soldiers, and other mundane professions as well as two fisted, sword swinging adventurers. Influenced by the work of Harold Lamb in particular, Howard was fascinated with the variety of exotic locations and situations suggested by history but, constrained by the markets available to him, devoted comparatively little of his time to historical fiction. During the early 1930s, he wrote several stories which made use of historical Oriental settings. He focused primarily on the interface between western Asia and bordering cultures, the clash of Christianity, Islam, and paganism, although it is evident that he attributed most of the conflict to baser motives than philosophical or even cultural differences. Howard's Orient consisted primarily of Syria, Persia, Iraq, Turkey, and Afghanistan, although his protagonists occasionally wandered further east. Howard wrote most of his historical Oriental fiction during a very short period, but in some cases years would pass before the stories were actually published. He abandoned that particular type of story in favor of more saleable fantastic adventures, although some of his contemporary adventure fiction returned to the Orient, which in his depiction had changed very little during the last several centuries..

One surprising aspect of Howard's historical fiction is that his protagonists are often scoundrels acting chiefly through self interest rather than to uphold some lofty principle. Some are outright scoundrels. They are all formidable fighters and maintain a certain degree of self respect, but they are almost always disenchanted with their own people, and often live in exile, self-imposed or forced. Although such characters might today be considered anti-heroes, it is likely that Howard was simply attempting to create more realistic characters than were commonly found in pulp fiction, people who are neither good nor evil but mixtures of both qualities.

Considering the volume of work that Howard wrote in a comparatively short career, it is not surprising that he employed several plot devices repeatedly including the use of disguises, surprise revelations of a character's true identity, temporary alliances between hero and villain ended, in most cases, by treachery, the search for a fabled treasure, and lengthy treks over hostile terrain. The same constraint may explain why his protagonists are for the most part interchangeable.

The earliest of Howard's Oriental tales is "Red Blades of Black Cathay," written in collaboration with Tevis Clyde Smith. The protagonist is Godric de Villehart, a Norman knight who was unhappy with the policies and behavior of his king. Searching for another cause to champion, he became swept up in a brief, misguided wave of fervor during the late Crusades. By then the initial success of the war against the infidel was only a distant memory, and Godric is further disillusioned to discover that the wealthy Christian merchants insist upon being paid before they will transport the newly recruited knights to the Holy Land. In order to raise the cost of passage, the would-be Crusaders become mercenaries fighting their fellow Christians, and the quest for power and money corrupts their purpose. Godric serves under Boniface de Montferrat, who lusts after power and wealth and has little interest in the avowed purpose of his commission. At his command, Godric takes one hundred men on a futile search for the kingdom of Prester John, a rumored Christian people who might be enlisted as allies, but whom Montferrat transparently wants to conquer. Nor is Godric free of the taint, because his plan is to seize the kingdom for himself.

After losing most of his followers, Godric leads the survivors in a suicidal attack on a band of barbaric Hians. Although he later asserts that he was motivated by the code of chivalry and sought to rescue the princess Yulita, it is evident from his comments about his fallen comrades that he more likely sought to end his own meaningless life in the process. In that he fails, because Yulita herself oversees his recovery and he discovers he has feelings for her. When a crisis forces Godric to make a difficult choice, he decides to abandon her small independent nation and sell his sword to Genghis Khan, their enemy, because "a warrior must pick the winning side." Although Godric feels shame about his decision, he is "weary of fighting for lost causes." Godric is probably Howard's most flawed hero, but he is not the only one who chooses pragmatism over principle.

Another recurring theme is revealed during his conversations with Yulita. She is convinced that Genghis Khan cannot defeat the more civilized cities arrayed against him, but Godric believes otherwise. He is convinced that higher civilizations are inherently doomed to succumb to the vigor of barbarism because they lack the will to defend themselves against a determined enemy. He compares Genghis Khan to the poorly equipped, "naked horde" of Crusaders who successfully conquered the theoretically impregnable city of Constantinople. It is in fact Godric's ability to shrug off the "civilizing French influence" which makes him so formidable in the battle that follows. In Howard's view, a peaceful civilization is a temporary aberration in the flow of history. It is the aggressors who will eventually triumph.

"Hawks of Outremer" follows much the same pattern. The story takes place shortly after the collapse of the Third Crusade. Outremer is that portion of the disputed lands still held by the Christian invaders, momentarily at peace while Saladin prepares a fresh assault. Cormac FitzGeoffrey is the Gaelic bastard of a foreign knight who found no welcome among the peoples of either of his parents. He had killed three men before he was twelve years old, and has led a violent, vindictive life ever since. FitzGeoffrey did not join the Crusade out of Christian fervor but simply to evade his enemies in Ireland. His shield bears a grinning skull and he is described as having a "sinister aspect," yet he is the hero of this story and a sequel.

Once again we learn that the Christian knights have begun to quarrel among themselves and are more interested in personal gain rather than the supposed ideals and goals of the Crusade. One of the Christian lords has been killed or abducted by unknown enemies, and FitzGeoffrey decides to rescue or avenge him to repay an old favor, refusing all assistance and riding off alone. Fairly standard swordplay follows with a maiden rescued and the villains slain, but FitzGeoffrey's apparent altruism is motivated by his sense of personal honor rather than his commitment to a higher ideal. He returns in the less interesting "The Blood of Belshazzar," which is structured in part in the form of a murder mystery. Having become even more alienated from the Christian armies, FitzGeoffrey travels to a den of thieves just in time to be wrongly accused of the murder of the local ruler and the theft of a legendary precious gem. Fabulous jewels or hordes of gold are another recurring element in Howard's Oriental tales, as well as his fantasy. It is FitzGeoffrey's sword and the intervention of another that saves him rather than his wits, and the solution to the puzzle is provided almost as an afterthought. In a third, never completed FitzGeoffrey story, "The Slave Princess," he enlists a young woman in a convoluted scheme of impersonation.

Cahal Ruadh O'Donnel of "The Sowers of the Thunder" is cast from the very same mold. Deprived on his Irish birthright by treachery, he travels among thirteenth-century Muslims en route to Jerusalem, alienated from his homeland and less than sanguine about his current surroundings. As did FitzGeoffrey in "The Blood of Belshazzar," so does O'Donnel also indulge in an unexpected and brief friendship with a Muslim. Howard's characters often forge pragmatic alliances with those who are theoretically their enemies in order to oppose villains from either the Christian or Muslim armies. This is perhaps Howard's most historically rich tale, filled with colorful images and descriptive passages that demonstrate the careful research that must have taken place before these stories were written. While most of the characters are larger than life, the physical setting—including details about clothing, weaponry, historical events, and customs—is portrayed in very detailed, realistic terms.

Once again, the weaknesses of the Christian leadership triumphs over its better nature. The ambition of the nobles and knights overwhelms their faith and sense of honor and they prove themselves to be no less corrupt than the worst of their enemies. Howard goes even further, indicating that even the best of men will bend under sufficient financial pressure. "Poverty drives men to desperate deeds." O'Donnel eventually falls in with Renault d'Ibrin, a Crusader who has turned outlaw and now preys upon the caravans of faithful headed toward Mecca. Paradoxically, he is one of the few people O'Donnel encounters who still maintains some sense of honor, if a somewhat twisted one. Their efforts to warn the people of Jerusalem, both Christian and Muslim, of the impending attack by a horde of Mongols fail and both men die during the course of the story. Their fate seems inevitable from the outset given the fact that neither man has a home or people, and their motives for sacrificing themselves are deliberately left unexplained. This is one of Howard's finest stories, despite an over reliance on coincidence—particularly his repeated encounters with the man who will eventually be his arch-enemy—and the rather unconvincing discovery that a mortally wounded knight is actually the woman who once wronged him, on a personal pilgrimage to expiate her own sins.

Donald MacDeesa, the Scot hero of "Lord of Samarcand," is clearly the same character in a slightly different guise. He too has been forever barred from his homeland because he chose the wrong side in a dispute, even though he acted from a sense of personal honor rather than crass ambition. Howard has moved forward in time to the late fourteenth century, but his view of the clash between civilization and barbarism is no less bleak. MacDeesa helps defeat a particularly brutal warlord, but through treachery and deceit rather than open conflict, and eventually he is in turn betrayed by his closest friends, Timour, the man for whom he has spent most of his adult years fighting and the only woman he ever loved, a Persian girl named Zuleika, who takes other lovers when he isn't looking and who is eventually executed for acting as a courier for their enemies.

Timour—aka Tamlerlane—is an empire builder, but the attitudes he holds toward conquest and rule are another reflection of the ascendance of barbarism. He considers such civilized subjects as philosophy and architecture nothing more than "mist and smoke conquest" and insists that he is a conqueror "before I am a builder." MacDeesa serves him almost to the moment of his own death, but his years in the Orient have not restored the happiness or sense of purpose he enjoyed in Scotland. He admits to himself that his life has been savage and futile and that his comforts are illusions. The reader senses that he has long wished to die in battle, that he has become weary of life. The story contains one of the rare anachronisms in Howard's historical fiction; Tamerlane is shot by a pistol, a technology not yet invented.

The protagonist of "The Lion of Tiberias" fares no better. John Norwald is the descendant of Danes living in northern Britain, his family ruined by the Norman conquerors. Although he fought for Christendom against the Turks, his life is spared by one of them, Achmet, and the two become close companions. When Achmet is murdered through treachery by Prince Zenghi, Norwald is sold as a galley slave, and survives years of hardship because of his determination to live long enough to avenge the death of the only man he ever called a friend. Even Zenghi is impressed by the baseness of his Christian enemies, who sell their loyalties for gold or other material value. Howard makes it clear that he believes that the Christian kingdom of Outremer failed not because the Crusaders were outfought but because they were more corrupt than the Moslems and Mongols. In fact, Zenghi's strategy for defeating the Franks is an alliance of convenience with the Greeks, who clearly feel no loyalty to their Christian brethren.

Not that Howard's infidel characters are any more noble. Zenghi is equally determined to slaughter his Moslem rivals to prevent anyone from interfering with his own ambitions. He uses trickery to avoid technically breaking his word in a dishonorable encounter, and later scorns all acts of mercy, comparing men to wolves—"a man must smite or be smitten." His reign of terror is finally ended by the reappearance of Norwald at an opportune moment, an ending which relies so much on coincidence that it feels both rushed and contrived, certainly the weakest of Howard's Oriental tales.

"The Shadow of the Vulture" is set near the low point for Europe, when the Turks are threatening to invade and the city of Vienna is under siege in the middle of the sixteenth century. The Austrians had earlier sent a delegation to try to influence Suleyman's decision about the future ruler of Hungary, which has fallen under his influence. Once again the Christian leaders are feuding among themselves and are unable to provide a united front, making each of them more vulnerable to Turkish pressure. Among that delegation is Gottfried von Kalmbach, an impressive fighter but a man who has lost faith in his leaders and who too often retreats into drunken stupors to escape awareness of his own failures. Gottfried survives the siege of Vienna by the Turks, largely due to the intervention of Red Sonja, a larger than life woman who fights as well or better than any of the other defenders. She is in fact the most interesting element in the story, and one of the more remarkable Howard characters.

Howard broke his usual pattern in "Gates of Empire" because its protagonist, Giles Hobson, is far from being an heroic figure or a member of the aristocracy. He is an English servant forced to flee to the Orient after a drunken practical joke gets out of hand. Following a string of lucky escapes, he finds himself right in the middle of the political and military maneuvering of Christian and Muslim lords for control of the Nile River, and he betrays one confidence after another in pursuit of personal gain. This time it is also the Muslims who are hampered by their inability to put aside personal interests for the common good as they indulge in an internecine struggle for control of Egypt. And Giles, more by chance than choice, precipitates a battle and ultimately finds a core of heroism within himself.

"The Road of the Eagles" (also known as "The Way of the Swords") pits a band of Christian Cossacks against Muslim pirates and other foes in a multi-sided battle for control of a potential claimant to the throne of Turkey. None of the male characters are portrayed in glowing terms this time; they are variously incompetents, rogues, or villains. Even Prince Orkhan, who seems at first an heroic figure, succumbs to fatalism and surrender, and is only saved from becoming a bargaining piece by Ayesha, his lover, who kills Orkhan to prevent him from falling into the hands of those who would use him for their own self aggrandizement. Ironically, had she held her hand only a short while longer, Orkhan would have been elevated to the throne by his own people, who had rebelled against the former regime, so even her attempt at a noble act is tainted by circumstance. This otherwise fine adventure story is marred by a contrived ending in which the two antagonists discover that they are not only both former Englishmen but that they knew one another during their youth.

Another Christian disguises himself as a Moor in "Hawks over Egypt," which takes place shortly before the beginning of the Crusades. Diego de Guzman is in almost all respects a typical Howard protagonist, a powerful but short tempered warrior exiled for one reason or another from his homeland, in this case Muslim dominated Spain. His purpose is initially the desire to avenge himself on an influential Muslim, which he manages with the assistance of a local man. De Guzman's ally is revealed as a prominent Muslim political figure in disguise, who is destined to become the power behind the throne of Egypt. Howard's frequent pairing of Christian and Muslim characters is probably meant to suggest that the soldiers of those two powers had more in common with each other than they did with their respective ruling classes. De Guzman helps the Muslim acquire political power, although as much for pragmatic purposes as friendship. Similarly, Sir Eric de Cogan, an English knight, makes common cause with Kosru Malik, a Muslim, in "The Road of Azrael" to foil a conspiracy between venial leaders of both faiths.

Howard later wrote several Oriental adventures set during the twentieth century, although at times the physical descriptions, sources of conflict, and other plot elements are virtually identical. They are in general less detailed, presumably because Howard was less familiar with the contemporary Mideast than he was with the historical one. The sparse detail resulted in a faster moving plot, but the texture of the prose is different. Several of them seem more hastily written as well, skipping over sequences that should have been expanded and there are sometimes less than entirely satisfactory endings.

The protagonists of these stories could well be the reincarnations of Howard's earlier heroes. Kirby O'Donnell, from "The Treasures of Tartary," is an American, but he is otherwise almost a carbon copy of Cormac FitzGeoffrey. He travels disguised as a Kurd, attacks his enemies with a sword in preference to a firearm, has only passing interest in women, and is advanced along his path through coincidence and luck as much as by planning. He has traveled to the remote city of Shahrazar in Afghanistan to steal a legendary treasure, impulsively intercedes in a one-sided fight, and through happenstance recovers a seal carried by one of the elite guardians of the treasure. He subsequently escapes one trap by finding a fortuitous secret passage, and survives another when a hostile force attacks just in time to divert his enemies. It is not one of Howard's better constructed tales, and lacks the close detail that brings so much of his work to vivid life.

O'Donnell reappeared in two further stories, one of which is among the best of the Oriental adventures. In that one, "Swords of Shahrazar," he continues his masquerade, but is now trapped by ill luck into leading a mission to seize a diplomatic dispatch. This proves more difficult than expected when a band of bandits intervenes but he prevails by means of his physical prowess as much as his quick wits, potentially preserving British rule of India in the process. His third appearance was in "The Curse of the Crimson God," which actually precedes the other two but did not see print until long after Howard's death. Another exciting treasure hunt story, it is marred by another succession of coincidences.

"The Brazen Peacock" is closer in tone and subject matter to Howard's supernatural fiction, and some of the action takes place outside the Orient. The protagonist hears the story of an adventurer who stole an idol from the temple of Asian devil worshippers, who have subsequently chased him into Africa to retrieve their property and avenge the insult. The ending is both predictable and perfunctory. "The Black Bear Bites" also has fantasy overtones—references to the Cthulhu Mythos of H. P. Lovecraft—but neither story involves any overt supernatural events. The latter describes the effort by a gang of villains to destabilize colonial China. The protagonist, John O'Donnell, is presumably some relation to the hero of "The Treasures of Tartary" and its sequels. In both of these, part of the conflict arises from the avarice of westerners disguised as Arabs, in the former a treasure hunter and in the latter an adventurer who hoped for personal gain amidst the chaos of a rebellion.

The modern stories continued Howard's theme of the corruption of western man by wealth and power. In "Blood of the Gods," we are told that "white men don't forget" in cases where there is "loot in the offing." Francis Gordon, yet another outsider disguised as a Muslim, races a band of thugs to the remote caves where lives a hermit who is supposed to possess a collection of fabulous gems. Gordon is the object of a search by Stuart Brent in "The Country of the Knife." Brent learns from a dying British agent that a Russian, inevitably disguised as a Muslim, has worked his way up to a powerful position within a secretive brotherhood of thieves and threatens to cause chaos in India. He attempts to convey this message to Gordon, who has disappeared in a remote part of Afghanistan, and is taken captive by those very same bandits before being rescued by Gordon himself, predictably wearing yet another disguise.

Howard re-emphasizes his contention that life in that part of the world had changed very little despite the passage of centuries. When a battle erupts in the bandits' stronghold, he tells us that except for the presence of firearms, "it might have been a riot in ancient Babylon." The story itself is well constructed except for a rather clumsy sequence in which the chief villain explains his entire plan to Brent because the American is "so unimportant." There is also an internal inconsistency. Abd el Khafid has converted to Islam "heart and soul" but later asserts that he intends to steal a horde of gold dedicated to Shaitan even though "not a Moslem in the world would touch a grain of it." The third Gordon story, "Son of the White Wolf," is relatively minor, set during World War I and involving a group of renegade Turkish soldiers who decide to abandon Islam and found a new empire. One oddity of the story is that a portion of it is told from the point of view of a female character, a supposed German spy forced into a temporary alliance with Gordon, a rarity for Howard, whose protagonists and narrators are generally very similar to one another. It is enlightening to note that one of the Arab leaders had associated with westerners for so long that he had lost his "primitive integrity," a reflection of Howard's dim view of civilized standards of behavior. The "surprise" ending is that the woman is a double agent and actually on Gordon's side.

Howard's Oriental adventurers are unusually indifferent to the opposite sex, or lack the opportunity for more than a passing relationship. Miles Du Courcey from "The Lion of Tiberias" does apparently have a close relationship with a woman whom he wrongly believes has died during the fall of Edessa, and they are reunited under less than pleasant circumstances later. Many of the female characters, almost all of whom play very minor parts in these stories, are just as dishonorable in their actions as are the men. Cahal O'Donnel lost his family holdings and high position in part because he developed feelings for the wrong woman, who betrayed him, though she subsequently regrets what she has done. MacDeesa takes some comfort in his concubine, Zuleika, but their relationship is, for her part at least, simply a matter of convenience and she takes her physical pleasure elsewhere when circumstances allow.

One of the few women who acts honorably in Howard's historical fiction is Ivga, a tavern wench in "The Shadow of a Vulture," who prefers to die with her people rather than flee when they are attacked by the Turks. She gets her wish. That same story features Howard's best known female character, Red Sonja. Sonja is, if anything, a more daunting warrior than Gottfried and is in many ways a more richly developed character than are most of Howard's male protagonists. Another formidable woman is Ayesha, the courtesan in "The Road of the Eagles," who risks her own life in an attempt to free a noble prisoner. There are two influential courtesans in "Hawks over Egypt," Zaida and Zulaika, but they have only peripheral roles, although it is Zaida who causes the insane Muslim ruler to believe himself Allah incarnate.

Howard made an effort to ensure that his stories were historically accurate. Although in most cases the actual events described were entirely fictional, he always set them within the context of actual events. He was not above taking literary shortcuts however. In "Red Blades in Black Cathay," for example, the Frankish wanderer has no language problems with the peoples among whom he travels, including Genghis Khan himself. Cormac FitzGeoffrey learns the truth about the treacherous death of his friend in "Hawks of Outremer" by conveniently coming across and rescuing one of the few people who knows the truth, then rescues a captive girl in the last few seconds before she is to be mutilated, and is finally rescued himself by the fortuitous and unexpected appearance of Saladin. Coincidental encounters are frequently used to redirect a story line or provide information required to advance the plot.

Unlike many of his contemporaries, Howard had a genuine feel for the flow of history and was particularly careful not just to avoid making obvious anachronistic or historical errors, but also to provide a detailed, highly textured context against which his characters could struggle and triumph, or occasionally fail. His heroes, even though flawed or perhaps because of that fact, seem rather larger than life, even when one of his imaginary characters stands next to one of the giants of history like Tamerlane or Genghis Khan, and by so doing he imparts to them a greater degree of humanity as well. Howard obviously felt that a single individual, no matter what his rank or background, could exert influence on the course of history, that no matter how inconsequential a person might appear, he or she could leave behind at least an anonymous legacy. His protagonists are not kings, but they are kingmakers. History was more than just a collection of dusty facts and old stories to Howard; they were a tapestry of human striving and accomplishment despite the sometimes overwhelming weight of chaos and barbarism.

Bibliography

"The Black Bear Bites" first appeared in *From Beyond the Dark Gateway*, April 1974.
"The Blood of Belshazzar," *Oriental Stories*, Autumn 1931
"Blood of the Gods," *Top Notch*, July 1935
"The Brazen Peacock," *REH: Lone Star Fictioneer*, Fall 1975
"The Country of the Knife," *Complete Stories*, August 1936
"The Curse of the Crimson God," first appeared in *Swords of Shahrazar*, 1978
"Gates of Empire," *Golden Fleece*, January 1939
"Hawks of Outremer," *Oriental Stories*, April-June 1931
"Hawks over Egypt," first appeared in *The Road of Azrael*, Donald Grant, 1979
"The Lion of Tiberias," *The Magic Carpet Magazine*, July 1933
"Lord of Samarcand," *Oriental Stories*, Spring 1932
"Red Blades of Black Cathay," *Oriental Stories*, February/March 1931
"The Road of Azrael," *Chacal* #1, 1976
"The Road of the Eagles," first appeared in *The Road of Azrael*, Donald Grant, 1979, as "The Way of the Swords."
"The Shadow of the Vulture," *The Magic Carpet Magazine*, January 1934
"Son of the White Wolf," *Thrilling Adventures*, December 1936
"The Sowers of the Thunder," *Oriental Stories*, Winter 1932
"Swords of Shahrazar," *Top Notch*, October 1934
"The Treasures of Tartary," *Thrilling Adventures*, January 1935

KING KULL AS A PROTOTYPE OF CONAN

by Darrell Schweitzer

Like so many Robert E. Howard's characters, Kull of Atlantis, is, as commentators from Sprague de Camp onward have noted, cut pretty much from the same cloth as the others. He is a huge, broad-chested man of almost superhuman strength and agility, a savage, exiled by his tribe and forced to wander and fight his way through foreign lands. The grim, outcast-with-a-grudge occurs again and again in the Howardian oeuvre, to some extent in the Conan series and to a greater extent in his crusading stories. Perhaps this figure is a fantasized projection of Howard himself, who often felt himself an outcast and virtually alone in an environment that constrained him without understanding him. What is the entire Howard canon if not a scream of rage and individuality against an uncaring, conformist world?

But Kull is not Conan. This is evident from the start. Conan's upbringing, such as we know of it, was that of a conventional tribal barbarian. It is not entirely certain why he left Cimmeria. In "The Phoenix on the Sword," he talks about what a gloomy place it is. Possibly he left out of sheer wanderlust, or, at first, an adolescent greed for the fabulous loot he'd heard could be had in civilized lands, which must have been well beyond anything available for thieving in backward, impoverished Cimmeria. But we are not told. We do not know.

Kull, on the other hand, is a feral man, closer to Tarzan than Conan. He was raised by tigers and wolves, and can almost make out their language. He fits into human society, even that of stone-age barbarians, uneasily. A classic Howardian individualist (unlike a most real-life primitives), he rebels against tribal customs and taboos. When he sees a woman about to be burnt at the stake for having married outside her tribe, he cannot save her, but he can spare her much pain with a deftly hurled flint knife, then escapes up a cliff amid a storm of spears. Thus, by an act of compassion, he has rejected the only human society he knows and becomes an exile. When we next see him, he is king of Valusia, a barbarian interloper in an ancient and decadent land. Quite a lot must have happened in the meantime, but Howard never wrote that part.

The Kull series as it has come down to us is a fragment, an incomplete work. Howard managed to sell only two Kull stories, "The Shadow Kingdom" and "The Mirrors of Tuzun Thune" in his lifetime, published in *Weird Tales* for August and September, 1929. A poem, "The King and the Oak," appeared in *Weird Tales* after his death. The rest remained among his unpublished papers until many years later, the first book edition being the 1967 *King Kull*, in which three fragmentary stories were completed by Lin Carter.

The unplanned nature of the series is quite obvious. Some of it is immature work. Many of the proper names seem clumsily chosen and unsystematic, certainly far less resonant than those Howard chose in later stories. (Zarfhaana, Kaanuub of Blaal, etc.) Some sound entirely too much like others. In the story in which we meet the dread sorcerer Thulsa Doom (who became Kull's perennial nemesis when the series was adapted into comic-books by Marvel) there is also someone called Julra Thoom.

No less than three of the stories begin with someone appealing to Kull to overrule custom and allow a forbidden marriage. *All* of the completed stories, with the exception of the prologue and two very short episodes, are about plots to remove Kull from the throne of Valusia. Two, "Swords of the Purple Kingdom" and "By This Axe I Rule!" are virtual reworkings of one another, neither with fantastic elements other than the setting, a prehistoric world which long predates even the Hyborian Age of Conan.

It is thus not surprising that the Lancer Books editor, who acquired the first Kull collection, would have wanted someone to complete the series and flesh it out. Readers of that paperback were not Howard scholars or purists who were interested in fragments. They wanted complete stories, particularly ones which might vary and balance the somewhat unsatisfactory structure of the overall series. Of course Lin Carter's completions are no more valid than anyone else's. Others would certainly be possible in the future, even as more than one writer has attempted an ending to Charles Dickens's *The Mystery of Edwin Drood*. Meanwhile, pure-text editions have been published. It is easy to obtain what Howard wrote and nothing else.

"The Shadow Kingdom" and "The Mirrors of Tuzun Thune" are strong stories by any standard, among Howard's best. The former, it may be further argued, holds a genuinely significant place in the history of fantastic literature as the first true sword-and-sorcery story. While there had been several prior stories of fantastic heroes swinging swords and doing deeds of daught in imaginary lands, notably Lord Dunsany's "The Sword of Welleran" and "The Fortress Unvanquishable, Save for Sacnoth" (both in *The Sword of Welleran*, 1908), there is something very different in Dunsany's tone and approach, his irony, his cynical and civilized heroes, and his undertones of black, cosmic comedy. There had been, too, many stories of Atlantis prior to Howard's—and the Kull series is a subset of the Atlantis mythos, though in Howard's version Atlantis is not the center of any lost civilization, but an outlying, barbaric realm.

What is different about "The Shadow Kingdom" is that in this story *all* of the elements we now recognize as sword and sorcery suddenly come together, even as there had been crime stories before, but the formal detective story begins with Poe's "The Murders in the Rue Morgue."

What "The Shadow Kingdom" most potently adds to the mix of fabulous antiquity, furious action, swordplay, eldritch magic (an elder race of Valusian serpent-men who can impersonate humans plot to depose King Kull) is the figure of the barbarian—Kull himself.

This was a new kind of fantasy protagonist, barbarian hero, unspoiled by the "disease" (as a character in another story phrases it) of civilization, strong enough to rule Valusia when the Valusians are too decadent to do so, a feral man who is closer to nature than others, whose half-animal instincts and sheer strength get him out of many a tight fix.

But he is not Conan. For one thing, as we are told over and over, Kull has no interest in women. Conan, it is implied, has done quite a bit of wenching here and there, and when he becomes king of Aquilonia, he even takes a queen. This is not because Kull is homosexual—an idea which would not have occurred to Howard, and which certainly could not have been expressed in a pulp-magazine story—but because he finds any romantic involvement an encumbrance. He is focussed on power and adventure and just staying alive. His total disinterest in sex or love or marriage echoes statements found in Howard's letters that he would probably not marry, because one who travels fastest travels alone. If this seems a slightly immature attitude, recall that Howard was about twenty-one when he was writing these stories. He hadn't met Novelyne Price yet.

The fascination of the series is with Kull himself, a powerful if (for Howard) slightly befuddled presence, who does not fit into the world in which he finds himself. Unlike Conan, who is quite a bit more down-to-earth, Kull is a dreamer, given to metaphysical speculations about the meaning of life and the nature of reality. In "Delcardes' Cat" he is beguiled, even played for a fool (almost fatally) by what seems to be a centuries-old, oracular cat, which can tell him things no man has ever known. He gazes into the mirrors of the wizard Tuzun Thune for the same reason, almost merging with a dream world, vanishing from this one, saved in the nick of time by the faithful and somewhat more realistically-minded Brule the Spear-Slayer, who recognizes that this is a trap to exploit the king's weakness. In story after story (some of which may be reworkings of one another) Kull is told that nothing is real, that "Time, place, and space are illusions, having no existence save in the mind of man" ("Delcardes' Cat"), or that there is no meaningful distinction between life and death: "What does it matter where you are, or whether you are dead, as you call it? You are a part of that great ocean which is Life, which washes upon all shores...." ("The Striking of the Gong"). Indeed, when Kull looks into the magic mirrors and sees a reflection of himself, he asks, "Which of us is the ghost of the other?"

These are existential questions, the sort of thing Philip K. Dick would write about if he'd ever turned his hand to sword-and-sorcery; but they are not the sort of thing which would intrigue, much less entrap the much earthier Conan of Cimmeria. At times we suspect Kull is in the wrong line of work and should have been a shaman.

Kull gathers around himself a cast of repeating characters, more than Conan ever does. Of course, other than in the brief prologue, we only see Kull as king. A king must have counselors and a core of supporters. For all Kull famously proclaims "By This Axe I Rule!"—*i.e.* that he is the state, above the laws, maker and breaker of laws by the strength of his arm and the sharpness of his blade—he must have a constituency if he is to rule for very long. He seems to command loyalty among the Valusian military (which is largely made up of foreign mercenaries anyway), but he also can rely upon Brule the Spear-Slayer, a Pict and stalwart companion; on Ka-nu the Pictish ambassador, who is an older man, more given to pleasure rather than heroism, but wise when it matters; on Lord Tu, a skeptical and cynical courtier who has survived many a plot and doesn't trust women any more than Kull cares for them; and on Kuthulos, a philosopher. These have the beginnings of an interesting ensemble cast. It is a pity that Howard was not more successful with the series and did not develop it further.

After selling the first two stories, Howard doubtless felt he was on a roll, but the series faltered. "By This Axe I Rule!" certainly did not fit into *Weird Tales*. We know it was submitted to, but rejected by, both *Adventure* and *Argosy*. It was too fantastic for them, by virtue of its setting, but not fantastic enough for *Weird Tales*, lacking any supernatural content.

This time, after Kull has once again been dragged into a controversy about a forbidden marriage and discovers that he cannot break the laws of Valusia, which are literally written in stone, various nobles plot to assassinate him, rushing him in his bedroom before he can fully arm himself. Sprague de Camp has pointed out that this seems based on the description of the death of Pizarro from Prescott's *The Conquest of Peru*, but of course Kull is (just barely) a match for the situation and survives. He then proceeds to smash the tablets of the law with his axe, though he is smart enough to proclaim something more than mere tyranny by force. The good laws he will keep, the obsolete ones, he will discard.

"Delacardes' Cat" has fantastic elements aplenty, a Beowulfian battle with monsters below a haunted lake, an elder race of inhumans, much more metaphysical speculation, and an undead, skull-faced sorcerer villain, but it doesn't seem to have clicked at *Weird Tales* either, possibly because it is too diffuse. At this point, after a few more short episodes, fragments, and failures, Howard abandoned the Kull series and went on to other things. We can even see him recycling the skull-faced sorcerer in "Skull-Face," in which the villain's name is Kathulos.

But the more significant recycling, or cannibalization of rejected material came when Howard rewrote "By This Axe I Rule!" into the first Conan story, "The Phoenix on the Sword."

The difference between the two is striking. "The Phoenix on the Sword" is aimed squarely at the *Weird Tales* market, with a good deal of supernaturalism: a hideous demon like a huge, half-mummified baboon, the dread Stygian sorcerer Thoth-Amon, who has lost his powers and been enslaved by a Aquilonian nobleman (but regains them, to wreak hideous vengeance), and even the ghost of a centuries-dead sage, who intervenes to save Conan from doom, because, barbarian or not, the Cimmerian's destiny is now tied to that of the kingdom.

It is a richer, more complicated story. The climax, wherein the conspirators rush a half-armored Conan in his bedroom, survives from the Kull version, as do some of the proper names, bits of the dialogue, and, most significantly, the scene in which the king is sitting at his desk, signing paperwork and yearning for the good old days of adventure.

Here is the Kull version:

> "I wish that I might ride with you to Grondar," said Kull enviously. "It seems ages since I had a horse between my knees, but Tu says that affairs at home require my presence. Curse him!
> "...Looking back now, over the hard path I followed, all those days of toil, slaughter, and tribulation seem like so many dreams. From a wild tribesman in Atlantis, I rose, passing through the galleys of Lemuria—a slave for two years at the oars—then an outlaw in the hills of Valusia, then a captive in her dungeons, a gladiator in her arenas, a soldier in her armies, a commander, a king!" (*Kull*, p. 129)

The Conan version is a virtual paraphrase. Both kings go on with the key observation (in Conan's words this time):

> "I did not dream far enough, Prospero. When King Numedides lay dead at my feet and I tore the crown from his gory head and set it on my own, I had reached the ultimate border of my dreams. I had prepared myself to take the crown, not to hold it. In the old free days all I wanted was a sharp sword and a straight path to my enemies. Now no paths are straight and my sword is useless." (*The Coming of Conan the Cimmerian*, p. 11)

The theme of all these barbarian-as-king stories is the hollowness of the victory. The throne of the barbarian king is never secure. He can never be fully accepted by civilized folk, and so finds himself in a treacherous web of flattery, lies, and assassination attempts. Such a king leads a paranoid, isolated existence. He is very fortunate indeed if he has any loyal friends of the calibre of Tu or Brule the Spear-Slayer. Howard expressed the king's plight very well in the verse quoted at the head of chapter II of "The Phoenix on the Sword:

When I was a fighting-man, the kettle-drums they beat,
The people scattered gold-dust before my horse's feet;
But now I am a great king, the people hound my track
With poison in my wine-cup and daggers at my back.

The few times something like this happened in real history, the results were similar. The Roman emperor Maximinus I, known as Maximinus the Thracian, who reigned A.D. 235-38, was as close to a real-life Conan as anyone ever came, a huge barbarian warrior who joined the Roman army and worked his way up by obvious merit, winning the esteem, even awe of the troops. Then, when faced with a weakling emperor (Severus Alexander) who compromised the soldiers' honor by a cowardly attempt to buy off the enemy, Maximinus seized the throne, only to find himself in a horrible situation, where he was despised by the Senate, hated by the people, surrounded by plots, and forced to bloody repression in a hopeless attempt to survive.

One doubts that Conan's or Kull's reigns would be very successful either, and neither is likely to die peacefully in his bed. It is not surprising to find such a figure reminiscing about the good old days, before he was a king.

This is the crux of the whole business, why the Conan series succeeded and the Kull series did not. Yes, Howard was a slightly more accomplished craftsman by the time he wrote the Conan stories, but the difference in technical excellence between the two is not great, certainly not decisive. "The Shadow Kingdom" and "The Mirrors of Tuzun Thune" are as good as anything Howard ever wrote.

The difference is that by the time Howard came to write the Conan series, he had realized that the hero's "good old days" made a better story than his kingship, which could only consist of (as it does in the Kull series) the barbarian king fending off one rebellion or assassination attempt after another.

It has always been a practical problem in plotting a sword-and-sorcery series that once the hero is "kinged and crowned" (to use Lin Carter's phrase) it is very hard for him to have any wide-ranging adventures. Edgar Rice Burroughs wrestled with this in his Martian series, ultimately settling on protagonists other than John Carter. Warlords of planets or even kings of fabulous lands don't get away that much. They are surrounded by servants, courtiers, and armies and are almost never alone.

After his success with "The Phoenix on the Sword," Howard briefly stumbled, with two Conan stories that Farnsworth Wright did not buy for *Weird Tales*, "The Frost Giant's Daughter" and "The God in the Bowl." Few would claim that these are the best Conan adventures, but what is significant about them is that both take place very early in Conan's career, in his youth or barely beyond it, long before he'd climbed up the ladder of thief, pirate, soldier, military commander, and king. The next Conan story Howard sold was one of the great ones, "The Tower of the Elephant," also about the barbarian's early days. "The Scarlet Citadel" followed, a return to Conan's kingship, and telling of yet another attempt to depose him, a theme Howard did not return to until a couple years later, when he recycled some of the earlier material into the novel, *The Hour of the Dragon*, aimed at the British book market and only published in *Weird Tales* when the book deal didn't work out.

But in the stories that came next and gave the series its momentum, "Queen of the Black Coast," "Black Colossus," "Iron Shadows in the Moon," "Rogues in the House," and so on, we are treated to the magnificent adventures Conan had *on his way* to the throne.

This is the one sense in which the Kull series can be seen as a try-out version of Conan. The character is different. Kull is a very different man from Conan. But in the Conan series, Howard broke out of the monotony of the king on the defensive, fighting for his life and his throne against a nefarious plot in every episode. Conan is able to roam far and wide, and so his saga, and the Hyborian Age, springs fully to life. Howard must have realized that in those few lines in which Kull muses about his days as outlaw, slave, gladiator, and soldier, he had tossed away the *real story*, and was, in the Kull stories he actually wrote, repeating the climax over and over.

When it came time to write Conan, he didn't repeat that mistake.

WORKS CITED

de Camp, L. Sprague. "Conan and Pizarro." In *The Conan Reader*. Baltimore, MD: Mirage Press, 1968.
Dunsany, Lord. *The Sword of Welleran and Other Stories*. London: George Allen, 1908.
Howard, Robert E. *The Coming of Conan the Cimmerian*. New York: Ballantine Books, 2003.
___. *Kull*. West Kingston, RI: Donald M. Grant, Publisher, 1985.
___, and Lin Carter. *King Kull*. New York: Lancer Books, 1967.

HOW PURE A PURITAN WAS SOLOMON KANE?

by Robert M. Price

GOD'S PALADIN

Robert E. Howard placed the adventures of his vigilante hero Solomon Kane in Elizabethan England, when Puritans were beginning to appear on the scene but well before the advent of the Cromwell regime. Nevertheless, he went to no great trouble to make the character into a genuine or convincing Puritan. Yet this is not a failure to carry through a theme consistently. It is as important as the setting itself that Kane does not fit the Puritan stereotype, a fact Howard more than once underlines.

What Michael Moorcock has since made explicit with the heroes of his own multiverse was already implicit in Howard's heroic tales. All the heroes seem to be reincarnations of the same elemental spirit in different times and climes. It is not that they are all the same character, for they have distinct personalities. The two closest-seeming Howard heroes, King Kull and Conan, are yet miles apart, the one mystical and brooding, the other pragmatic and elemental. Bran Mak Morn has little in common with his royal predecessor in Atlantis, brooding though he is. Bran is the incarnation and guardian of his people, whose fate rests upon his shoulders, whereas Kull is an interloper who, almost despite himself, rejuvenates an archaic people and culture. Kane is the solo adventurer like Conan, but he ultimately evades the entanglements of throne and crown, and, while Conan sought his own fortune and glory, Kane seeks but to follow his Arjuna-like dharma, the ineluctable path of the bloody-handed warrior—as a service for his God.

Obviously the Howard heroes, like the Moorcock heroes, share the same role as the mythic hero, but a role is not the same as a character. It is, however, somewhat analogous to the Hindu concept of *atman*, the spark that clothes itself ever and again in flesh and blood and personality. It is a consistent core that travels through history. Howard uses Kane's nominal Puritan identity to symbolize the alienation of that "eternal champion" *atman* from the world around it. He is *in* the world but barely *of* it, a stranger in a strange land. Puritanism symbolizes this well, since the Puritans set themselves stolidly against the spirit of their age, stubbornly refusing to allow the world and its ways into the church. Kane, too, is at odds with the world in which he finds himself, whether England or darkest Africa. He is equally foreign to both. But as for actual, historical, theological Puritanism, Kane hardly fits the picture. Even if Kane does not recognize it, Howard does: "If he thought of it at all, he considered himself a fulfiller of God's judgment, a vessel of wrath to be emptied upon the souls of the unrighteous. Yet in the full sense of the word Solomon Kane was not wholly a Puritan, though he thought of himself as such." (*Red Shadows*, p. 48).

Beyond a basic moral absolutism, Kane's ostensible Puritanism is solely a veneer, the closest-fitting garment available to him in the age he occupies. To convey the point Howard uses Kane's clothing as an explicit metaphor:

> The stranger's clothing was simple, severely plain and suited the man. His hat was a black slouch, featherless. From heel to neck he was clad in close-fitting garments of a somber hue, unrelieved by any ornament or jewel. No ring adorned his powerful fingers; no gem twinkled on his rapier hilt and its long blade was cased in a plain leather sheath. There were no silver buttons on his garments, no bright buckles on his shoes, Strangely enough the drab monotone of his dress was broken in a novel and bizarre manner by a wide sash knotted gypsy-fashion about his waste. This sash was silk of Oriental workmanship; its color was a sinister virulent green, like a serpent's hide, and from it projected a dirk hilt and the black butts of two heavy pistols.... His appearance suggested the Puritan, yet—("The Blue Flame of Vengeance," p. 186)

The gypsy sash, of course, is the ineradicable influence of his many adventures. He wears their trace like a dueling scar, and they have left their mark upon his soul. His association with the shaman N'longa, for instance, went way beyond the pale of what Cotton

Mather would ever countenance, but experience has shown Kane that the world is wider than his creed. He carries the ancient juju staff, though he knows good and well that, according to the confines of his Puritan faith, he should not. But then so much for Puritanism.

Howard has Solomon Kane make precious few statements of faith, or at least of theology. When he does, he sometimes gets it right, sometimes wrong. Kane curses an opponent as "offal of Purgatory" ("Blue Flame of Vengeance," p. 206) which he probably would not do, since Puritans repudiated all such vestiges of Papist dogma, believing in only heaven and hell. On the other hand, Kane has a lively sense of creaturely humility, right out of both Puritan devotionalism and the Deuteronomic theology of the Old Testament. Human strength in and of itself is a snare and a delusion; only when the self-abnegating soul resolves, with John the Baptist, "He must increase and I must decrease" (John 3:30) will divine energy flow. "'Nay, alone I am a weak creature, having no strength or might in me; yet in times past hath God made me a great vessel of wrath and a sword of deliverance." ("The Moon of Skulls," p. 168).

Kane seems not so sure of his salvation: "I come out of the sunset and into the sunrise I go, wherever the Lord doth guide my feet. I seek—my soul's salvation, mayhap" ("The Blue Flame of Vengeance," p. 220). At first such uncertainty may seem odd, given the ringing certainties of Reformation faith, according to which one focused on the objective saving work of Jesus Christ, and not upon one's own good works.

But in fact Puritanism did foster terrible introspection and melancholy. John Calvin, whose theology Puritanism imbibed, had imagined that the belief in divine predestination would be a great comfort for the average Christian, since it should assure him that his salvation was safe with God, who had elected him, and did not rest on his own fickle, feeble efforts. What the Puritans saw that Calvin had not seen was that one could scarcely just assume one's membership among the elect. If God's choice of the saved at the dawn of time was truly a matter of "unconditional election," not predicated on any foreseen righteousness, then mustn't even the piety of the Christian life be deemed equally irrelevant? God might have predestined one to hell anyway, and no amount of pious good works could change that! It was a perverse and yet consistent reading of Calvin. But many Puritans reasoned that prosperity might count at least as a sign of election, for why would God waste his blessings on those he had already written off? We might understand Solomon Kane's career of wreaking the vengeance of the Lord as a similar attempt to secure, if not divine grace, then at least evidence of God's calling.

Kane also dares to court heretical beliefs when his inherited creed proves itself inadequate to account for the wonders of the wider world. For instance, what is he to make of the bat-winged vampire-men of Africa? They can scarcely be the demons of the Bible since they bleed and die. "Perhaps they were the offspring of a forbidden and obscene mating of man and beast; more likely they were a freakish offshoot on the branch of evolution—for Kane had long ago dimly sensed a truth in the heretical theories of the ancient philosophers, that Man is but a higher beast." ("Wings in the Night," p. 318).

What's this? Was evolutionism a known option in Kane's time? In fact, it was. As Howard says, it had already been surmised by ancient natural philosophers (notably the pre-Socratic Ionian philosopher Anaximander) that all life had emerged from the sea and that human beings must have descended from some hardier species whose young did not pass through so long a period of infant vulnerability as we do. What Darwin discovered so much later was the *mechanism* of evolution, namely natural selection. As far as I know, the Puritans had nothing to say on the matter. Did they even know some form of evolutionism had been espoused by St. Augustine, he whose predestinarianism Calvin had inherited?

EXILE FROM CHRISTENDOM

Solomon Kane's greatest departure from Puritanism is his solitary existence and his lonely mission of exacting God's justice. Puritanism was above all else a corporate affair. It was all about the proper order for the faith community. Puritanism was both a program of Congregationalist (anti-episcopal) Church government reform and a theocratic system of civil government. Christian existence took place in the congregation. It was there that the preaching of the saving message went forth, there that the individual met God and tasted of divine grace. And in the church the individual stayed, like a plant receiving its needful nourishment in a hothouse.

The Puritans had inherited the chief dilemma of the so-called Magisterial Reformation. Protestant Reformers taught that all believers must receive for themselves the saving grace of Christ. It must be an individual crisis experience of New Birth. Such preaching tends naturally toward individualism. But at the same time neither the Lutherans, Calvinists, or Zwinglians wanted to give up the medieval Catholic notion of "Christendom," a Christian civilization and society into which everyone entered through the gate of infant baptism. In this the individual had no choice. As Martin Luther eventually rationalized it, one's conscious, volitional decision for grace was a subsequent actualizing or appropriation of the baptismal sacrament chosen for one by one's Christian parents. The Anabaptist wing of the Reformation was more consistent in simultaneously dropping infant baptism and Christendom, advocating instead the separation of church and state. But not the Puritans! It was not as if theocratic regimes like that of Calvin in Geneva or the slightly later Puritans of Cromwellian England or of Massachussetts Bay Colony let the church run the state's affairs. No, church and state were twin arms of Christendom, rather like two of our three branches of government.

To the New England Puritans, the problem of a corporate Christian community as a whole versus a band of true believers, self-selected on the basis of individual conversion experiences, was no merely abstract dilemma. They had to decide who would have what status in church. Solomon Stoddard created the compromise theology of the "Halfway Covenant." On this widely adopted understanding, every colonist was baptized into the Puritan Christian community and therefore could and must attend church. But if one had somehow not experienced the grace of God through a crisis of conversion, one was not eligible for taking communion. But all citizens were Christian enough to be rightful subjects of Old Testament law, which the Puritans made the basis for civil society in the New World.

Solomon Kane is completely oblivious to all this. He does not even bother attending church, as far as we know, much less being a steady member of a home church. He wanders the earth like the Wandering Jew, or like his biblical namesake Cain. And as for adherence to the biblical statutes governing the Puritan community, they are nothing to Solomon Kane. Granted, there were witch-finders and inquisitors among the Puritans, but Solomon Kane, a fanatical vigilante, is of a totally different breed. Here is a man who knows himself intuitively for the angel of death, the living sword of the Lord. It does not occur to him either that he requires civil authorization for his one-man vengeance crusades or that he is usurping God's prerogative: "'Vengeance is mine,' saith the Lord, 'I will repay'" (Deuteronomy 32:35). No, Solomon Kane looks in the mirror and sees the angel of judgment ready to unleash burning plagues on the sinners of the earth. He is divine judge and jury.

> "It hath been my duty in times past to ease various evil men of their lives—well, the Lord is my staff and my guide and methinks he hath delivered mine

enemy into mine hands." ("Blue Flame of Vengeance," p. 189)

"I work the will of God. While evil flourishes and wrongs grow rank, while men are persecuted and women wronged, while weak things human or animal, are maltreated, there is no rest for me beneath the skies" (*ibid.*, p. 221).

That his sense of calling to be what Luther called "the left hand of God" does not quite fit the religion he thinks he belongs to is hinted in "The Hills of the Dead," where Howard reads Kane's subconscious mind: "Kane could not have analyzed this call; he would have attributed it to Satan, who lures men to their destruction. But it was but the restless turbulent spirit of the adventurer, the wanderer" (p. 229).

But maybe it is a little more than that. In Solomon Kane, Howard has drawn a parallel with Kierkegaard's "knight of faith." In his essay "Fear and Trembling" Kierkegaard sought to explain Abraham's motivation and his justification in the moment he sought to sacrifice his son Isaac at the seeming command of God. What business did the patriarch have setting aside the command of God, "Thou shalt not kill"? (Better, "Thou shalt do no murder.") He was no simple transgressor of the law. Rather, he understood implicitly that God's command addressed not to the nation of Israel through Moses, but directly aimed at him personally, elevated Abraham above the level where general laws apply. The lesson Kierkegaard drew was that, if one hears the existential call of God in one's soul, one sees that *the individual is exalted above the absolute*. Israel must not kill. Man must not kill. But if God tells him to, Abraham must kill. And so must Solomon Kane, in sovereign freedom from the strictures of Oliver Cromwell or Cotton Mather. Solomon Kane is a poor Puritan because he is the sword of the living God. If there is a Howardian type of Christianity, I'd say that's it.

* * * * * * *

{All quoted passages come from Robert E. Howard, *The Savage Tales of Solomon Kane* (NY: Del Rey/Ballantine Books, 1998.

BALTHUS OF CROSS PLAINS

by George H. Scithers

The story "Beyond the Black River" is, to me, one of the best stories of the Conan series. Like all of Howard's stories, this one is a rousing adventure. It introduces a bit of mythology—demonology if you prefer—that is surprisingly Lovecraftian. And it gives an insight into the character of Howard himself.

As a story, it contains defeat as well as victory, and tragic death as well as thrilling rescue. There are the Picts, the bloodthirsty wild men of western Hyboria (whom some people see as cognates of the Amerinds, although in fact some of the Amerinds went in for far more diabolical tortures than anything Howard ever wrote), implacable enemies of the more civilized Aquilonians. Stealth, swordplay, and slaughter play their part in the story, as does magic, defeated at last by the agility and power of the Cimmerian's iron-muscled physique. And there is more:

> My brother had not whispered your name to the black ghosts that haunt the uplands of the Dark Land. But a bat has flown over the mountains of the dead and drawn your image in blood on the white tiger's hide that hangs before the long hut where sleep the Four Brothers of the Night.... Thunder rumbled through the black Mountain of the Dead and the altar hut of Gullah was thrown down by a wind from the Gulf of Ghosts. The loon which is a messenger to the Four Brothers of the Night flew swiftly and whispered your name in my ear.... Your head will hang in the altar hut of my brother. Your body will be eaten by the black-winged, sharp-beaked Children of Jhil. (*King Conan*, Gnome Press, p. 110)

But where is this Dark Land? Who are the Four Brothers of the Night? What is Jhil? Howard never says. They are sufficient to themselves and are not seen again; a happy contrast to Howard's somewhat tiresome habit of reusing the same names for entirely unrelated persons and places in his stories. There are *swarms* of Valerii.

But the most important element in the story is the characterization of the secondary hero, Balthus, originally of the Tauran, and the resemblance between Balthus and Howard.

Consider Balthus's appearance:

> "He was a young man of medium height, with an open countenance and a mop of tousled, tawny hair.... Though not tall, he was well built, and the arms that the short, wide sleeves of his tunic left bare were thick with corded muscle.... [A young man with] frank countenance and strongly knit frame." (p. 58.)

Consider Balthus's homeland: the Tauran, a rural section of Aquilonia, though long settled, is close enough to the frontier to be steeped in the traditions of the border and he wars and feuds with both Picts and Cimmerians.

But all this, except of course for the detail of Balthus's tawny hair, is a fairly good description of the black-haired Robert E. Howard himself and the post oak region of Texas where he lived. And although it has been pointed out by a number of writers that Conan was an idealized version of Howard, Balthus seems to me to be a more accurate characterization of his author. The contrast between the man from the Tauran and the barbarian from Cimmeria brings this out even more clearly.

Conan is basically feral; his experience with civilization has produced no real change in his essential wildness. Balthus was born and raised in settled, relatively stable surroundings; his woodcraft is a deliberately learned thing. Well learned craft, it is true, but still a craft, instead of the almost instinctive behavior of the Cimmerian. Then too, under stress, Conan becomes wholly wild, while Balthus tends towards more civilized behavior. Certainly Balthus is more dependent on the people around him than is Conan, the self-sufficient and altogether self-reliant barbarian.

Yet nowhere in all this is there any suggestion that Balthus is any weakling—on the contrary, he is a fighter and an athlete in his own right—even as Howard himself was. Balthus seems small only when measured against Conan's mighty frame and almost superhuman strength and agility. "Among the settlements of the Tauran [Balthus] was accounted a good runner, but Conan was leaving him behind with maddening ease." And so it is in almost all respects; Balthus is good, Conan is better.

Through all this, Balthus emerges as the more identifiable character, and not entirely because the majority of the story is told from his viewpoint. Balthus is closer to what we—and Howard—are or can be. He is the product of civilization, as are most of us. For him, the wilderness can be a place of menace, and of loneliness. He is not, as was Conan, "concerned only with the naked fundamentals of life...Bloodshed and vilolence and savagery were the natural elements of the life that Conan knew...," and in this he is a contrast to Balthus, who is deeply affected by death, even as Howard tragically was.

Here is one further detail: Slasher, the dog that Conan and Balthus meet near the Black River itself. Howard's dog, Patch, had been with him for twelve years; he died only a few years before this story was written, and his death was one of the greatest losses Howard suffered. Slasher, the dog of the story, joins Conan and Balthus, but it is Balthus who pats him and it is Balthus that Slasher stays with until the end.

I suggest, then, that it is Balthus of the Tauran who is really Robert E. Howard; they are more alike, both physically and mentally, than are Conan and his chronicler. When, in this story, Balthus first meets Conan:

> ...[Balthus] emerged dubiously and stared at the stranger. He felt curiously helpless and futile as he gazed on the proportions of the forest man—massive iron-clad breast, and the arm that bore the reddened sword, burned dark by the sun and ridged and corded with muscles. He moved with the dangerous ease of a panther; he was too fiercely supple to be a product of civilization, even of the fringe civilization which composed the outer frontiers. (p. 60)

Here we have Howard-as-he-really-wished-to-be.

I think this meeting was very real to Robert E. Howard. Certainly the principal characters, Balthus and Conan, have come to life in the pages of this story. Much of the aliveness is, I believe, simply due to the fact that Howard *had* put himself into the story; had given himself an opportunity to get to know Conan.

It is in this story then, "Beyond the Black River," that Conan and his creator get acquainted; and their meeting makes a wonderful tale.

FICTIONALIZING HOWARD

by Gary Romeo

Before L. Sprague de Camp's full-length biography, *Dark Valley Destiny*, Robert E. Howard fans had to rely on snippets from letters, reminiscences from his acquaintances, and book introductions for any facts relating to his life.

The key introduction was the Arkham House volume *Skull-Face and Others* published in 1946. August Derleth writes in his foreword that Howard "had in him the promise of becoming an important American regionalist...only to have this promise cut short by the curious complex which caused him to take his own life...." H. P. Lovecraft follows with his "Robert E. Howard: A Memoriam." Here we get some standard biographical information: birth date, birth location, and family background. We learn that Howard starting writing at age fifteen. Howard was interested in ancient history, particularly Celtic history. Lovecraft states that Howard's westerns reflected his "growing ability and inclination to reflect the backgrounds with which he was directly familiar." Lovecraft praises Howard's writing ability, restates his love of sports, history, and travel. He also states that Howard was politically liberal and concerned with civic injustice. Lovecraft concludes that Howard "suggested more than casually his own famous character—the intrepid warrior, adventurer, and seizer of thrones, Conan the Cimmerian."

E. Hoffmann Price adds more to the discussion. Price tells us of the Howard and Lovecraft correspondence and mentions his own letters from Howard. Price recalls meeting Howard face to face. (The only fellow *Weird Tales* writer to do so.) "The meeting is still clear in my memory: that broad, towering man with a bluff, tanned face and a big, hearty hand, and a voice which was surprisingly soft and easy, instead of the bull-bellow one would expect of the creator of Conan and those other swashbucklers."

Howard's father and mother impressed Price with their welcoming manner. Price mentions Howard's quirks and feelings of being an outsider in this conventional small town. Price says Howard would mention being slighted by some in the town and talked of enemies. Price says, "During his thirty years of life, I believe that he lived in two worlds, and if, as they tell us, there is not only an afterlife but a retention of identity, it must have been very easy and natural for Robert E. Howard to step from this lane to the next."

Price goes on to tell of Howard's final days and how his mother's failing health was bothering him and later we learn of Howard's "permanent departure to avoid facing the tragedy of life and home without his mother." Price's friendship with Howard's father continued after Howard's suicide. It is through Dr. Howard's correspondence with Price that we learn of Howard's love of poetry, his sojourn to Brownwood to avoid the burying of his dog Patch, and being a victim of bullying as a young boy. Price sums up: "I repeat, I have wished many a time that Robert had had somewhat more of his father's courage to resist and strength to endure."

It was the Lancer Conan series that introduced Howard to millions. The volume entitled simply *Conan*, published in 1967, retold this standard biography with a few updates. As pedestrian a life as it was, it fascinates enough to be the source of argument and discussion to this very day. De Camp sometimes seems deliberately provocative.

De Camp wrote: "His personality was introverted, unconventional, moody, and hot-tempered, given to emotional extremes and violent likes and dislikes." He later wrote, "Howard was maladjusted to the point of psychosis. For several years before his death, he talked of suicide. At thirty, learning that his aged mother—to whom he was excessively devoted—was on the point of death, he ended a promising literary career by shooting himself."

Despite, or most likely because of, this somewhat sensationalist talk fans became so interested in Howard's life that Sprague finally put together his full-fledged biography *Dark Valley Destiny* published in 1983. Starting in 1989 collections of Howard's letters appeared in chapbooks by Necronomicon Press. Spurred by Sprague's interviews and inquiries some of Howard's friends began writing their own books. Tevis Clyde Smith was only able to give us bits and pieces of Howard's life and these reminiscences were undoubtedly colored by Smith's very conservative politics. Smith's Howard comes across as more racist than we'd like. *Report on a Writing Man* (a collection of various articles spanning the years 1928-1986) was published in 1991. While interesting, it is uneven and choppy.

Better, and lengthier, was Novalyne Price Ellis's *One Who Walked Alone* published in 1986. This book and the following movie *The Whole Wide World* released in 1996 are the new standard. While not very different from previous accounts in total, fans really take to this "romantic" version of Robert E. Howard. Novalyne is now the fan favorite expert on Howard. The movie is also a favorite among Howard fans and their wives.

Reading the various book introductions, de Camp's biography, and the reminiscences of his friends still fails to give us a complete picture of Robert E. Howard. Several authors have turned to fiction since all else has left us wanting.

The very first author to fictionalize Robert E. Howard was Robert E. Howard. Howard wrote an autobiographical novel later entitled *Post Oaks and Sand Roughs* when he was twenty-three. The manuscript was believed lost for a time. It was finally published in 1990.

Howard's alter ego is named Steve Costigan. Steve loves sports, particularly football and boxing. The more violent, the better. Steve is uncomfortable with mankind in general and his friends in particular. Steve greets his best friend and thought "there seemed a slight restraint between them...." Steve thinks about the fellows rooming with him at the boarding house, "barred from the companionship of the rest of the boys by his instinctive reserve he fell back more and more on his writing." Steve is, to borrow an opinion, "introverted, unconventional, moody, and hot-tempered, given to emotional extremes and violent likes and dislikes." He doesn't seem overly dependent on his mother though. He mentions regret at not being able to buy her a nice Christmas present due to lack of funds and mentions getting most of his extra spending money from her while attending school in Redwood. He mentions his mother as encouraging his writing and indulging his "laziness" at finding employment. Perhaps meaningful, he barely mentions his father at all. Steve likes nothing better than boxing with friends, even when getting the worst of it. He takes pride in his cuts and bruises. He is highly critical of both his boxing and writing skills. Most of the self-criticism is so overdone it suggests self-esteem issues. Yet, at the same time, Steve delights in his eccentricities.

One of the funniest lines in the book appears when Steve is discussing literary themes with Lars Jansen. One isn't quite sure if Howard meant this to be funny or not. In either event it is classic Howard.

Lars asks:

"I bought me some books and took a correspondence course in scenario writin'. It's a great help. It tells you all the twenty dramatic situations. What do you think is the greatest dramatic situation?"

"Sacrifice," said Steve. "A man givin' up his life to kill his enemy by dyin'."

"That's what they say, only they say sacrifice to save somebody."

The novel rambles on with Steve's introspection and musing. There is a long middle section concerning a prank that Clive and Spike play on Steve. Clive introduces his girlfriend Gloria to Steve. The girl was instructed to be heavily flirtatious with him. Spike and Clive assumed Steve's flustered inexperience with girls would be amusing. Steve turns the tables and out flirts the girl and kisses her several times over the course of the night. This causes a rift between the boys that eventually gets settled.

The oil boom comes to Lost Plains and Steve hates the roughnecks and hates the promoters. Recognizing the literary drama inherit in all this, Steve just "hated them all too much to write about them." Steve plods on writing for "Bizarre Stories" all the while. Steve seems most happy when discussing poetry with Clive.

Throughout the book Steve talks of adding enemies to his list. Most of the enemies are simply employers who fired him. Steve gets friendlier with the oil-boom crowd while working as a soda jerk. "A boom town drugstore is an ideal place to study humanity. Steve became acquainted with, and sometimes friendly to, whores, bootleggers, gamblers, dope fiends, and yeggs...." Steve notices an oil tough stuffing a magazine down his shirtfront. Steve asks the man, "Are you pregnant?" The man returns the magazine, apparently amused at Steve's question. Howard narrates that Steve was ready to drive a hidden ice pick through the man's heart.

The book ends with Steve finally giving in to his red rages and black moods. Steve arrives late to a new job and the employer derides him by making jest of his writing poetry. Steve proceeds to savagely beat the fellow. It is all wild fantasy and reflects a real immaturity about life. The novel comes to its dead end conclusion and has Steve leaving Lost Plains intent of traveling around and experiencing life *à la* Jack London.

It is undoubtedly a mistake to take this novel too seriously as a literal look into Howard's soul. After all, he was still quite young when he wrote it. And while it is an interesting look at the author it is far too self-critical and fanciful to really be a reflection of his actual life.

Novalyne Price Ellis wrote a radio play in 1947 featuring a fictionalized REH. The play, *Day of the Stranger*, was reprinted by Necronomicon Press in 1989. Howard, the Stranger, is described thusly: "Underneath the gay, whimsical speech of the Stranger is a keen knowledge of the desires and loves that motivate the lives and actions of human beings. He is one of those gifted and charming persons who seem destined to be forever on the outside watching and imagining, rather than actually experiencing the things they observe."

The play features a waitress, Jeanne, who loved a young man who is believed to have died during the war. This Stranger shows up at her lunch counter and is a dead-ringer for the young man. Their love is almost rekindled but Jeanne chooses the more practical Jerry. This REH doppelganger comes across as a romantic dreamy figure and a bit forlorn.

L. Sprague de Camp's "Far Babylon" first appeared in 1976. W. Wilson "Willy" Newbury, de Camp's alter-ego, who is constantly elbow-rubbing the supernatural but seems otherwise a prosaic banker, meets Robert E. Howard building sand castles on a Texas shore. Newbury asks about the sandcastle and is told that it is a model of Babylon. REH then waxes forth with a poem about Babylon. Newbury tells REH that he has traveled to Babylon and that, "It looks like the place in your poem, except where they've excavated the remains of the ancient buildings. These seem to have been all made of plain brown mud bricks. Must have been a pretty monotonous-looking place when it was alive." REH responds, "Reckon I'd prefer my dream Babylon to the real thing. But that's life. Still, I wish I could have seen it. I thought, when the change came, that at least I'd be able to go. It didn't seem much to ask." Puzzled, Newbury asks REH to explain, but he is only given a rather oblique reply. The next day, Newbury remembers a conversation he had with a mechanic about a local writer:

> "He didn't look like my idea of a writer," said the mechanic. "Writers ain't nothing but skinny little characters who couldn't punch their way out of a paper bag. This was a big, two-fisted guy. I think he was a little touched, always talking about old ruins and fooling around with stories instead of getting a regular job."
> "What happened to him?" [Newbury] asked.

"Dead. Shot hisself."

De Camp has Newbury realize he has seen a ghost. End of story. De Camp sets an effective mood with his poetic opening sentence, "Under the lucent moon, a man in a black cowboy hat was squatting by the stream, making a castle of sand." And the cliché ending works. It all seems "right" after the immediate read. However if you think about it too long, it loses the mood. No one wants to think of REH trapped on this earthly plane forever resigned to only dreaming about ancient ruins.

Richard A. Lupoff's *Lovecraft's Book* was published in 1985. It is a "what-if" story about H. P. Lovecraft and Nazi sympathizers. Howard is brought into the story to get information about a transplanted Texas dentist who heads a Ku Klux Klan outfit in Georgia. Howard is depicted as a tough-minded borderline psychopath who loves his mother. Before heading out on his adventure, Howard arms himself, hugs his mother, and checks his car for booby-traps left by his enemies. Bob liquors up a bit and proceeds to intimidate his friend Lindsay Tyson for information. According to the story, Lindsay is a local Klan leader and REH is willing to pull a loaded gun on his friend for the needed information.

The REH presented here is probably not too off-putting for some fans. This is sort of the "Two-Gun Bob" of Lovecraft's imagination coupled with the Doc Howard's crazy son of Cross Plains and E. Hoffmann Price's reminiscences. Howard is rather racist but not a Klan member. Howard is close to his mother but not weak or effeminate. He comes across mainly as a crazy tough guy.

Robert Silverberg won a Hugo for his novella "Gilgamesh in the Outback" in 1987. That story became the basis for the expanded novel *To the Land of the Living*. The novel seems derivative of Phillip Jose Farmer's Riverworld series that started with the brilliant *To Your Scattered Bodies Go*, but petered out to an unsatisfying conclusion. Both books feature an afterlife where all of Earth's citizens, famous and non-famous, are resurrected. It is a nice concept that allows the author to have famous people from different eras comingle.

In this story Robert E. Howard and H. P. Lovecraft are reunited in the afterworld and are working for King Henry VIII. Howard is described a big barrel-chested man with powerful arms and a deep tan. Howard drives recklessly through the landscape all the while mentioning the beauty of Texas. Howard and Lovecraft come upon the powerful and heavy muscled Gilgamesh. Howard looks

"...up with awe and something like rapture in his eyes at the towering huntsman."

"A look of adoration, almost the sort of look a woman might give a man when she has decided to yield herself utterly to his will."

Howard wrestles with feelings for Gilgamesh. Silverberg has Howard think about a true-life incident he wrote upon viewing bathers at the Cisco Dam. "For a while he looked at them and reveled in their physical perfection. And then as he listened to them shouting and laughing and crying out in their foul-mouthed way he began to grow angry, seeing them as mere thoughtless animals who were the natural enemies of dreamers like himself." Silverberg presents Howard as a latent homosexual.

The men are attacked and Howard freezes in battle. Lovecraft brokers the peace. Howard continues to agonize over his lustful thoughts for Gilgamesh. Complications ensue, lots of famous names are tossed out, and Gilgamesh is reunited with Enkidu. They leave Howard and Lovecraft behind. Howard pines:

"He had wanted to be Gilgamesh's brother, or perhaps—he barely comprehended it—something more than a brother. But that could never have been, knowing that the man who seemed so much like his Conan was lost to him forever, Howard felt tears beginning to surge uncontrollably within him."

There is probably nothing more anger-inducing among Howard fans than suggesting that he or some of his characters were homosexual. But voluminous knee-jerk reactions of personal prejudices are not facts in and of themselves. Until *Dark Valley Destiny* and *One Who Walked Alone* were published very little was known about Howard's social life. We knew he had his literary minded friends in Brownwood and that he was a loner. The mere speculation that he might have been a homosexual should not be off-putting, but Silverberg's Howard rings false.

In any event, *Dark Valley Destiny* and *One Who Walked Alone* establish Howard firmly in the (would-be) breeder camp.

Quest for Riverworld published in 1993 was a collection of short stories set in the previously mentioned Riverworld created by Phillip Jose Farmer. David Bischoff and Dean Wesley Smith's story "Nevermore" is primarily about Edgar Allan Poe. REH features as a bit player:

"A heavyset, powerful-looking fellow with a square face and short hair worked hard at a stack of kindling. He was singing some song in a low voice that would alarmingly bellow out for a verse, then die down to a whisper. Some ditty about a 'Yellow Rose of Texas.'"

Howard and Lovecraft are back together, along with Edgar Rice Burroughs, Lester Dent, Frederick Faust, and other authors publishing works in the afterlife. It is a pulp fan's dream. Most Riverworld stories feature the protagonist trying to find his or her former wife/girlfriend/etc. These short story collections reused this idea to tedium. This story is no exception. Poe is looking for his ex-wife. Howard says:

"First thing I did was look for Maw. Found her too, but took a while. She's got herself a home now and I know just where to go visit her.... But you know, Mister Poe, now that I got my buddies here and this publishing house...well, I don't think about Maw so much any more."

Most Howard fans would probably like the Howard portrayed here. He is described as a big strapping guy. His "maw" fixation cured by having some mutually minded friends in the afterlife that help get him laid regularly. The story has a turn of events where Nazis takeover the presses. Howard is suitably heroic in resisting them. There is next to nothing be upset by in this portrayal.

The latest novel featuring Howard is *Shadows Bend* by David Barbour and Richard Raleigh published in 2000. Most Howard fans seem to like this novel well enough, even though it follows de Camp's views in the main. It is fun to think of Howard and Lovecraft as this iconic team of pulp authors sharing in bizarre adventures.

The details are off at times; they mention "an upstairs" for the Howard house, for instance but the authors clearly like the characters and put them through their paces without any undue potshots at their foibles. Perhaps, more unforgivable, for Howard purists is a later reference to Red Sonja as a "counterpart of Conan the barbarian." It rankles some that this character created by Roy Thomas for the Marvel Comic has been passed off as a genuine Howard creation in comics, books, movies and TV.

Howard is very close to his mother and there is friction between him and his father. The dialog rings true-enough while reading along. Howard reluctantly agrees to going on a trip with Lovecraft to meet up with Clark Ashton Smith. Strange things have been happening since Lovecraft was mailed an ancient artifact. Smith's knowledge of the arcane is needed. Howard doesn't want to leave his mother alone but Lovecraft's artifact might have healing powers. Howard's father bullies him into going on the trip. Howard doesn't want to leave his sick mother but finally agrees.

The road trip is amusing at times. The authors have a good deal of fun with Howard's "big" Texas personality and Lovecraft's "proper" New England one. Howard is presented as a man of action. He gets into a fistfight with some toughs harassing a pretty girl. Howard, while shy, comes across as suitably interested in the girl. The novel pads out the road trip with various incidents that get a little repetitious. When the trio arrives at Clark Ashton Smith's house, the girl, Gloria McKenna is instantly attracted to Smith.

McKenna discusses Howard with Smith: "He rebuffed me that night pretending he was morally outraged, but I think it was really because he was scared.... Do you think he might be a virgin?"

Smith answers: "Given the deportment of his heroes in his writing, that wouldn't surprise me at all. We really can't hide our true selves even in our most fantastic work."

Smith is apparently thinking of Solomon Kane and King Kull instead of Conan and Wild Bill Clanton.

Howard and McKenna get a little closer later in the novel and Howard discusses his mother's dislike of his girlfriend, Novalyne. McKenna explains: "Mother is always the central woman in a man's life. You're always her baby, no matter how old you are. It's natural for any mother to feel like her baby's girlfriend is an intruder After all, who's going to take better care of her baby than she could?"

Eventually the trio leave Smith behind and they resume their adventure. They enter a cave and Cthulhu and his minions attack the trio in dreams and visions. Howard imagines his father using an aspirator to pump out his mother's congested lungs. His father starts pumping out not just congested mucus but blood and guts. Blood and mucus become snakes and snakes become his father's attacking penis. Lovecraft and McKenna confront their own psychological horrors.

McKenna is the first to snap out of it. She wakes Lovecraft who in turn wakes Howard. McKenna inserts the artifact they had been carrying into its magical slot and all gets set aright. There is another attack as they leave the cave and McKenna dies saving the two men.

The novel concludes with the men promising to stay in touch and keep writing. There is a final postscript where Howard's suicide is retold and Lovecraft dies of cancer.

Howard is definitely heroic in the novel, a fit writer for adventure stories. The author's captured some of what we know about Howard's demeanor and personality. While trying for some psychological horror angles they latched on to the obvious oedipal themes inherent in Howard's suicide. The book was apparently popular enough in its original release to warrant a mass-market paperback to be published later this year.

There are, most likely, plenty of fictionalized Howards that haven't been as widely published as those listed above. De Camp bibliographer and writer, Charlotte Laughlin, together with Bill Crider, wrote a novel, *The Heart of Ahriman*, which teamed a resurrected Howard with others fighting a supposedly real life Conan villain. Only a few REHupa members have read this unpublished manuscript. Small fan publications have published fictional stories featuring REH and Cross Plains as characters. This author's own "REH in Cross Plains" published in REHupa is a good example of fan fiction that will probably never escape its fan bound origins.

The Dark Horse *Conan* comic book featured REH as character in issue #28. The script by Kurt Busiek has Howard as Rovann, the town storyteller. The town's ruffians consider him somewhat of a joke. Rovann dreams of being a warrior but stays on with parents to take care of the family farm. He shadowboxes while doing his chores. At the mead hall Rovann captures the attention of the crowd and they enjoy his stories. But they call him a mama's boy when he mentions his chores. Conan rides into town followed by a pack of demons. The townspeople set to fighting the demons trying to keep them from entering through the city gates. Rovann joins the fight and is pushed away by a town warrior. Rovann remembers a hidden cave and fears the demons will enter that way. Everyone fights off the demons until sunrise banishes them. Rovann had singlehandedly fought them from entering the city through the cave all night long. Apparently perishing from his wounds Rovann is finally found and called "madboy" and "mama's boy." The final scene shows him doing his play shadow boxing in the great hereafter.

While certainly this was meant as a tribute to REH it falls flat. Howard is suitably heroic and intelligent but Howard as misfit and outsider doesn't work in this context. Howard fans can readily accept that Howard was considered a misfit by provincial church-going town folk and was odd by regular societal standards but to be insulted by the hardened ruffians that *heartily enjoy* his stories is akin to saying his readers can't take Howard seriously. The final scene with Howard imaging great battles in the hereafter rings false after his real battle with demons. It would have been far better to have Howard telling of his great battle surrounded by a group of dedicated listeners.

Mark Finn, the latest Howard biographer, wrote at least two online magazine stories featuring Howard that are somewhat insightful to his views on Howard. The first published story "Afterlife" has Howard resurrected in the service of Arthur Conan Doyle. Howard tells Doyle, "For a long time, I sat in my car, holding that gun, trying to see if I had the courage to pull the trigger, only to find out that I didn't have the courage not to."

Howard is upset at the resurrection. He says he didn't want to stay on this plane of existence anymore. "I don't care about anyone else. You don't understand. The only reason I stuck around for as long as I did was because Momma needed me to take care of her." There is a boxing match to decide Howard's fate. Howard wins but decides to work for Doyle anyway. His job is to run a bar and be a caretaker of a library for dead authors. Finn has set the stage for future adventures.

Finn's next story is "A Whim of Circumstances." The story is about a would-be Conan movie being done in 1972. It is a Charles Schneer/Ray Harryhausen production. L. Sprague de Camp and Lin Carter are on the set as technical advisors. Patrick Wayne stars as Conan. There is a murder on the set and chaos ensues. Turns out the ghost of Howard influenced a mentally unstable starlet to kill someone so this travesty of a movie would not be filmed. This story doesn't give any real insight into Howard. It does show how emotional some fans are about pastiches and adaptations. Turning Howard into a murderer's accomplice is probably the worst violation of his character to date.

All in all these stories featuring REH as character are no substitute for REH's own words and the words of those that knew him. At best they give us a look into whatever thoughts about Howard were prevailing at the time of their writing. They, no doubt, tell us more about the story's author than they do about Robert E. Howard.

WORKS CITED

Barbour, David, and Richard Raleigh. *Shadows Bend.* New York: Ace Books, 1990.

Bishoff, David, and Dean Wesley Smith. "Nevermore." In *Quest to Riverworld* ed. Philip Jose Farmer. New York: Warner Books, 1993.

De Camp, L. Sprague. "Far Babylon." In *The Purple Pterodactyls*. New York: Ace Books, 1980.

Ellis, Novlyn Price. *Day of the Stranger: Further Memories of Robert E. Howard*. West Warwick, RI: Necronomicon Press, 1989.

Finn, Mark. "Afterlife." Published: www.clockworkstorybook.com. No longer available on this site.

___. "A Whim of Circumstance." Published in the World Fantasy Convention book for 2006.

Howard, Robert E. *Post Oaks and Sand Roughs*. Hampton Falls, NH: Donald M. Grant, Publisher, 1990.

Lupoff, Richard. *Lovecraft's Book*. Sauk City, WI: Arkham House, 1985.

Silverberg, Robert. *To the Land of the Living*. New York: Warner Books, 1990.

JOURNEY TO CROSS PLAINS

by Howard Waldrop

What can I tell you?
This article was written eighteen years ago [in 1966—Ed.], *by a kid who was nineteen years old and in the last throes of some kind of hero worship (though he didn't know he was in the last throes) he would soon shake off. And, sorry to say, that kid was me.*
Ed Bryant thinks this article has some kind of historical value or something, since no one seems to have had the success at much the same thing in years since. So, damn Ed's eyes, here it is, exactly as it was written then. Except....
Except, taking my cue from the Canuck poet Leonard Cohen, I've gone back and added impertinent footnotes, generally castigating my younger self for its crimes against humanity, its writing, etc. What Cohen did in Death of a Lady's Man *was to provide, on one page, a poem from 1969-1972, and on the facing page what his 1975 self thought about the person who had written those lines. An act of self-immolation, folks, before your very eyes.*
Another couple things you should remember as you read this. I was heavily under the influence of James Agee's Now Let Us Praise Famous Men, *and the Paul Williams-Chester Anderson-edited days of* Crawdaddy *magazine in its first incarnation.*
Also, the Robert E. Howard boom hadn't developed yet at all; there were maybe ten or twelve of his stories in reprint paperback anthologies, and a couple of hardcovers. It wasn't until late in the year that the Conan books came back into print and started the whole thing.
And, that this article was done to the best of my then ability for a general audience. (US Magazine/paperbook—not the People *ripoff, of a little later—or* Countdown, *or magazines like that come to mind as markets I had in my mind then.) How I ever hoped to sell it, or what I was thinking when I wrote it, well, damned if I know.*

I'll shut up now, and leave you to the gentle tortures of this wild-eyed, style-deaf, uncultured young punk, who used to be one of me, tells you about his....

JOURNEY TO CROSS PLAINS

June 11, 1966: A clear day that should come off hot.[73] It is 6:30 in the morning, and my father tells me to use his car rather than my old '51 Chevy for the trip. A trip that will take me a hundred and fifty miles there and a much longer way back, it seemed.

I set out west on US 80, through Ft. Worth and Weatherford, and out into the bleary, hilly land beyond. The sun keeps its promise and comes up hot.[74] I wore a yellow, short-sleeved shirt, slacks, and tennis shoes. I looked like the All-American boy.[75] Beside me on the seat were a couple of themebooks, a state map, and three paperback books. My shirt pocket was full of Bic pens, from the look of the notes I have here before me, blue medium points.[76]

I was going out in search of a part of American and Texas gone exactly thirty years to that day. The three books on the seat were *Worlds of the Weird*, and *Weird Tales* edited by Leo Margolies, and *Swords and Sorcery* edited by L. Sprague de Camp. All contained stories from the old pulp *Weird Tales*, stories written by Robert E. Howard:

> Born 1906, Peaster, Texas. Only child of Dr. and Mrs. I.M. Howard. Moved to Cross Plains, Texas, 1915. First sale to *Weird Tales* at the age of nineteen. In eleven years old more than 160 stories and novelettes to such magazines as *Argosy, Strange Stories, Magic Carpet, Oriental Stories, Fight Stories,* and *Ghost Stories.* Unmarried. Died, 1936.[77]

You get to Cross Plains, Texas (pop. in 1936—1100; pop. in 1966—1100) by going out Highway 80 to Cisco and turning south

---

[73] You will see references to this again. Pay attention.
[74] See footnote 73.
[75] I looked like the All-American nerd.
[76] Aren't you really interested in this kid with his pocket full of pens and what he might have to say to you? Do you have any idea what this article is about, already? Do you care?
[77] At last, a clue as to what the author might be writing about!

on US 183 to Rising Star and west on State 136 for six miles, and you are there.

It was 10:30 Sunday morning when I got there after following trucks up and down hills all the way out 80. Sunday mornings in this part of the state means most people are in church. I had only a vague idea of what to do or where to go, that in the form of the name of the town's newspaper editor. My only hope was to wait till after church, look him up, introduce myself, and hope for the best.[78]

Cross Plains is small. It consists of three or four gas stations (two of them Encos[79]), a few grocery stores, some merchandise houses, a bank; the rest are houses. There are two stoplights, and one of them wasn't working.[80] The town was still, resting under the sun, and there were seven or eight cars in the downtown area.

I decided there was nothing to do but find some shade and wait, so I pulled into a Gulf station that looked like the only thing open in town. It was across from one of the churches. I stopped and climbed out.

The attendant got up from his straightback chair and came out to me. "Can I help you, son?"

I told him that I only wanted a coke. Then I tried an outside shot, asked him if he had ever heard of a writer named Robert E. Howard, who lived in Cross Plains in the thirties.

"Bob Howard?" he asked. "A writer here a long time ago?"

I said yes.

"Yeah. I knew him. You should ask my brother, he used to run with him when they were boys. D. C. Lee."[81]

I asked where I could find him. He said at the Coffee Cup, or some such restaurant name. I started to ask directions to the place.

"Here he comes now," the attendant said.

A pickup pulled in on the gravel near the cement of the station driveway. Two men got out; one looked vaguely like the attendant. I went to him, introduced myself.

---

[78] His oaflike kid really knew how to prepare for an interview, know his subjects, arrange introductions beforehand, didn't he. Presumptuous brat. "I think I'll drive over to Oxford today and interview all the people who knew Faulkner."

[79] Let's see the hands of all those over the age of thirty.

[80] The author has changed tense in this sentence.

[81] I'll get around to telling you later that this was J .H. Lee. See, I thought back then you had to write articles like they were happening *right then*. I'd been reading too many *Crawdaddy*s for my own good.

Mr. D. C. Lee had graying hair and warm eyes over which he wore dark-rimmed glasses. He was wearing work clothes and a khaki cap.[82]

"Do you work for a newspaper?" he wanted to know.

It was thirty years to the day after Howard died. We sat down between the pumps, Mr. Lee drinking a cold drink of some kind while I rummaged around with my pens and notebooks. It was hot and getting hotter.[83]

Mr. Lee thought Howard in a class by himself among all the people he had ever known, thought him to be also the most ambitious person he had ever met. He was sports-minded, loved to hunt, fish, and ride on horseback, although he never went for athletics at school. He was quiet and studious, and had a limited number of friends. He stayed home most of the time as he got older, with his writing and caring for his mother, who had become a semi-invalid while Howard was still young. He did not go for women much until the last four or five years of his life.

When they had been younger, he and Lee sometimes spent the night at each other's houses. Robert would tie his right hand to the bed because he had violent dreams and would wake up swinging.

Robert had written an article on Camp Colorado, a ghost town stuck back in the brush miles away from Cross Plains. A photograph was used to illustrate it, showing D. C. Lee standing beside a statue commemorating the first Hereford brought into West Texas. He, Robert, and some friends had spent some time where while Robert was researching the article.

During the Depression, the money Howard got from his writing made him the richest man in town, even though editors sometimes went as long as a year before paying him for a story.

Mr. Lee once had some of Howard's magazines and such. He and his wife donated them to Cisco Junior College.

Dr. Howard was a country doctor, gone most of the time on his rounds and house calls. Robert had been essentially raised by his mother, and he worried himself about her illness all the time he was writing. In his thirtieth year, in June, his mother went into a comatose state.

On June 11, 1936, D.C. met Robert coming out of the post office with his mail. They talked for nearly an hour. Howard was despondent about his mother; he talked that death and sickness were

---

[82] He was at work. What else would he be wearing?
[83] See footnote 73.

unfair to older people who had lived lives and had memories. Mr. Lee talked with him about it, then Robert went home.

"They called me thirty minutes later," Mr. Lee said.[84]

From the newspaper accounts:

> Howard went home and spoke to the nurse who attended his mother. He asked her if she thought his mother would ever come out of the coma. The nurse told him she didn't think his mother would ever wake up again. Robert went to his typewriter, wrote out a paraphrase from Dowson's "Cynara":
>
> All fled—all done, so lift me on the pyre;
> The Feast is over and the lamps expire.
>
> He went through the house and out to his car. He sat down in the front seat, opened the car pocket and took out his revolver.[85]

He shot himself in the head. He was taken to the hospital, where he died the next day. His mother died the same afternoon, never having come out of the coma.

When Mr. Lee had finished I asked directions to the Howard home. Mr. Lee's brother-in-law lived there, it turned out. I thanked Mr. Lee and his brother J.H. for the interview, and gave them the paperbacks; they didn't know Howard's works were beginning to be reprinted and hadn't seen any of them. I waved goodbye to them.[86]

THE HOUSE

Second from the corner at the intersection of 36 and FM 880. In the front, cactus plants, three of them, stand beside the road. The front: the yard and low picket fence and two short pecan trees. A walk leads up to the porch, from the ceiling of which hangs a porch swing. The house itself: T-shaped, the long part off-center from the middle of the house but not far enough to be L-shaped. The roof is

---

[84] I've been fairly quiet here, as I got most of the interview right, and these are about the only interesting things about Robert E. Howard you will learn from this whole article.

[85] It wasn't a revolver, it was a Colt .32 caliber automatic.

[86] The casualness of this interview still strikes me as too good to be true, eighteen years later.

covered with hexagon shingles; a chimney projects up out of one of the front rooms.

At the door I'm met by Mr. Eugene Grider, the owner. I explain why I'm here. He says fine, go ahead and have a look. Mrs. Grider is not home. Yes, he knows this is the old Howard home, but he did not know Howard or the family.

There are five rooms and a bath: two hall bedrooms, a living room, a kitchen, a dining room. The long part of the house is an entirely screened-in back porch. I move through the house slowly, trying not to be curious.[87] I go out on the screened porch then into the back yard. At the far back, two sheds. A fence extends the back and side yards. The yard itself has shrubs and trees—peaches and cedars. Near the back fence: a garden, rows of different vegetables. Coming around off the highway and to the back of the house is the driveway (where thirty years and some hours before Robert Ervin Howard ended his life).

I thank Mr. Grider and walk across the street to the car. I stand there and look both ways down the road and around the house. A few other houses, a grocery store. The road going away to the left and right. Heat coming up off the road, with the sun beating down.[88] I drive away, back to Rising Star, but instead of left I cut right at the stoplight. One more place to go.

You turn out the highway to Coleman once you get to Brownwood, twenty-eight miles from Cross Plains. Left four or five blocks, then out the Brownwood-Brady highway for a mile or two. At the entrance you turn in. Greenleaf Memorial Cemetery.

I parked the car, got out, and began to walk. Row on row of stones, marble, granite. Most are old, the marble is grayed or black, the raised letters are beginning to wear. The cemetery is huge, extending nearly a half-mile down the front-road, at least that wide back from the road.

The groundskeeper's house is near the entrance, but I didn't go there.[89] I began to walk through the paths between the headstones. There are trees here, some large, some small, shrubs and bushes.

Up above and behind the cemetery is a gravel works. Every few minutes a rockcrusher roars like a dragon from the hill.[90]

---

[87] This was possibly the understatement of *this* century, anyway.
[88] See footnote 73.
[89] That's because I was stupid.
[90] This is the first bit of more than see-cat-go writing in this article. Also the last.

Two-thirds of the way back, near the center, I came on the marker, a big one. HOWARD. In Roman Block. On the side facing the entrance.

From Mr. Lee:

> "It was the saddest funeral I've seen in my life. It was Cross Plains' first double funeral. I was one of the pallbearers for Bob. Dr. Howard stood there talking to both coffins for forty-five minutes."

I went around and stood in front of the graves. It was headed by a triple headstone which said:

HOWARD

Robert E.	HESTER ERVIN	ISAAC M.
Author & Poet	Wife & Mother	Physician
1906-1936	1870-1936	1871-1944

> "They were lovely and pleasant in their lives and in their death they were not divided."

There were footstones at Robert's and his mother's spaces.

I stood for a while, went back to the car, turned around and left.[91]

---

[91] There were three more paragraphs to the article, but, boys and girls, they were cheesy.

WEIRD TALES AND THE GREAT DEPRESSION

by Scott Connors

Hugo Gernsback may well be forever known as the "Father of Science Fiction," but it is likely that he will also be remembered for just as long as "Hugo the Rat" for his habit of "forgetting" to pay his writers, or paying them only upon lawsuit. (There was actually a New York attorney, Ione Weber, who specialized in suing Gernsback [Ashley, 243].) But consider the following:

> I always hate to write a letter like this, but dire necessity forces me. It is, in short, an urgent plea for money. It is nothing new for me to need money, but the present circumstances are different from those in which I generally found myself in the past.

The author of this poignant *cri de cœur* was Robert E. Howard, and the recipient was Farnsworth Wright, editor of Howard's primary market, *Weird Tales*. Howard continued in his letter of May 6, 1935:

> For some time now I have been receiving a check regularly each month from *Weird Tales*—half checks, it is true, but by practicing the most rigid economy I have managed to keep my head above the water that I was able to do so was largely because of, not the size but the regularity of the checks. I came to depend upon them and to expect them, as I felt justified in so doing. But this month, at a very time when I need money so desperately bad, I did not receive a check. [...] As you know, it has been six months since "The People of the Black Circle" (the story the check

for which is now due me) appeared in *Weird Tales*. *Weird Tales* owes me over eight hundred dollars for stories already published and supposed to be paid for on publication—enough to pay all my debts and get me back on my feet again if I could receive it all at once. Perhaps this is impossible. I have no wish to be unreasonable; I know times are hard for everybody. But I don't believe I am being unreasonable in asking you to pay me a check each month until the accounts are squared. [...] Necessity drives me. A monthly check from *Weird Tales* may well mean for me the difference between a life that is at least endurable— and God alone knows what.

Just over thirteen months later, Wright would learn how Howard, overcome by grief at the impending death of his mother, took his own life.

It is not my intention to cast Farnsworth Wright as the villain responsible for Howard's death. It is, however, my hope to illuminate the realities of the pulp magazine *business*—for such it was, regardless of how much we might extol the virtues of such writers as H. P. Lovecraft and Clark Ashton Smith who espoused an attitude of *ars gratia artis*—during a Depression that is not called Great without justification. It is significant that writers such as Manly Wade Wellman, who according to his friend and literary executor David Drake regarded Gernsback with contempt for his business practices, during this same period held Wright in high esteem.

A complete history of the self-styled "Unique Magazine" is beyond the scope of this article, but here are some highlights: founded in 1923 by Chicago entrepreneur J[acob]. C[lark]. Henneberger, *Weird Tales* failed to achieve the success of his earlier magazine *College Humor*. Henneberger was convinced that the magazine could become a great success, and sold both *College Humor* and *Detective Tales* in order to continue publishing. The magazine's first reader, Farnsworth Wright, replaced founding editor Edwin Baird after H. P. Lovecraft turned down the position, and remained in the post until shortly before his death in 1940. *Weird Tales* owed many thousands of dollars in printing bills, so in order to continue publication, Henneberger sold a majority interest to the printer, B. Cornelius, with the rather optimistic proviso that should the magazine become profitable Mr. Cornelius would be repaid and the stock revert to Henneberger. As a result Wright did not have to concern himself greatly about paying the printer, but he was greatly circumscribed in his editorial actions and always under pressure to increase circulation and control costs.[92] (Weinberg 4)

Weird Tales, like all pulp magazines, was at the mercy of the distributors who supplied the news stands and drug stores of the nation. Jerry Westerfield, in a 1940 *Writer's Digest* feature, describes how they would typically purchase the entire print run of a magazine at half the cover price (at 25¢ an issue *WT* was already one of the more expensive pulps on the stands, with most pulps costing 20¢ in the early 1930s according to a 1932 article in *Author & Journalist*, a trade paper for writers [Bamber 51]), with the publisher buying any unsold copies back at a slightly higher price to compensate for the return shipping (87). In the case of *Weird Tales* the news company held "back payment always for three full issues, a sum which we cannot tap" (Wright to I. M. Howard, Sept. 6, 1936). It is not known what the magazine's circulation was precisely, but according to August Derleth it may have been as much as 100,000 copies (18).

The Twenties roared as much for the magazine business as for any other, and like any other business it suffered greatly after the stock market crash of October 1929. The prolific fictioneer H. Bedford-Jones described "The Changing Market" in an article for *Author & Journalist*:

> The new year dawned with a crash. The safes were full of manuscripts; everybody had lost money, circulation was dropping to the danger point, advertising was thin. Money was being rapidly lost, not made. Extinction threatened. [...] The magazine market was—and is—flooded with publications that had far passed the saturation point; anyone with a little backing was putting out new magazines. [...] During the flush days of 1929, the editors had bought largely and at high prices. (p. 36)

For instance, Wright paid writers such as H. P. Lovecraft and Abraham Merritt, and presumably Seabury Quinn, the munificent sum of 1½ cents a word, "but the depression forced that down to one

---

[92] Unfortunately this also left Wright at Cornelius' mercy when issues of quality control arose. When Clark Ashton Smith first began illustrating his own stories for *WT*, Wright warned him to "keep the illustration as open as possible [...] for the cuts have a tendency to fill up with ink if the lines are too close together. [...] Such blurring would not be good printing, of course; but as the printer is the principal owner of the magazine, we are helpless in this respect." (Wright to CAS, Dec. 7, 1933)

cent" (Wright to August W. Derleth, April 19, 1937). It was *at this time* that Wright launched a new pulp, *Oriental Stories*, that featured tales of adventure in the Levant and the Far East. (This was possibly related to a suggestion made by Bedford-Jones in his 1929 book *This Fiction Business*, which Wright may have read, since not only did the writer submit to Wright [both for *WT* and for *OS!*], but they also shared a mutual friend in Chicago bookman and journalist Vincent Starrett.) He explained the reasoning behind this rather breathtaking display of optimism in Charles D. Hornig's fanzine *The Fantasy Fan*:

> Wright blames the failure of *Oriental Stories* on ex-president Hoover. After listening to one of Hoover's speeches in which he stated that prosperity was just around the corner, Wright thought that it would be an opportune time to launch a new magazine.... You, we, and Farnsworth Wright know what happened (Schwartz and Weisinger, 14; ellipses in original).

The first issue of *Oriental Stories* (later renamed *Magic Carpet*) had a cover date of October-November 1930. Unfortunately, as Wright wrote to Derleth, this meant that "*Weird Tales* has to carry all the expenses of *Oriental Stories* for a few months, for we get nothing from the News Company until we deliver our fourth issue to them" (October 8, 1930). The added burden meant that *Weird Tales* was forced to switch to a bimonthly schedule, which Wright paradoxically asserted would actually *help* the magazine because "a sixty-day sale will increase the circulation of the magazine quite materially" (Wright to Derleth, December 3, 1930). The market for the stories of Howard and Smith and others was thus cut in half, and Wright already had "enough Smith and Howard stories on hand to use one in each issue for more than a year" (Wright to Derleth, Dec. 16, 1930). Fortunately, negative reader response to this change convinced Wright to resume a monthly schedule starting with the August 1931 issue "to prevent fans from getting out of the habit of reading the magazine" (Wright to Derleth, Jan. 13, 1931). According to former Arkham House editor Peter Ruber, the magazine was still in dire straits, with Cornelius ordering Wright to shut it down, but Wright was able to convince him that two serials, *Tam, Son of Tiger* by Otis Adelbert Kline (June-July to December 1931 [Price 32]), and *The Devil's Bride* by Seabury Quinn (February to June 1932

[Ruber 335]), would boost circulation enough to justify its continued publication.

Up until this point *Weird Tales* had been able to pay its writers on publication, but in September 1932 Wright warned Derleth that "my business office [business manager William Sprenger] informs me that for the next two or three months the cheques will be somewhat late" (Sept. 1, 1932). However, in March 1933 all bank accounts were frozen, first by order of state governments (beginning with Michigan and followed closely by Indiana, home of the Fletcher-American Bank where the bulk of Popular Fiction Co.'s funds were deposited), and then by order of newly inaugurated President Franklin Delano Roosevelt. However, as Wright wrote to Derleth on March 30, 1933:

> After the national bank holidays were ended, all the banks in Indianapolis were opened on a 100% liquid basis—except the Fletcher-American Bank. It finally opened for business on a 5% basis. Of all the banks in Indianapolis, we picked on the only one that was not sound. Our funds are tied up securely in that bank. We are informed that our money is perfectly safe, and that we will get it when the bank's frozen assets are thawed out; but how long that will take, we do not know.

While *WT* soon found another bank, the funds deposited were limited to recent remittances from the news distributors. During the bank holiday the magazine industry came to a virtual standstill, with sales falling off drastically. Soon *WT*'s contributors were discovering to their shock that their checks were bouncing. An embarrassed Wright apologized to Clark Ashton Smith, insisting "We want you to know that the non-payment of the check we sent you in payment for your story 'The Mandrakes' is no fault of ours. The money was in the bank at the time and is still in the bank—but the bank will not release it because they are still on a restricted withdrawal basis" (April 13, 1933). But the bank never reopened, and the Popular Fiction Publishing Co. lost most of its assets. While Wright made some business decisions that in retrospect seem to have been unwise, such as launching a new magazine at the worst possible time that proved to be "a drag on *Weird Tales*" (Wright to Derleth, April 22, 1932), it is a testimonial to his managerial skills that he was able to keep the magazine afloat at a time when his competitors, most notably William Clayton's *Strange Tales*, went under.

Ripples from this financial crisis spread rapidly. Veteran pulpster Hugh B. Cave wrote to his fellow *Weird Tales* contributor Carl Jacobi that July that "I don't know what to make of *Weird Tales*. The magazine is a good one to play with when checks are coming in promptly, but this business of waiting months and months for money isn't conducive to good work" (41). Jack Williamson says in his memoirs that Wright owed Edmond Hamilton over $700 (97), which he paid off in installments of $25 a month, and that he himself waited several months to receive the check for his popular serial *Golden Blood* (83).

In examining the surviving letters that Wright and Sprenger wrote to Clark Ashton Smith and August Derleth, we can form an objective impression of how long the gap between publication and payment was for two of Wright's most dependable authors. Smith wrote to August Derleth on July 2, 1933 that *WT* owed him the sum of $200. As mentioned above, Smith's check for "The Mandrakes" (*WT* February 1933) bounced in April, but he received two payments starting in August. As the following chart illustrates, the gap gradually increased from five to twelve months until 1938 saw a resumption of payment upon publication, or even slightly in advance of publication.[93]

Table 1. Monies Owed to Clark Ashton Smith

Item	*$$*	*Issue*	*Paid*
The Saturnienne	7	December 1927	10/31/27
The Nightmare Tarn	10	November 1929	11/16/29
Shadows	8	February 1930	01/14/30
The Last Incantation	15	June 1930	04/30/30
The Phantoms of the Fire	20	September 1930	07/29/30
A Rendezvous in Averoigne	56	April-May 1931	06/24/31
Justice of the Elephant	14	*OS*, Autumn 1931	10/28/31
The Tale of Satampra Zeiros	48	November 1931	10/28/31
The Weird of Avoosl...	33	June 1932	05/28/32
Maker of Gargoyles	56	August 1932	07/27/32

---

[93] However, as late as 1941, somebody apparently still owed Smith a significant sum of money, since in a letter to a friend he complained that "I wish to hell the Government would give me power to collect what's due me" (335).

The Mandrakes	45	February 1933	08/29/33
The Isle of the Torturers	60	March 1933	04/21/33
The Seed from the Sepulchre	45	October 1933	02/23/34
The Holiness of Azederac	80	November 1933	03/30/34
The Weaver in the Vault	45	January 1934	05/29/34
drawing for above	7	January 1934	05/29/34
The Charnel God	42.5	March 1934	08/29/34
The Tomb-Spawn	35	May 1934	11/30/34
drawing for "Colossus...	7	June 1934	03/30/35
In Slumber	7	August 1934	05/31/35
Xeethra	68	December 1934	10/25/35
The Last Hieroglyph	60	April 1935	03/31/36
The Black Abbot of…	39	March 1936	02/25/37
Necromancy in Naat	73	July 1936	03/29/37
Hymn to Beauty	7	June 1937	10/29/37
The Garden of Adompha	37	April 1938	02/28/38
The Maze of Maal Dweb	47	October 1938	07/25/38

Derleth received payment the same month a story was published until October 1932. Payment for stories typically lagged three months behind publication until 1938. (The difference between the regularity of payments between Smith and Derleth may be attributable to the fact that most of Derleth's stories were short "fillers.")

Table 2. Monies Owed to August W. Derleth

Item	*$$*	*Issue*	*Paid*
Across the Hall	10	June 1930	4/30/30
The Captain Is Afraid	15	October 1931	9/25/31
In the Left Wing	65	June 1932	5/28/32
The Sheraton Mirror	45	September 1932	9/22/32
A Battle Over the Tea-Cups	20	*OS, Summer 1932*	10/6/32
Red Hands	25	October 1932	10/31/32
The Return of Andrew	70	September 1933	1/30/34

Colonel Markesan	60	June 1934	8/30/34
Feigman's Beard	27	November 1934	2/28/35
A Matter of Faith	35	December 1934	3/30/35
The Metronome	20	February 1935	5/31/35
Two Gentlemen in Black	40	August 1938	7/23/38
The Drifting Snow	43	February 1939	12/23/38
The Return of Hastur	100	March 1939	2/1/39

The attentive reader will notice that the gap between payment and publication spiked to almost a year in 1935. This may have been attributable to the failure of one of Wright's pet projects, his own edition of the works of the Bard of Avon, *Wright's Shakespeare Library*. Issued as a "tie-in" to the release of Max Reinhardt's production of *A Midsummer Night's Dream*, it failed to find an audience with his core readership despite the wonderful illustrations by Virgil Finlay.

Curiously enough, H. P. Lovecraft did not wait for his check for "Through the Gates of the Silver Key" (July 1934), although this may have been an effort on the part of Wright to lure Lovecraft back into regular submission, as witness his rapid receipt of checks late in 1936 for "The Haunter of the Dark" (December 1936) and "The Thing on the Doorstep" (January 1937).

It is rumored that Seabury Quinn, arguably the most popular contributor to *Weird Tales* among its contemporary readers (a distinction which has not endured), boasted that he always received his money up front, although in the opinion of *Weird Tales* historian Robert Weinberg this may have been just so much hot air.

This brings us at last to Robert E. Howard. Like Smith and Derleth, Howard was a prolific contributor to the magazine, appearing in twenty issues between February 1933 (when the Indiana bank holiday froze *WT*'s assets at the Fletcher-American Bank) until May 1935, when he composed his dunning letter to Wright. When Wright failed to respond quickly enough for him, Howard wrote the following to his agent, fellow *WT* contributor Otis Adelbert Kline, on May 13, 1935:

> For over a year, as I remember, I've received just half a check each month—just barely enough to keep me alive, but I didn't kick, because I knew times were hard, and I believed Wright was doing his best

to pay me. But this month there was no check forthcoming—and this check would have been much bigger than any check I've gotten for a long time from *Weird Tales*. I wrote Wright, telling him the trouble I'd been in, and explaining my desperate need for money, and up to now he's coolly ignored my letter. No check—and not the slightest word of explanation. The case is simple enough: *Weird Tales* owes me over $800, some of it for stories published six months ago. I'm pinching pennies and wearing rags, while my stories are being published, used and exploited. I believe Wright could pay me every cent he owes me, if he wanted to. But now, when I need money worse than I ever needed it in my life before, he refuses to pay me anything, and ignores a letter in which I beg him to pay me even a fraction of the full amount. What's his game, anyway? Is *Weird Tales* still a legitimate publication, or has it become a racket?

Wright was apparently able to convince William Sprenger to loosen his grip on the corporate purse strings, since by February 15, 1936 Howard could report to E. Hoffmann Price that "I've been able to just about break even on expenses, thanks to a fortunate sale or so, and comparatively generous payments from *Weird Tales*—which, I'll admit, I demanded urgently." This continued for several months, since another letter to Price, dated April 21, 1936, reports that REH was "in better shape financially than I was when you saw me last, in spite of my heavy expenses. *Weird Tales* has been paying regularly lately...."

It is difficult to determine precisely what Howard's feelings were towards Wright and *Weird Tales*. As he expanded his markets and began to sell regularly to such markets as *Action Stories, Fight Stories, Top Notch,* and *Argosy*, Howard wrote less for *Weird Tales*, although he told Price on February 15, 1936 that "I would, if payments could be made a little more promptly. I reckon the boys have their troubles, same as me, but my needs are urgent and immediate." This, along with a note written shortly before his death on June 11, 1936, that indicated certain of his unpublished manuscripts should be submitted to Wright, would indicate that he had accepted whatever apologies Wright had offered for their arrears. On the other hand, Howard's one-time girlfriend Novalyne Price Ellis provides the following in her memoir *One Who Walked Alone*, which apparently dates to the spring of 1936:

> Like Truett [Vinson, a mutual friend of Novalyne and REH], I don't understand Bob anymore. From the way he talks, he's making a good many sales to *Argosy*, sales to *Action Stories*, but the thing that seems to upset him is that *Weird Tales* still owes him about a thousand dollars and doesn't pay.
> He appreciates Wright for giving him a start in selling stories, but sometimes he calls Wright a two-bit editor; a man who can't recognize anything good; a dyspeptic; a small man who gags at a gnat and swallows a camel. Although he uses such barbed epithets, *he really doesn't mean to be malicious* [emphasis added]. (278)

At the time of his death Howard was owed some thirteen hundred dollars from *Weird Tales*. Many have speculated as to whether Wright's failure to reward Howard for the fruit of his labor might have contributed to his death. It is apparent that Howard suffered from depression most of his life, and this condition was worsened by a number of external stressors, of which the impending death of his mother was but the precipitating factor. Another factor was the failure of Robert's relationship with Novalyne. All of these various stresses, financial, physical and emotional, wore away at him constantly and without remission. Howard was in fact suffering from a condition referred to variously as caregiver burden or caregiver stress syndrome, where a family member who assumes the responsibility for insuring that a loved one's activities of daily living, such as eating, drinking, and personal hygiene, begins to experience chronic fatigue, difficulty sleeping, decreased immunity to illnesses, increased susceptibility to conditions such as high blood pressure and heart disease, and increased anxiety. As these continue, the caregiver can come to resent the loved one for being ill, which can result in feelings of guilt. Depression is a common concurrent condition (Taylor *et al.*, p. 137). Howard biographer Rusty Burke offers this assessment:

> Through 1935 and 1936, Howard's mother's health deteriorated rapidly. Increasingly, she had to be taken to sanitariums and hospitals, and even though Dr. Howard received a discount on services, the medical bills began to mount. Robert was faced with a dilemma—his need for money was more acute

than ever, but he had little time in which to earn it. *Weird Tales* owed him around $800, and payments were slow. With his own meager savings exhausted, Dr. Howard moved his practice into his home, which meant that patients were now coming and going day and night. Father and son finally hired women to nurse and keep house, but this further filled their home with people and provided Robert little opportunity to be alone and concentrate on his writing. This, combined with the despair he felt as his mother inexorably slid towards death, placed enormous stress upon the young writer, and he resurrected an apparently long-standing plan not to outlive his mother.

Patrice Louinet points out that at the time of his death Howard had $2,000 in savings and argues from this that the monies owed by *Weird Tales* were immaterial to his decision to kill himself. Don Herron offers a counter-argument. He asserts that it was the type of story he wrote for *Weird Tales* that best allowed Howard to express his ideas, especially those concerning the grand sweep of historical eons. Wright's failure to pay for these stories made it difficult for Howard to continue writing them. Despite all of the money Wright owed him, Howard continued to write weird fantasies, with two of his best, the regional horror "Black Canaan" and the last Conan story, "Red Nails," appearing in 1936. We should recall that Howard was a southerner, a Celt, and a member of a "honor culture" as described in Richard E. Nisbitt and Dov Cohen's 1996 study *Culture of Honor: The Psychology of Violence in the South.* They assert that in such a culture a person's economic and social survival depended upon his reputation. Howard was already viewed with some suspicion by his fellow inhabitants of Cross Plains, Texas, who wondered when he would give up this "writing foolishness" and settle down to a real job like clerking in a store or bookkeeping. So long as he could point to a degree of success at what he loved to do most, Howard could keep his self-respect in the face of this philistine indifference. But when it appeared that he was being cheated like a country bumpkin, Howard's ego took a major bruising. Consider the following conversation between Novalyne and Robert, which took place in March 1936, three months before his death:

> "We've got a couple of goats now," he said. "We thought goat's milk would be better for Mother than

cow's milk. Well, those goats have proved something to me."

I didn't have to ask him what it was, for he was so excited he'd tell me anyway.

"One of our goats is bigger than the other one," he said. "I have to watch her closely. She won't let the little one eat. She gobbles up most of her food, then moves over and runs the little one off and begins on her food. It's the nature of animals to dominate the ones they can. I understand that. Human beings are the same way. They dominate the ones they can dominate. Wright won't pay me what he owes me, because he's got the upper hand. His salary is assured; therefore, I can work my guts out, and it doesn't mean a damn to him. He's the dominant one. It's the animal in him. We're one...man and animals."

"We're not one with the animals," I said. "We're civilized."

He shrugged that aside. "When one man can dominate another man...or dominate a woman, he does it,"Bob insisted. (p. 279)

It is charged that Wright, like Hugo Gernsback, subsidized his own salary at the expense of his writers. As evidenced in this conversation with Novalyne, Howard certainly believed that Wright had the ability to pay him what was due to him, but did not just to show that he was the "alpha male," and this point of view was apparently passed along to his father, Dr. I. M. Howard. Several months after Howard's death, on September 4, 1936, Dr. Howard vented some of his grief and anger at Wright, ostensibly because of the failure of the magazine to honor REH's passing in a manner consistent with "thirteen years [sic] hard work, self denial, often begging you to pay him what you owed him, waiting for months on you for what you sold stuff and put in your pockets and let him go hungry." In a dazzling example of how the Postal Service has declined since the 1930s, Wright responded two days later that:

> I must correct the impression that I or anyone else connected with *Weird Tales* "put in our pockets" the money that was due your son during the period when *Weird Tales* was in the throes of the depression. Fact is, I often did not know from one month to

the other whether I would receive any money at all from the magazine; and I often received nothing (a serious condition, with my wife and son Robert to take care of); and it has been years since I received more than a fraction of the salary I used to get. My wife and I had borrowed on our life insurance up to the limit of the policy's capacity; and when I got my veteran's bonus this year it all had to be applied on repayment of the loan from my life insurance. These are personal details that will probably not interest you, but I don't want you to think that we have profiteered at the expense of the authors. It is only in the last few months that we have been able to begin closing the gap between publication of stories and payment for them. But there has always been a sufficient balance at the news company (which holds back payment always for three full issues, a sum that we cannot tap) to pay off the authors in full in case the magazine went under; though the funds would not be available for that purpose until all the copies outstanding with the magazine-dealers had been called in. Your son understood this state of affairs with the magazine, for both Mr. Sprenger and I explained it to him in our letters. (I did not, however, tell your son the personal details which I have told you in this letter; and the only way I am telling them to you is that I do not want you to think I have profited at your son's expense.)

According to Robert Weinberg, Wright's statements were corroborated by statements made by the artist Hannes Bok, who knew Wright after he and the magazine both relocated to New York City, in an interview with John Vetter, but he discounted these as a fan legend based upon the recollections of E. Hoffmann Price. He cites a letter from E. Hoffmann Price, who reported that Wright drew a monthly salary of $600 in 1927 and that at the last time he saw Wright in November 1933 he gave no evidence of financial pressures, and in fact had purchased a costly Spanish buffet for either $600 or $800 (the amount varied depending upon when Price was telling the story). Price went on to cite a statement by Edmond Hamilton that shortly before his death Wright was "living comfortably, though not luxuriously" (Weinberg 5). (It should be remembered that at the time of Wright's death in 1940 the nation was finally shaking off the last of the depression in the industrial retooling fueled by World War II.)

Price goes further in his memoirs, reporting that Wright drew $80 weekly writing a music column for a Chicago newspaper, and mentions that when he asked Wright's son if he noticed anything, "He laughed heartily, and denounced the yarn as hogwash" (15). But Robert Wright had not even been born at the time of the Crash of 1929, so his evidence as to his parents' financial status up until REH's death is questionable at best: children generally do not think of themselves as poor or rich until they have something with which to compare their families' prosperity. Perhaps most damning is a statement Price added to his memoir of Howard when he revised it for publication in *The Book of the Dead*, posthumously published in 2001 by Arkham House:

> A good many years after this dialogue [between Price and Dr. Howard during the former's first visit to Cross Plains in April 1934], I learned from an employee of the bank which had handled *W.T.* funds from the beginning and on until another outfit bought the magazine, that the publisher had money by the ream. The outfit always pleaded poverty, and had found the "Great Depression" a handy device to exploit writers who could not, or who fancied they could not write salable yarns for any other than *W.T.* (p. 72)

I find it very difficult to believe this statement. Leaving aside the breathtaking violation of fiduciary trust involved in a banker discussing the financial affairs of a client, and not even raising the issue as to whether this supposed employee was accurate in his recollections, the reader will recall earlier it was established that the Fletcher-American Bank of Indianapolis, "the bank which had handled *W.T.* funds from the beginning," failed in 1933. I suspect that Price may have been trying to justify to himself his decision to forsake the "unique magazine;" in his later years Price became increasingly jealous of the attention paid to writers like Howard, Smith, and Lovecraft, the latter two of whom he regarded as failures for their inability to crack the bigger markets. Price was most proud not of his early stories from *Weird Tales*, for which he is most likely to be remembered, but of his achieving a rate of two cents a word for "real magazines" like *Argosy* and *Short Stories*.

Was the money owed to Howard a contributing factor in his death? Insomuch as *Weird Tales'* debt to Howard intensified the financial pressures brought on by his mother's condition, it may be said to have contributed to the events of June 11th. But was Wright culpable for the death? *Weird Tales*, like many businesses during the 1930s, almost fell victim to the Great Depression, but between *W.T.*'s editor and business manager, William Sprenger, it was able to keep the magazine afloat despite being bound to a printer-publisher who had no interest in the magazine outside of what he could squeeze out of it, and despite such poor business decisions as *Oriental Stories* and Wright's *Shakespeare Library* that leeched capital from the magazine. Howard's death was not a foreseeable consequence of those business decisions. Its continued publication provided a venue for what Howard regarded as his most important work, and led him to associations with such fellow writers as Lovecraft and August Derleth, who collected this work posthumously for future generations to discover.

WORKS CITED

Ashley, Mike and Robert A. W. Lowndes. *The Gernsback Days: A Study of the Evolution of Modern Science Fiction from 1911 to 1936.* Holicong, PA: Wildside Press, 2004.

Bamber, Wallace R. "Let's Face the Facts, Pulp Writers!" *Pulp Fictioneers: Adventures in the Storytelling Business.* Ed. John Locke. Silver Spring, MD: Adventure House, 2004. 49-54.

Bedford-Jones, H. "The Changing Market." *Pulp Fictioneers: Adventures in the Storytelling Business.* Ed. John Locke. Silver Spring, MD: Adventure House, 2004. 36-39

Burke, Rusty. "A Short Biography of Robert E. Howard." *The Robert E. Howard United Press Association.*
<http://www.rehupa.com/short_bio.htm>.

Cave, Hugh. *Magazines I Remember.* Chicago: Tattered Pages Press, 1994.

Derleth, August. "The Making of a Literary Reputation." *A Century Less a Dream: Selected Criticism on H. P. Lovecraft.* Ed. Scott Connors. 2nd ed., Rockville, MD: Wildside Press, 2007. 16-25

Drake, David. *Drake's Potpourri.* "Esoteric Order of Dagon" mailing 95, Lammas (August) 1995.

Ellis, Novalyne Price. *One Who Walked Alone.* West Kingston, RI: Donald M. Grant, 1986.

Howard, I. M. Letters to Farnsworth Wright, 4 September 1936 and 7 September 1936. Mss., private collection.

Howard, Robert E. Letter to Farnsworth Wright, May 6, 1935. *Runes of Ahrh-Eih-Eche*. Lamoni, IA: Jonathan Bacon, 1976. pp. 16-17.

___. Letters to E. Hoffman Price, February 15, 1936 and April 21, 1936. *The Ghost* no. 3 (May 1945): 51-53

___. Letter to Otis Adelbert Kline, May 13, 1935. Ms., private collection.

Nisbett, Richard E. and Dov Cohen. *Culture of Honor: The Psychology of Violence in the South*. Boulder, CO: Westview Press, 1996.

Price, E. Hoffmann. *Book of the Dead. Friends of Yesteryear: Fictioneers & Others*. Ed. Peter Ruber. Sauk City, WI: Arkham House, 2001.

Ruber, Peter. "Seabury Quinn." *Arkham's Masters of Horror*. Ed. Peter Ruber. Sauk City, WI: Arkham House, 2000. 335-339.

Schwartz [Julius] and [Mort] Weisinger. "Weird Whisperings." *Fantasy Fan* 2 (September 1934): 14-16.

Smith, Clark Ashton. *Selected Letters*. Ed. David E. Schultz and Scott Connors. Sauk City, WI: Arkham House, 2003.

___. Letter to August W. Derleth, July 2, 1933. Ms., August Derleth Papers, State Historical Society of Wisconsin, Madison, WI.

Tailor, Carol, Carol Lillis and Patricia LeMone. *Fundamentals of Nursing*. 2nd ed. Philadelphia: J. B. Lippincott, 1993.

Weinberg, Robert. *The Weird Tales Story*. West Linn, OR: FAX Collector's Editions, 1977.

___. Personal communication, June 23, 2006.

Westerfield, Jerry K. "The Sky's No Limit." *Pulp Fictioneers: Adventures in the Storytelling Business*. Ed. John Locke. Silver Spring, MD: Adventure House, 2004. 86-93.

Williamson, Jack. *Wonder's Child: My Life in Science Fiction*. NY: Bluejay Books, 1984.

Wright, Farnsworth. Letters to Clark Ashton Smith. Smith Papers, John Hay Library, Brown University, Providence, RI.

___. Letters to August Derleth. August Derleth Papers, State Historical Society of Wisconsin Library, Madison, WI.

___. Letter to Dr. I. M. Howard, 6 September 1936. Private collection.

The author gratefully acknowledges the assistance and encouragement of Glenn Lord, Leo Grin, Rob Roehm, Jim Rockhill, Robert

Weinberg, Don Herron, and Rusty Burke in the writing of this article.

AFTER AQUILONIA, AND HAVING LEFT LANKHMAR...

Sword-and-Sorcery Since the 1980s

by Steve Tompkins

The subgenre of modern fantasy with which Robert E. Howard is nearly synonymous died down in the mid-1980s but did not die out. Far from it; sword-and-sorcery proved to be as difficult to kill as many of its protagonists. But before we can celebrate Robert E. Howard's legacy by following the subgenre's fortunes for the last several decades, we need to establish what we mean by sword-and-sorcery. For starters, what is meant is an approach to heroic fantasy that *became aware of itself* when Howard decisively expanded on the promise and premise of Lord Dunsany's 1908 story "The Fortress Unvanquishable Save for Sacnoth" with "The Shadow Kingdom" in 1929.

The verb "expanded" is chosen with no disrespect whatsoever intended toward Dunsany's story; it is possible that during his long involvement with sword-and-sorcery, L. Sprague de Camp never did the subgenre more of a favor than when he selected "The Fortress" for his anthology *The Fantastic Swordsmen* (1967). The young swordsman Leothric and the sorcerer Gaznak, "the greatest magician among the spaces of the stars," meet in a climactic duel as so many swordsmen and sorcerers have done ever since, but the special FX and local color (vampires slumbering in the stronghold's rafters, a pet dragon hand-fed "tender pieces of man") have rarely been as dazzling. Still, hero and setting leave room for expansion if not necessarily improvement, and in "The Shadow Kingdom" Kull, who questions reality as he would a captured conspirator, is too singular a character to be contained by a single story. Leothric is barely even a character, being merely a means to an end, the end of Gaznak. Kull possesses a past—he's haunted by his younger, wilder self, another spectral presence in a story full of them—and a future, at least a little of which *Weird Tales* readers got to see in "The Mirrors of Tuzun Thune" and "Kings of the Night."

"The Fortress Unvanquishable" offers a village, Allathurion, in "a wood older than record," and a "Land Where No Man Goeth," the site of Gaznak's lair when he isn't riding comets. Other than that, a suspicion that Dunsany's backdrop exists only as far as the story's first and last paragraphs is not unwarranted. By way of contrast the world of the Seven Empires (which Howard would only later name the Pre-Cataclysmic Age) extends across the "green roaring tides of the Atlantean sea" to "the far isles of the sunset," and is lavishly backstoried, what with its "sudden glimpses into the abysses of memory" and account of the aeons-abiding struggle to make human history human, or the "ghosts of wild wars and world-ancient feuds" that whisper to Kull and Brule the Pict. Sword-and-sorcery's geography is "designed for more to happen," as the subgenre's entry in *The Encyclopedia of Fantasy* (1997) emphasizes, which means that the characteristic protagonist, from Kull onward, is he or she to whom that "more" happens. The resulting stories are epic in eventfulness rather than in length; after all, the next adventure is impatiently awaiting its cue. So the difference between Dunsany's Leothric and Howard's Kull of Atlantis is not only the arrival of a frontier-fashioned, if educated, American voice with a Texas accent, but a changeover from self-contained to sequel-sustained storytelling.

It is important to keep in mind that Fritz Leiber, arguably second only to Howard as a tutelary deity for sword-and-sorcery, foresaw that any quest for definitional exactitude would involve scrambling after a will-o'-the-wisp. Even as he proposed the cloak-and-dagger, blood-and-thunder analog as a playful or placeholder name for stories like the Conan series or his own Fafhrd and the Gray Mouser in the second, April 1961 issue of the fanzine *Ancalagon*, he noted "Of course there will always be wide fringes of borderland around a story-area like this," and warned that too much pedantry, too much misuse of broadswords and battle-axes to split hairs rather than more dignified and deserving targets, might "result in a kind of nonsense." (Case in point, the aforementioned *Encyclopedia of Fantasy* "sword-and-sorcery" entry, which unhelpfully suggests that both S & S and heroic fantasy "are aspects of adventure fantasy")

Thus cautioned, we are now ready to call some expert witnesses, the first of whom, J. R. R. Tolkien, revolutionized *Beowulf* studies on behalf of Grendel, Grendel's mother, and the dragon in his 1936 lecture "Beowulf: The Monsters and the Critics," while also saying essential things about heroic fantasy as powerfully and poetically as they can be said. Tolkien speaks of "a man faced with a foe more evil than any human enemy of house or realm," and of "battle with the hostile world and the offspring of the dark." When he stresses that "the monsters do not depart, whether the gods come or go," we have our justification for the sword-and-sorcery imperative that humankind be able to clear a little space for itself, torch-lit and steel-shielded, in an environment that is ceaselessly and outrageously hostile.

Tolkien, of course, is almost always seen as the grandsire of another sort of fantasy, "epic" or "high," although some of the peak moments in the Christopher Tolkien-compiled *History of Middle-earth* demonstrate that his father was quite capable of being a great heroic fantasist whenever he wanted. Still, this might be as good a place as any to state of the thematic overlap between Howard-descended and Tolkien-descended fantasy that sharks might move through the same waters as whales, but they do so at a different speed and in pursuit of different sustenance while covering different distances. Sword-and-sorcery is rarely about restoration but frequently about upheaval and overthrow. Much muscular effort is expended on keeping the past in the past, and Old Orders are no more welcome than any other revenants. Dark Lords, those half-dictator/half-*diabolus* progeny of John Milton's Satan like Tolkien's Morgoth and Sauron, Stephen R. Donaldson's Lord Foul in *The Chronicles of Thomas Covenant*, or Guy Gavriel Kay's Rakoth Maugrim in *The Fionavar Tapestry*, are usually habitués of epic fantasy. They would unbalance sword-and-sorcery stories, where just surviving against archmages like Xaltotun in Howard's lone Conan novel *The Hour of the Dragon* is hard enough without having to take on fallen angels hellbent on enslaving or exterminating all forms of life.

Our second expert witness is Howard himself, by way of a boast of his to his friend Tevis Cyde Smith in December of 1932: "My heroes grow more bastardly as the years pass." This tells us something of the subgenre's scapegrace and seldom shining-armored nature, its pragmatic willingness to side with the lesser and *more human* of two evils, especially when Good is nowhere to be found or preoccupied with its hierarchies and hypocrisies. Grittiness coexists with what the otherwise unsmitten science fiction writer Damon Knight conceded was "dreamdust sparkle."

Our final witness, Karl Edward Wagner, identifies sword-and-sorcery as "a fascinating synthesis of horror, adventure, and imagination, displayed to best effect in "a universe in which magic works and an individual may kill according to his personal code." The fact that horror is listed first in Wagner's "fascinating synthesis" and his pointed mention of code-governed killing are only to be expected from the creator of that First Manslayer and Eden escapee Kane, who wanders accursedly through the collections *Death Angel's Shadow* and *Night Winds* and the novels *Bloodstone, Darkness Weaves,* and *Dark Crusade.* Although Wagner objected to the term sword-and-sorcery, which he believed to be belittling, he also insisted, crucially, that the subgenre "can command the reader's attention on multiple levels of enjoyment." The fact that the levels of enjoyment do indeed have the potential to be *multiple* has been lost on some other commentators.

Having been careful not to lock ourselves into a single definition or a set of rules begging for exceptions to show up and show them up, we are now in a position to borrow Fritz Leiber's imagery of "wide fringes of borderland" and conceive of sword-and-sorcery as a border kingdom ruthlessly carved out of the frontier provinces of fantasy, horror, and historical adventure fiction. In *The Hour of the Dragon* the conspirator Orastes assesses the Cimmerian who rules Aquilonia as ripe for overthrowing: "He is not part of a dynasty, but only a lone adventurer." Steadfast vassal Servius Galannus reinforces the point by telling Conan "You have no heir to take the crown." But Howard, unlike Conan at the time of *HOTD*, was a dynasty-founder in the border kingdom he'd created. Heirs duly appeared to take his crown and preserve a succession, albeit one based upon worth rather than birth. After a few *Weird Tales* pretenders to the throne like Clifford Ball and Henry Kuttner, there arrived in Leiber a successor who would rule with a more elegant roguishness than Howard's for many years. Michael Moorcock, a prince from across the water who came close to mastering the kingdom if not his own ambivalence, dominated the subsequent interregnum with his Eternal Champion avatars Elric of Melniboné, Dorian Hawkmoon, and Corum Jhaelen Irsai, and then the young march-wardens Karl Edward Wagner, Charles R. Saunders (*Imaro, The Quest for Cush,* and *The Trail of Bohu*) and David C. Smith (*Oron, The Sorcerer's Shadow, Mosutha's Magic*) seized new territory in audacious campaigns on multiple fronts.

Unfortunately, their conquests were not followed by consolidation; venturesome characters like Kane, Imaro, and Smith's Oron never quite gained their creators the resources and recognition they had more than earned. Instead, for sword-and-sorcery by the early 1980s, the best of times commercially was too often the worst of times creatively. Drugstore racks and bookstore displays were a

Muscle Beach of Braks, Jariks, Jandars, Kandars, Kothars, Thongors, Wandors, and Odans, but the formulaic and the forgettable held sway—too many statues came to life (often more convincingly than the heroes they menaced), too many tentacles groped to no great effect, too many graves surrendered skeletons that clattered into combat, too many towers proved to contain not anything like the secret of "The Tower of the Elephant" but merely confirmation of the author's inventive shortfall. Iconoclasm, which did exist, was obscured by an iconography that begged to be trivialized or burlesqued, and was, in the lumbering movies of the period.

But to impose a '70s boom/'80s bust storyline is to oversimplify. 1984 can be described as a tale of two nadirs: the cinematic nadir of *Conan the Destroyer* and the Nadir, the continent-overrunning crypto-Mongol nomads of David Gemmell's *Legend*. That first of thirty heroic fantasy novels was given a U.S. tryout as *Against the Horde* (1988), but until the late '90s Americans were mostly denied what critic John Clute singled out as an "ability to press ahead with revelation and action at a pace whose intensity can seem at times almost surreal." Clute's words call to mind an earlier, Texan heroic fantasist about whose work Gemmell, who never ceased remembering the Alamo, was unfailingly complimentary. The circumstances that produced *Legend* (1984) have become as legendary as the adamant non-surrender of the Nadir-engulfed defenders of Dros Delnoch within the book's pages. Misdiagnosed as being terminally ill, Gemmell opted to work out his feelings about the death sentence in a manuscript. His determination to stare down his own mortality and fascination with few-against-many clashes like Thermopylae and Rorke's Drift inspired a siege as epic as, and more episode-rich than, Tolkien's Helm's Deep and Minas Tirith or Karl Edward Wagner's melding of Troy and Verdun in his harrowing *Night Winds* tale "Lynortis Reprise."

Druss, A.K.A the Captain of the Axe or Deathwalker, made his debut and met his demise in *Legend*, but prequels appeared by genuinely popular demand until Gemmell's tale-telling was cut short in mid-career by his death on July 28, 2006. Druss emerged from a blood-red gene pool; his father having recoiled from the carnage his grandfather reveled in, and in the axeman's relationship with his weapon Snaga as in that of Elric and Stormbringer the question of who wields whom remains unsettled. Right on up through the decidedly non-Virgilian Aeneas of *Lord of the Silver Bow* (2005), who burns captured Mycenaean pirates alive in upheavals just prior to the outbreak of the Trojan War, Gemmell depicted men who cannot escape from violence and indeed have often previously escaped *into* violence. He drew upon past stints as a silver-tongued rather than iron-fisted bouncer, day laborer, and investigative journalist; not since Howard famously built Conan from "the dominant characteristics of various prize-fighters, gunmen, bootleggers, oilfield bullies, gamblers, and honest workmen" has a heroic fantasist watched how certain men live, and live with themselves, so attentively.

Besides Druss, who partners Skilgannon the Damned, another killer of killers hounded by memories as well as unrelenting pursuers, in *White Wolf* (2003) and *The Swords of Night and Day* (2004), Gemmell's creations include assassin nonpareil Waylander and Jon Shannow, the Jerusalem Man of *Wolf in Shadow* (1987), *The Last Guardian* (1989), and *Bloodstone* (1994), a post-apocalyptic paladin whose sixgun-and-sorcery adventures are more efficiently told but just as Eastwoodian as those of Stephen King's Roland the Last Gunslinger. Gemmell devised a Matter of Britain variant, Utherian fantasy, with two novels of the embattled Pendragon, *Ghost King* (1988), and *Last Sword of Power* (1989). *The Sword in the Storm* (1998) and *Midnight Falcon* (1999) take up the old quarrel of William Morris (in *The House of the Wolfings*), Talbot Mundy (in the Tros of Samothrace series), and Robert E. Howard with Rome as Connavar the Demonblade and the Keltoi tribes he unites are caught between the all-annexing legions of imperial Stone and the longships of Vars sea wolves. *Ravenheart* (2001) and *Stormrider* (2002) revisit Connavar's kinsmen in a later, *Rob Roy*-esque age in which "Varlish" oppressors strive to break the spirit and erase the culture of the proud highlanders. Gemmell's own blood boasted a touch of tartan, and in other novels (*Morningstar*, *Hawk Eternal*) indomitable clansmen also preserve their cattle-thieving, claymore-brandishing ways in defiance of overweening outsiders. No higher praise exists in his work than to say of someone "He's a man to walk the mountains with."

Gemmell's weaknesses? The demons that trouble his characters from within are more convincing than those that do so from without, and he was always more interested in monstrous deeds than monstrous beings, although *Dark Moon* (1996), *Winter Warriors* (1997), and *Hero in the Shadows* (2000) escalated the efforts of pre-human or inhuman forces to regain hegemony. A preoccupation with redemption and expiation as bad men manage to come to good ends occasionally risked sententiousness. But quantity never endangered quality, despite the staggering productivity that made Gemmell a bestselling heroic fantasist for three consecutive decades.

Gemmell has been denied a chance to challenge Fritz Leiber's half-century of work in the subgenre, and it is unlikely that the latter's genre-flouting coup of 1970 will ever be matched. That year his "Ill Met in Lankhmar," a novella about the newly-teamed Fafhrd and the Mouser's loss of, if not innocence then at least youthful insouciance, won *science fiction's* Hugo and Nebula Awards. By *The Knight and Knave of Swords* (1988), later incorporated in *Farewell to Lankhmar* (1998), the two "dubious heroes and whimsical scoundrels" are balancing on the cold knife's-edge between the late autumn and early winter of their careers. Repairing to Rime Isle, which is reminiscent of a post-saga Iceland, they resolve (mostly) to accentuate the merchant half of being merchant-adventurers, and Leiber cannily folds predictable reader resentment of their we'll-go-much-less-a-roving melancholy into *Knight and Knave*. At one point Fafhrd is "perversely lonely for Lankhmar with its wizards and criminal folks, its smokes (so different from this bracing northern sea air) and sleazy grandeurs," while the Mouser admits to being "tired of killing." But more than winding down and settling in is going on; the showpiece novella "The Mouser Goes Below," in which the principal battlefield is the boudoir, renders explicit the extent to which the Small Gray One might have been a much darker shade of gray had he never met up with his noticeably better half Fafhrd.

Another signature character was reactivated as Michael Moorcock summoned the old magic in *The Fortress of the Pearl* (1989), which recounts Elric's crimson reckoning with Quarzhasaat, a desert city unwise enough to challenge his ancestors. *The Revenge of the Rose* (1991) initially sustains the momentum as the Prince of Ruins salvages a symbiosis with a relict Melnibonéan dragon graceful as "a wind-dancing kestrel" and has an Elsinorean encounter with the ghost of his royal father Sadric. But *Rose* progresses by digressing, a trend that escalates in *The Dreamthief's Daughter* (2001), *The Skrayling Tree* (2003), and *The White Wolf's Son* (2005). Not-quite-invisible quotation marks seem to be flapping their batwings around characters and events, while the Moorcockian multiverse is now a wilderness of mirrors, reflections gesturing to reflections with no underlying realities in sight. The recent Elric is himself more transparent than albino; when he does appear, we suspect the wan honoring of a contractual obligation.

An expansive rather than contractive or constricted take on what is heroic fantasy and what isn't permits us to claim works by Michael Shea and Tanith Lee, writers at home throughout the fantastic genres. Shea's *Nifft the Lean* (1982), *The Mines of Behemoth* (1997) and *The A'rak* (2000) show again and again that he is qualified to join Dante and Bosch in brainstorming Infernos, and his at-times feline sensibility recalls the claw-tipped caresses of Clark Ashton

Smith and Jack Vance. Lee launched sword-and-sorcery sequences that exceeded, and subverted, readers' expectations with *The Birthgrave* (1975) and *The Storm Lord* (1976), and whenever she returns to heroic fantasy, she functions as a coldly candid wind blowing up the subgenre's kilt, or a source of searing scrutiny in which anything facile shrivels and the fulfillment of such wishes as are fulfilled can startle those who do the wishing. That is the case with *Cast a Bright Shadow* (2004) and *Here in Cold Hell* (2005), the first two novels of a Lionwolf Trilogy set in a winter-entranced Ultima Thule, northern without being Norse. Barbarians ride snow-mammoths and fish-horses, an "icon of bronze and fire" leads a tribal Gullahammer, a "hammer of a million heads," against fading cities, pseudo-saurian parasites scavenge in the skin-folds of a continent-sized whale, and enmity is sworn in a fell afterworld "till time *itself* is dead and rotting in some hell."

The second half of the 1980s saw a shamrock-trampling stampede of cheapjack Celticism, to which the work of the Australian Keith Taylor was a rebuke and a reminder of what could be done with Northern European themes. His five *Bard* novels, set on the same seas and shores frequented by Cormac Mac Art and Wulfhere the Skull-splitter, play with Howard's piratical pairings of not only the Gael and Dane but also Conan and Bêlit in the *amour fou* of harpist Felimid mac Fal and reaver Gudrun Blackhair. Taylor commuted surefootedly between Tir Nan Og, Camelot, and Valhalla. for three books, and although Felimid's artistic prowess never prevents him from also making his sword sing, his humor and humane tendencies confer upon him a unique status, half-in and half-out of the Celtic and Germanic warrior ethos. Then came the fourth Felimid novel, *Raven's Gathering* (1987), which is the standout. Gudrun's Valkyrie veneer is sorely tried as Odin *and* rival sea-wolves turn on her in a Ragnarok-writ-small that vies with Poul Anderson's reconstruction of *Hrolf Kraki's Saga* (1973) as an evocation of what Tolkien called the Old North's "potent but terrible solution in naked will and courage" to the inevitable victory of dark powers. The same ethos gleams a chilly blue in Stephan Grundy's *Rhinegold* (1994), dedicated to Richard Wagner and Tolkien but sure to delight many sword-and-sorcery devotees with its wargs and Walsings, hordes and hoards. As for Anderson himself, *War of the Gods* (1997) reaffirmed the stature *The Broken Sword* (1954) had won him as an honorary frost giant, the greatest American exponent of "the Northern thing." The primal Midgard of *War* still reels from the repercussions of the war between the Aesir and Vanir as Hadding of the

Skjoldungs rises to kingship in northlands not wholly relinquished by jotuns, nicors, trolls, night-gangers, and land-wights.

The ever-darker delights of the 1990s, which often seemed likely to cause a scarcity of black ink, were heralded by Glen Cook's *The Tower of Fear* (1989), in which the city of Qushmarrah, suggestive of Punic Carthage and Roman-garrisoned Jerusalem, seethes with necromancy and incipient intifada under its Herodian occupiers. Darrell Schweitzer's *The White Isle* (revised 1989) sends Prince Evnos of Iankoros on an errand like that of Orpheus to a caperingly cruel underworld. The even more harrowing second half of the novel is given over to a war of wills between father and daughter on Iankoros, an island turned death's other kingdom. In Australian Andrew Whitmore's *The Fortress of Eternity* (1990) characters enduring the "agonizing rack of being" race to forestall a malign theophany in a world "dwelling at the gutter-end of Time." A forest kingdom's rangers and outlaws in Simon Green's *Down Among the Dead Men* (1993) are drawn to a border fort beneath which something older and fouler than any demon dreams unspeakably. The ensuing pyrotechnics avoid the facetiousness with which Green has been known to self-sabotage his many other swashbucklers and space operas.

Generous helpings of horror make the heroism in heroic fantasy more heroic, and who better to supply them than a modern master like Ramsey Campbell? *Far Away and Never* (1996) collects his 1970s sword-and-sorcery, including four stories of Ryre, in the author's words "as much of [a hero] as I could believe in," and a sole exemplar of initiative, however mercenary, in sun-stunned, dust-choked regions of squalor and torpor where slavering mouths and vampiric wings are all-but-disembodied but no less voracious for it. *Engor's Sword Arm* (1997), an expanded version of one of David C. Smith's Attluma stories, is a sort of epilogue or afterword to the history of humankind on that island continent: the gods are dead and the pretense that men rule men is dying. Smith sends the central tableau of the subgenre, the eventual confrontation between swordsman and sorcerer, spinning off into the Outer Dark, which is exactly where the major weird fiction event of the late 1990s, Brian McNaughton's *Throne of Bones* (1997), made its lair. The linked stories of *Throne* are mostly a danse macabre of sportive ghouls, but "The Return of Liron Wolfbaiter" features a Fomorian Guardsman named Crondard Sleith whose misadventures after killing his captain might have had Howard and Leiber smiling while swallowing hard: "The blood of demon-haunted barbarians screamed that he had blundered into a blackness deeper than the night beyond a northern hearth."

Interviewed by Gabriel Chouinard in 2001, Matthew Woodring Stover said of his fiction "They used to call it swords and sorcery...I really, truly, profoundly believe that swords and sorcery (fantasy, SF, whatever) ought to be more than just junk food." Stover's *Iron Dawn* (1997) introduces Barra, a Pictish warrior-woman who trained with the bulldancers of Knossos and soldiered as one of the Pharoah's Shardana. In a nod to Leiber's only non-Nehwonian Fahrd/Mouser novella "Adept's Gambit," Barra is based in Tyre, but hers is the earlier Tyre of the late Bronze Age; both *Iron Dawn* and its sequel *Jericho Moon* (1998) are awash in empty-eyed veterans of the Trojan War who have never really left the plains before Priam's city. In the second book Barra throws in with the Jebusite defenders of what is not yet Jerusalem against the Habiru tribes led by the tormented Joshua, "a man used hard in the service of his god." We learn why the ruins of the fallen Jericho are no place for the living and are treated to the most all-out assault on Yahwist or Jehovan omnipotence since Harlan Ellison's "The Deathbird." All four of Stover's heroic fantasies offer fight scenes of such crippling power that they risk hospitalizing incautious readers: the original, transcendently apposite title of *Heroes Die* (1999) was *Acts of Violence,* described by Stover as "a piece of violent entertainment that is a meditation on violent entertainment." In this novel sword-and-sorcery, as it is enacted by both the natives of, and Earthly "Aktiri" transported to, the transdimensional Overworld, is the opiate, the Soma, of the masses back home, the bread and circuses that keep consumers consuming. Peter Beagle's well-known words about Tolkien—"Let us now praise the colonizers of dreams"—start to seem very sinister indeed the deeper one reads in *Heroes Die* and its even more unsparing sequel The *Blade of Tyshalle* (2001).

It might seem strange to speak of the increasing militarization of a subgenre largely built on the Nemedian invasion of Aquilonia, Poul Anderson's great northern war between elves and trolls in *The Broken Sword,* and the titular event of Wagner's *Dark Crusade,* but vast campaigns and defenses-in-depth have all but driven out the incidents and vignettes of yore. Fewer barbarians steal into temples to steal from sorcerers and villages see fewer wanderers who save maidens from being sacrificed to the local godling. Glen Cook told Jeff VanderMeer that "The conflict between fantasy and real medieval warfare is stark" in a 2005 interview, but combined-arms operations relying on swords *and* sorcery have become a staple not only in Cook's much-loved Black Company series but also in Steven

Erikson's Cook-endorsed *Malazan Book of the Fallen* sequence, which applies the Canadian author's training as an archaeologist and anthropologist to hailstorms of falling empires and battles as seismic as the grindings of tectonic plates. The Malazan novels thus far are *Gardens of the Moon* (1999), *Deadhouse Gates* (2000), *Memories of Ice* (2001), *House of Chains* (2002), *Midnight Tides* (2004), and *The Bonehunters* (2006). The outputs of Gemmell, Stover, Cook, and especially Erikson, who threatens the livelihood of doorstop manufacturers, reflect the way market realities have forced sword-and-sorcery into a dependence on novels that is at variance with its pulp and paperback heritage. Like horror, the subgenre is "at ease in shorter lengths," as David Pringle once put it, thriving in novellas and novelettes—think "The People of the Black Circle," "Adept's Gambit," or Wagner's "Raven's Eyrie" in the *Night Winds* collection. But with the best of the new swordmasters, the pages turn just as quickly even if there are more of them.

Like Gemmell and Erikson, Northern Ireland's Paul Kearney has been known to speak knowledgeably and enthusiastically about Howard's classic heroic fantasy characters. His *The Monarchies of God* combines the immemorial power structures honeycombed with shapeshifting infiltrators of "The Shadow Kingdom" and the titanic grudge-match between an onrushing East and an unyielding West of "The Shadow of the Vulture." The sequence consists of *Hawkwood's Voyage* (1995), *The Heretic Kings* (1996), *The Iron Wars* (1999), *The Second Empire* (2000), and *Ships From the West* (2002). Kearney has moved on to *The Mark of Ran* (2004), and *This Forsaken Earth* (2006), in which the scion of a pre-human pariah race becomes the most audacious captain of a hidden pirate city, but his Normanni-versus-Merduk clash of civilizations in *The Monarchies of God*, which echoed the Ottoman attempts on Vienna *and* the Balkan wars of the 1990s, anticipated the barely-disguised crosses and crescents that bludgeon each other in several twenty-first-century series. Having already courted a fatwa with a secular study of an empire-affrighting Mohammed-figure in his *The Fire in His Hands* (1984) and *With Mercy Toward None* (1985), Glen Cook further disturbed the "peace" of militant monotheisms with the *Instrumentalities of the Night* sequence. In leadoff installment *The Tyranny of the Night* (2005), the Holy Land of a world in which magic is on the wane and fanaticism is on the boil is torn between adherents of a Patriarch and a "Kaif." *The Warrior Prophet* (2005) and *The Thousandfold Thought* (2006) the second and third novels of R. Scott Bakker's *Prince of Nothing* series, fantasticate the First Crusade as we remember it from Harold Lamb's histories to chronicle a Holy War even more apocalyptically destructive than the real thing.

Encouragingly, revivals have restored some of sword-and-sorcery's missing—and much-missed—memories. Chaosium's *The Scroll of Thoth: Tales of Simon Magus and the Great Old Ones* (1997) did aficionados of Richard Tierney's studiously syncretic weird fiction an incalculable favor by assembling most of the stories about ex-gladiator and Julio-Claudian bugbear Simon of Gitta in one volume; Wagner's Kane makes an unbilled guest appearance. Night Shade Books' *A Cruel Wind: A Chronicle of the Dread Empire* (2006) gathers the original three novels of Glen Cook's first heroic fantasy sequence: *A Shadow of All Night Falling* (1979), *October's Baby* (1980), and *All Darkness Met* (1980). *Exorcisms and Ecstasies* (1997) is a bittersweet assemblage of Wagneriana. The references in its Kane fragment to "the broken ruins of prehuman dream" and the "flaming death of Eden" induce a state of longing on the far side of tantalization as we contemplate all that we will ever read of *In the Wake of the Night*, sword-and-sorcery's greatest story never told. Regrettably, *Gods in Darkness: The Complete Novels of Kane* (2002) and *The Midnight Sun: The Complete Stories of Kane* (2003) were indifferently packaged and even more indifferently proofread by Night Shade, yet it is difficult to hold a grudge against publishers who have also coaxed Charles Saunders out of premature retirement. His 1970s stories and 1980s novels about Imaro of Nyumbani, the most wounded warrior since Philoctetes, showcased his passion for, and pride in, the vibrance of African history and myth, and also constituted sword-and-sorcery's most notable attempt at self-correction and slur suppression. *Imaro* (2006) entices with two new novellas, and future volumes will present both reconceived and never-before-published material.

So nowadays a devotion to word-and-sorcery need not entail tomb-robbing and fossil hunting; the subgenre has a presence outside used bookstores and cyber-conclaves of graying fans. Millions of potential readers were exposed to the tried-and-true trappings, computer-conjured but acted and directed with more brilliance and bravura than ever before, in Peter Jackson's *LOTR* films. Howard, the most Howardian Howard ever made available, is back in bookstores courtesy of the Wandering Star team and their Del Rey partners. *Bran Mak Morn: The Last King*, *The Bloody Crown of Conan*, and *Kull: Exile of Atlantis* are alphabetically adjacent to a warrior-king's-ransom of Gemmell novels, and within browsing distance of Stover, Kearney, and up-and-comers like Scotsman William King, another Howard admirer whose rip-roaring Gotrek & Felix novels include *Trollslayer* (1999), *Beastslayer* (2001), and *Giantslayer* (2003), and who recently introduced a brooding Highlands swordsman with the not unfamiliar name Kormak. Heroic fantasy isn't going anywhere—except forward into a future in which its swords will continue to cut through the clutter and its sorcery will continue to spellbind.

WORKS CITED

Anderson, Poul. *The Broken Sword* (Fantasy Masterworks Edition). London: Victor Gollancz, 2004.
___. *Hrolf Kraki's Saga*. New York: Ballantine Books, 1972.
___. *War of the Gods*. New York: Tor Books, 1997.
Bakker, R. Scott. *The Darkness That Comes Before*. Woodstock, NY: Overlook Press, 2004.
Bakker, R. Scott. *The Thousandfold Thought*. Woodstock, NY: Overlook Press, 2006.
___. *The Warrior Prophet*. Woodstock, NY: Overlook Press, 2005.
Campbell, Ramsey. *Far Away and Never*. West Warwick, RI: Necronomicon Press, 1996.
Cook, Glen. *A Cruel Wind: A Chronicle of the Dread Empire*. Newberg, OR: Night Shade Books, 2006
___. *The Fire in His Hands*. New York: Pocket Books, 1984.
___. *An Ill Fate Marshalling*. New York: Tor Books, 1987.
___. *Reap the East Wind*. New York: Tor Books, 1988
___. *The Swordbearer*. New York: Pocket Books, 1982.
___. *The Tower of Fear*. New York: Tor Books, 1989.
___. *The Tyranny of the Night*. New York: Tor Books, 2005.
___. *With Mercy Toward None*: New York, Baen Books, 1985.
Erikson, Steven. *The Bonehunters*. London: Bantam Press, 2006.
___. *Deadhouse Gates*. London: Bantam Press, 2000.
___. *Gardens of the Moon*. London: Bantam Press, 1999.
___. *Memories of Ice*. London: Bantam Press, 2001.
___. *House of Chains*. London: Bantam Press, 2002.
___. *Midnight Tides*. London: Bantam Press, 2004.
Gemmell, David. *Bloodstone*. London: Legend Books, 1994.
___. *Dark Moon*. London: Bantam Press, 1996.
___. *Dark Prince*. London: Legend Books, 1991.
___. *Echoes of the Great Song*. London: Bantam Press, 1997.
___. *The First Chronicles of Druss the Legend*. London: Legend Books, 1993
___. *Ghost King*. London: Legend Books, 1988.

___. *Hawk Eternal*. London: Legend Books, 1995
___. *Hero in the Shadows*. New York: Del Rey Books, 2000.
___. *Ironhand's Daughter*. London, Legend Books, 1995
___. *The King Beyond the Gate*. London: Legend Books, 1985.
___. *Knights of Dark Renown*. London: Legend Books, 1989.
___. *The Last Guardian*. London: Legend Books, 1989.
___. *Last Sword of Power*. London: Legend Books, 1989.
___. *Legend*. London: Century, 1984.
___. *The Legend of Deathwalker*. London: Bantam Press, 1996.
___. *Lion of Macedon*. London: Legend Books, 1990.
___. *Lord of the Silver Bow*. New York: Del Rey Books, 2005.
___. *Midnight Falcon*. London: Bantam Press, 1999.
___. *Morningstar*. London: Legend Books, 1992.
___. *Quest for Lost Heroes*. London: Legend Books, 1990.
___. *Ravenheart*. New York: Del Rey Books, 2001. .
___. *Shield of Thunder*. London: Bantam Press, 2006.
___. *Stormrider*. New York: Del Rey Books, 2002.
___. *Sword in the Storm*. London: Bantam Press, 1998.
___. *Swords of Night and Day*. New York: Del Rey Books, 2004.
___. *Waylander*. London: Century, 1986.
___. *Waylander II: In the Realm of the Wolf*. London: Legend, 1993.
___. *White Wolf*. New York: Del Rey Books, 2003.
___. *Winter Warriors*. London: Bantam Press, 1996.
___. *Wolf in Shadow*. London: Legend Books, 1987.
Green, Simon R. *Down Among the Dead Men*. London: Victor Gollancz, 1993.
Grundy, Stephan. *Rhinegold*. New York: Bantam Books, 1994.
Howard, Robert E. *The Bloody Crown of Conan*. New York: Del Rey Books, 2004.
___. *Bran Mak Morn: The Last King*. New York: Del Rey Books, 2005.
___. *The Coming of Conan the Cimmerian*. New York: Del Rey Books, 2003.
___. *The Conquering Sword of Conan*. New York: Del Rey Books, 2005.
___. *Kull: Exile of Atlantis*. New York: Del Rey Books, 2006.
Kearney, Paul. *Hawkwood's Voyage*. London: Victor Gollancz, 1995.
___. *The Heretic Kings*. London: Victor Gollancz, 1996.
___. *The Iron Wars*. London: Victor Gollancz, 1999
___. *The Mark of Ran*. London: Transworld Publishers, 2004
___. *The Second Empire*. London: Victor Gollancz, 2000.
___. *Ships From the West*. London: Victor Gollancz, 2002.

___. *This Forsaken Earth*. London: Transworld Publishers, 2006.
King, William. *Beastslayer*. Nottingham, UK: Games Workshop, 2001.
___. *Daemonslayer*. Nottingham, UK: Games Workshop, 2003.
___. *Dragonslayer*. Nottingham, UK: Games Workshop, 2003.
___. *Giantslayer*. Nottingham, UK: Games Workshop,
___. *Skavenslayer*. Nottingham, UK: Games Workshop, 2003.
___. *Trollslayer*. Nottingham, UK: Games Workshop, 1999.
___. *Vampireslayer*. Nottingham, UK: Games Workshop, 2001.
Lee, Tanith. *The Birthgrave*. New York: DAW Books, 1975.
___. *Cast a Bright Shadow*. London: Pan Macmillan, 2004.
___. *Here in Cold Hell*. London: Pan Macmillan, 2005.
___. *The Storm Lord*. New York: DAW Books, 1976.
Leiber, Fritz. *Farewell to Lankhmar*. Clarkston, GA: White Wolf, 1998.
___. *The Knight and Knave of Swords*. New York: William Morrow & Company, 1988.
Moorcock, Michael. *The Dreamthief's Daughter: A Tale of the Albino*. New York: Warner Books, 2001.
___. *The Fortress of the Pearl*. New York: Ace Books, 1989.
___. *The Revenge of the Rose*. New York: Ace Books, 1991.
___. *The Skrayling Tree: The Albino in America*. New York: Warner Books, 2003.
___. *The White Wolf's Son: The Albino Underground*. Boston, MA: Aspect, 2005.
McNaughton, Brian. *The Throne of Bones*. Black River, NY: Terminal Fright, 1997.
Saunders, Charles. *Imaro*. Newberg, OR: Night Shade Books, 2006.
___. *Imaro*. New York: DAW Books, 1981.
___. *Imaro II: The Quest for Cush*. New York: DAW Books, 1984.
___. *Imaro III: The Trail of Bohu*. New York: DAW Books, 1985.
Schweitzer, Darrell. *The White Isle*. King of Prussia, PA: Owlswick Press, 1989.
Shea, Michael. *The A'rak*. New York: Baen Books, 2000.
___. *The Mines of Behemoth*. New York: Baen Books, 1997.
___. *Nifft the Lean*. New York: DAW Books, 1982.
Smith, David C. *Engor's Sword Arm*. North East, PA: Forgotten Ages Press, 1997.
___. *The Ghost Army*. New York: Zebra Books, 1983.
___. *Mosutha's Magic*. New York: Zebra Books, 1982.
___. *Oron*. New York: Zebra Books, 1978.
___. *The Sorcerer's Shadow*. New York: Zebra Books, 1978.
___. *The Valley of Ogrum*. New York: Zebra Books, 1982.

Stover, Matthew Woodring. *Blade of Tyshalle*. New York: Del Rey Books, 2001
___. *Heroes Die*. New York: Del Rey Books, 1998.
___. *Iron Dawn*. New York: Roc, 1997.
___. *Jericho Moon*. New York: Roc, 1998.
Taylor, Keith. *Bard*. New York: Ace Books, 1981.
___. *Bard II*. New York: Ace Books, 1984.
___. *Bard III: The Wild Sea*. New York: Ace Books, 1986
___. *Bard IV: Ravens' Gathering*. New York: Ace Books, 1987.
___. *Bard V: Felimid's Homecoming*. London: Headline Book Publishing, 1991.
Tierney, Richard. *Scroll of Thoth: Tales of Simon Magus and the Great Old Ones*. Oakland, CA: Chaosium, 1997.
Tolkien, J. R. R. "Beowulf: The Monsters and the Critics." *The Monsters and the Critics and Other Essays*. Boston: Houghton Miflin Company, 1984.
Wagner, Karl Edward. *Bloodstone*. New York: Warner Books, 1975.
___. *Dark Crusade*. New York: Warner Books, 1976.
___. *Darkness Weaves*. New York: Warner Books, 1978.
___. *Death Angel's Shadow*. New York: Warner Books, 1973.
___. *Exorcisms and Ecstasies*. Minneapolis: Fedogan & Bremer, 1997.
___. *The Gods in Darkness: The Complete Novels of Kane*. Newberg, OR: Night Shade Books, 2002.
___. The *Midnight Sun: The Complete Stories of Kane*. Newberg, OR: Night Shade Books, 2003.
___. *Night Winds*. New York: Warner Books, 1978.
Whitmore, Andrew. *The Fortress of Eternity*. New York: Avon Books, 1990

ABOUT THE CONTRIBUTORS

POUL ANDERSON (1926-2001) was a leading writer of science fiction and fantasy from the late 1940s. His contributions to heroic fantasy are mang and distinguished: *The Broken Sword, Hrolf Kraki's Saga, Three Hearts and Three Lions, The Merman's Children, The War of the Gods,* etc. He also wrote several historical novels set in the Viking age, most notably the three volume *The Last Viking.*

DON D'AMMASSA has been book-reviewer for *Science Fiction Chronicle* for many years and is also a prolific writer of short fantasy and horror fiction. He has also published novels, including *Blood Beast, Servant of Chaos,* and *Scarab.*

L. SPRAGUE DE CAMP (1907-2000) was trained as an engineer, lost his job in the Great Depression, and wrote for a living for the rest of his life. He was a leading contributor to *Astounding Science Fiction* and *Unknown Worlds* in the 1940s, publishing in the latter such classic fantasies as *Lest Darkness Fall,* and, in collaboration with Fletcher Pratt, *The Incomplete Enchanter, Castle of Iron,* and *Land of Unreason.* He was a world-traveler, and the author of non-fiction books on many subjects, including *Great Cities of the Ancient World* and *The Ancient Engineers.* He discovered Robert E. Howard's works in 1950 and became a great Conan enthusiast, ushering the Conan series into mass-market paperback in the 1960s. His biography, *Dark Valley Destiny: The Life and Death of Robert E. Howard* (with Catherine Crook de Camp and Jane Whittington Griffin) appeared in 1983.

SCOTT CONNORS has edited a book of essays about H. P. Lovecraft, *Lovecraft: A Century Less a Dream* and is also a leading expert on Clark Ashton Smith, having edited Smith's *Selected Letters* and the recent symposium about Smith *The Freedom of Fantastic Things.* Arkham House will be publishing his upcoming biography of Smith.

He reviews books for *Weird Tales*, *The New York Review of Science Fiction*, and *Publishers Weekly*.

MARK FINN is the recipient of the 2005 Cimmerian Award for Outstanding Achievement in Robert E. Howard studies, and author of a new biography, *Blood and Thunder: The Life and Art of Robert E. Howard*. He is an expert on twentieth-century pop culture and genre studies, and Creative Director of the Violet Crown Radio Players.

LEO GRIN was editor of *The Cimmerian*, a discontinued semiprofessional journal dedicated to the study of Howard and his works.

MARK HALL graduated with his doctorate in Anthropology (Archeology emphasis) from the University of California at Berkeley in 1992. After graduation, he held a variety of curatorial posts in museums in Japan and California. In 2003, he began editing *The Dark Man: The Journal of Robert E. Howard Studies*. He is currently employed as an archeologist with the Bureau of Land Management.

CHARLES HOFFMAN became an early pioneer of Howard studies with the publication of his essay, "Conan the Existential" in the mid-1970's. He has contributed further essays on Howard's writings to *The Dark Man: The Journal of Robert E. Howard Studies*, *The Cimmerian*, and *Spectrum*. With Marc Cerasini, he co-authored the book-length critical study, *Robert E. Howard*, which was published by Starmont House in 1987. Hoffman has also contributed articles, fiction and reviews to *Crypt of Cthulhu*, *Risque Stories*, *Rave Reviews*, *Romantic Times*, *Wrapped in Plastic*, *S.W.A.T.*, *Law & Order*, and other publications. His biography for young adults, *Bruce Lee, Brandon Lee, and the Dragon's Curse* was published by Random House in 1995. A new, revised edition of Cerasini and Hoffman's book, now titled *Robert E. Howard: A Critical Study*, will be available from Wildside Press.

S. T. JOSHI is an expert on, among others, H. P. Lovecraft, Lord Dunsany, Ambrose Bierce, and John Dickson Carr. In the Lovecraft field he has single-handedly established the corrected texts, written the standard biography (*H. P. Lovecraft: a Life*), edited the collected poems (*The Ancient Track*), compiled the standard bibliography, edited the leading journal for many years (*Lovecraft Studies*), edited the Penguin Classics editions of Lovecraft, and produced numerous other volumes of interest, many of them in recent years from Hippocampus Press. He is the author of *The Weird Tale*, *The Modern Weird Tale*, and many others.

FRITZ LEIBER (1910-1992) was, after Robert E. Howard, the leading American sword-and-sorcery writer of the twentieth century, and the very person who coined the term. He was the son of a leading actor, but after a few bit parts in movies of his own, he turned to writing in the late 1930s. He continued his Fafhrd and Gray Mouser series throughout most of his life, his last book being in that series, *The Knight and Knave of Swords* (1988). He is also the author of *Gather, Darkness!*, *Conjure Wife*, *The Big Time*, *Our Lady of Darkness*, and numerous other classics. He was a correspondent of H. P. Lovecraft, and certainly the one member of the Lovecraft Circle to become a literary peer to the master himself.

MICHAEL MOORCOCK is one of the world's leading authors of imaginative fiction, most famous in the heroic fantasy field for his Elric series. Among his many books in the genre are *Stormbringer*, *The Stealer of Souls*, *The Warhound and the World's Pain*, *The City of the Autumn Stars*, *The Jewel in the Skull*, *The Sorcerer's Amulet*, *Count Brass*, *The Eternal Champion*, *The Skrayling Tree*, and many more. His other works are as diverse as *Behold the Man*, *Blood: A Southern Fantasy*, and *Mother London*. In the 1960s he edited the ground-breaking SF magazine, *New Worlds*. He now lives in Texas.

ROBERT M. PRICE edited and published *Crypt of Cthulhu* for many years. He has edited many books of a Lovecraftian nature for Fedogan and Bremer and for Chaosium. A former clergyman of a more orthodox sort, he has uplifted the faithful with memorable sermons at the Cthulhu prayer-breakfasts at the Necronomicon conventions. These will soon be published as *The Sermon on the Mound and Others* by Zadok Allen: Publisher. Price was also editor of *Strange Tales* magazine, when it was briefly revived by Wildside Press.

GARY ROMEO is the author if the booklet *In Search of Cimmeria* about Robert E. Howard's travels in the Southwest, and a frequent contributor to *The Cimmerian*.

DARRELL SCHWEITZER is a fiction-writer, author of three fantasy novels, *The Mask of the Sorcerer*, *The White Isle*, and *The Shattered Goddess*. These, plus many of his over 250 published stories (especially those in the story-cycle *We Are All Legends*) have distinct sword-and-sorcery elements. He has written critical books about H.

P. Lovecraft and Lord Dunsany, edited numerous critical symposia, including *The Neil Gaiman Reader*, *Discovering H. P. Lovecraft*, *Discovering Classic Fantasy*, etc. He has contributed to *Amra* and *The Cimmerian*. He reviews books for *The New York Review of Science Fiction*, *Publishers Weekly*, and elsewhere. He was co-editor of *Weird Tales* from 1987-2000, and is thus a little humbled to realize he held in the position longer than Farnsworth Wright, although admittedly not for as many issues.

GEORGE SCITHERS'S swordly accomplishments included editing *Amra* magazine, a leading journal devoted to Robert E. Howard and related matters, for many years. For this he won two Hugo Awards for best fanzine. He won two more, as best professional editor for editing *Isaac Asimov's Science Fiction Magazine*. He was also the editor of *Amazing Stories* and co-editor (with John Betancourt and Darrell Schweitzer) of *Weird Tales*. He published books under the Owlswick Press imprint for many years, including fine, illustrated editions of books by Lord Dunsany, L. Sprague de Camp, and Avram Davidson. He died in 2010.

STEVE TOMPKINS is a Cimmerian Award winning essayist, and the editor of Robert E. Howard's *The Black Stranger and Other American Tales* from Bison Books.

HOWARD WALDROP is a Texas writer of mighty peculiar books and stories, including *The Texas-Israeli War: 1999* (with Jake Saunders), *Them Bones*, *Howard Who?*, *All About Strange Monsters of the Recent Past*, *A Dozen Strange Jobs*, *Night of the Cooters*, *Going Home Again*, *Dream Factories and Radio Pictures*, *Custer's Last Jump and Other Collaborations*, *Heart of Whitenesse*, and, most recently, *Things Will Never Be the Same: A Howard Waldrop Reader*. He won both the Nebula and the World Fantasy Award for "The Ugly Chickens" in 1980. He has been nominated for other Hugo, Nebula, and World Fantasy Awards.

ROBERT WEINBERG is an expert on pulp fiction and pulp authors, a prolific anthologist, and the author of such novels as *The Devil's Auction*, *The Armageddon Box*, *The Black Lodge* etc. His total score includes nearly 100 short stories, 16 novels, 17 non-fiction books (including *The Weird Tales Story*), and more than two dozen comic scripts. One of his most recent books is *The Occult Detective*, a collection of stories. He has won two Stoker Awards, and two World Fantasy Awards.

INDEX

Action Stories, 30, 170, 171
Acts of Violence (Stover), 188
"Adept's Gambit" (Leiber), 188, 189
Adventure, 28, 31, 34, 129
"The Adventure of the Dying Detective" (Doyle), 25
"Afterlife" (Finn), 153
Against the Horde (Gemmell), 183
All Darkness Met (Cook), 189
Almuric (Howard), 34
An Amateur Flagellant, 105
Amra, 7, 72
Anaximander, 136
Ancalagon (fanzine), 180
Anderson, Chester, 155
Anderson, Poul, 186
Antelope Valley Press, 18
"The Apparition in the Prize Ring" (Howard), 28
The Arabian Nights, 12
The A'rek (Shea), 185
Argosy, 31, 129, 156, 170, 171, 175
Arkham House, 17, 52
The Aryans: a Study in Indo-European Origins (Childe), 87
"At the Mountains of Madness" (Lovecraft), 85
Augustine (of Hippo, Saint), 136
Austin, Mary, 89
Author and Journalist, 164
Baen Books, 20
Baird, Edwin, 163
Ball, Clifford, 182
Ballantine Books, 7
"The Barbarian" (Anderson), 39
The Barbaric Triumph (ed. Herron), 21
Bard series (Taylor), 186
Baudelaire, Charles, 65
Beastslayer (King), 191
Bedford-Jones, H., 164, 165

Beowulf, 12, 180
"Beowulf, The Monsters and the Critics" (Tolkien), 181
"Beyond the Black River" (Howard), 32n, 47, 47, 139-142
Billy the Kid, 72
The Birthgrave (Lee), 186
Bison Books, 7, 20
"The Black Bear Bites" (Howard), 121
"Black Canaan" (Howard), 28n, 172
"Black Colossus" (Howard), 97, 107, 132
The Black Pirate (film), 25
"The Black Stranger" (Howard), 24
"Black Wind Blowing" (Howard), 104
"The Blade of Tyshalle" (Stover), 188
Blood and Thunder: The Life and Art of Robert E. Howard (Finn), 21
"The Blood of Belshazzar" (Howard), 116-117
"The Blood of the Gods" (Howard), 121
The Bloody Crown of Conan (Howard), 190
Blosser, Fred. 107
Blue Book, 31
"The Blue Flame of Vengeance" (Howard), 134, 135, 137-138
Bok, Hannes, 174
The Bonehunters (Erikson), 189
Bran Mak Morn series (Howard), 21, 34
Bran Mak Morn: The Last King (Howard), 190
"The Brazen Peacock" (Howard), 121
Brando, Marlon, 12
Breckenridge Elkins series, 34
The Broken Sword (Anderson), 186, 188
Brundage, Margaret, 44, 104
Bryant, Edward, 155
Burke, Rusty. 80
Burroughs, Edgar Rice, 12, 14, 24, 26, 34, 94, 95, 131, 150
Burton, Sit Richard Francis, 24
Busiek, Kurt, 152
Byron, Lord, 15
"By This Axe I Rule!" (Howard), 25, 31, 48, 126, 129-130
Caldwell, Erskine, 89
Calvin, John, 135, 137
Camus, Albert, 12, 14
Carter, Lin, 126, 131, 153
Cast a Bright Shadow (Lee), 186
Cave, Hugh B., 167
Chambers, Robert W., 24
Chandler, Raymond, 22, 107
Chaney, Lon, Sr., 25
"The Changing Market" (Bedford-Jones), 164

Chouinard, Gabriel, 188
The Chronicles of Thomas Covenant (Donaldson), 181
La Chute (Camus), 12
The Cimmerian, 7, 21
Clark, John D., 32, 39
Clute, John, 183
Cohen, Leonard, 155
College Humor, 127, 128, 131-132, 163
Conan (comic book), 152
Conan (Howard; Lancer book), 152
Conan series (Howard), 11, 12, 13, 14, 16, 17, 18, 21, 22, 31-33, 39-41, 43-44, 54, 125
Conan the Adventurer (Howard, et al.), 94, 97
Conan the Conqueror (Howard), 12, 25, 32, 35-36, 41 (See also *The Hour of the Dragon*.)
Conan the Destroyer (film), 183
Conger, Alice, 51
"The Conquest of Granada" (Dryden), 25
The Conquest of Peru (Prescott), 129
Conversations with Texas Writers, 22
Cook, Glen, 187, 188, 189
Cooper, James Fennimore, 11
Corbett, Jim, 68-69, 70
Costain, Thomas, 35
Countdown (magazine), 155
Cormac Mac Art series (Howard), 27, 35
Cornelius, B., 163, 165
Crawdaddy (magazine), 155
Cromwell, Oliver, 138
A Cruel Wind: A Chronicle of the Dread Empire (Cook), 190
Cthulhu Mythos, 33, 121
The Culture of Honor: The Psychology of Violence in the South (Nisbitt & Cohen), 172
"The Curse of the Crimson God" (Howard), 121-122
"Cynara" (Dowson), 159
The Dark Barbarian (ed. Herron), 18, 21
Dark Crusade (Wagner), 182, 188
The Dark Man (magazine), 7
Dark Moon (Gemmell), 184
Darkness Weaves (Wagner), 182
Dark Valley Destiny (de Camp, de Camp, & Griffin), 21, 143, 144, 149
Darwin, Charles, 136
Day of the Stranger (Price-Ellis), 147
Death Angel's Shadow (Wagner), 182
Deadhouse Gates (Erikson), 189
"The Dead Remember" (Howard), 28n

Dean, James, 12
"The Deathbird" (Ellison), 188
Death of a Lady's Man (Cohen), 155
de Camp, L. Sprague, 13, 17, 18, 47, 123, 128, 143, 144, 145, 150, 153, 179
de Sade, Marquis, 101
"Delcardes' Cat" (Howard), 128, 129
Del Rey Books, 20
Dempsey, Jack, 61-62
Dennis Dorgan series, 30, 31, 37
Dent, Lester, 150
Derleth, August, 51-52, 143, 165, 165, 166, 167, 168, 169, 176
"The Devil in Iron" (Howard), 25, 108, 109
The Devil's Bride (Quinn), 165
Dick, Philip K., 128
A Discourse on the Origins and Foundations of Inequality Among Men (Rousseau), 26
The Dreamthief's Daughter (Moorcock), 185
Doc Savage, 98
Doctor Satan series, 104
Donaldson, Stephen R., 181
D'Onofrio, Vincent, 19
Down Among the Dead Men (Green), 187
Doyle, Arthur Conan, 22, 153
Drake, David, 163
Dryden, John, 25
Dumas, Alexandre, 27
Dunsany, Lord, 127, 179
Dyalhis, Nictzin, 65
Eddison, E.R. 41, 43
Elric series (Moorcock), 13-14
The Encyclopedia of Fantasy (Clute & Nichols), 180
Engor's Sword Arm (Smith), 187
Erikson, Steve, 189
Eugenics, 89
Exorcisms and Ecstasies (Wagner), 190
Fables of Identity (Frye), 85
Fafhrd and Gray Mouser series (Leiber), 16-17
Fairbanks, Douglas Sr., 25
Fantastic Universe, 13
The Fantastic Swordsmen (ed. De Camp), 179
The Fantasy Fan, 165
Far Away and Never (Campbell), 187
"Far Babylon" (de Camp), 147-148
Farewell to Lankhmar (Leiber), 185
Farmer, Philip José, 148

Fatu Hiva (Heyerdahl), 26
Faust, Frederik, 150
The Fortress of Eternity (Whitmore), 187
The Fortress of the Pearl (Moorcock), 185
Fear and Trembling (Kierkegaard), 138
Fight Stories, 30, 156, 170
Finlay, Virgil, 169
Finn, Mark, 21, 153
The Finovat Tapestry (Kay)
The Fire in His Hands (Cook), 189
Fleming, Ian, 22
"The Fortress Unvanquishable, Save for Sacnoth" (Dunsany), 127, 179-180
France, Anatole, 99
Francis X. Gordon series (Howard), 34
Frye, Northrup, 85-86
Frazetta, Frank, 22, 97
"The Frost Giant's Daughter" (Howard), 25, 33, 99, 131
"The Garden of Fear" (Howard), 35, 99, 110
Gardens of the Moon (Erikson), 189
"Gates of Empire" (Howard), 119
Gemmell, David, 183-184, 189, 190
Genghis Khan, 41
Gernsback, Hugo, 162, 163, 173
Ghost Stories, 156
Giantslayer (King), 191
Gibbon, Edward, 70, 87
"Gilgamesh in the Outback" (Silverberg), 148
Girasol Books, 20-21
Gnome Press, 13
"The God in the Bowl" (Howard), 25, 108, 131
Gods of the Darkness (Wagner), 190
"The Gods of the North" (Howard), 33, 99n
Golden Fleece, 35
Ghost King (Gemmell), 184
Gor series (Norman), 102
"Graveyard Rats" (Howard), 104
"The Great God Pan" (Machen), 25
Grider, Eugene, 160
Grin, Leo, 7
Guest, Edward, 65
"Guns in the Mountains" (Howard), 33n
Guthrie, A.B., 37
Guthrie, Woody, 12
Haddon, A.C., 88
Haggard, H. Rider, 94, 95

Hammett, Dashiell, 7, 9, 22
Hamilton, Edmond, 167, 174
The Hand of Fu Manchu (Rohmer), 25
Hardin, John Wesley, 72
"The Haunter of the Dark" (Lovecraft), 169
"Hawks of Outremer" (Howard), 120, 123
Hawkwood's Voyage (Kearney), 189
Hawthorne, Nathaniel, 17
Hays, H.R., 17, 36
"The Heart of Ahriman" (Laughlin & Crider), 152
Hemingway, Ernest, 25
Henneberger, J.C., 163
Here in Cold Hell (Lee), 186
The Heretic Kings (Kearney), 189
Hero of the Shadows (Gemmell), 184
Heroes Die (Stover), 188
Herron, Don, 172
Heyerdahl, Thor, 26
"The Hills of the Dead" (Howard), 138
"The Historical Text as Literary Artifact" (Frye & White), 83
The History of Middle-Earth (Tolkien), 181
The History of the Conquest of Peru (Prescott), 25
A History of the Rod, 105
"The Home of Thunder" (Skimmer), 25
Horror Stories, 104
The Hour of the Dragon (Howard), 32, 99-100, 107, 132, 181, 182 (see also *Conan the Conqueror*)
The House of the Wolfings (Morris), 184
The Howard Collector (magazine), 7
"Howard's Fantasy" (Leiber), 95
Howard, Isaac M., 51, 144, 156, 158, 172, 173, 175
Howard, Robert E.
    correspondence with Lovecraft, 51-81
    education of, 28
    detective stories of, 34
    income of, 29
    misconceptions about, 8, 19-20
    racial views of, 27-28, 53-54
    suicide of, 8, 38
    western stories of, 37-38
Howlin' Wolf, 12
Hrolf Kraki's Saga (Anderson), 186
The Hunchback of Notre Dame (film), 25
"The Hyena" (Howard), 29
"The Hyborian Age" (Howard), 82-90
"Hyborian Genesis" (Louinet), 83, 95, 111

Imaro (Saunders), 182, 190
"Ill Met in Lankhmar" (Leiber), 185
The Incredible Adventures of Denis Dorgan (Howard), 30
Instrumentality of Night sequence (Cook), 189
In the Wake of the Night (Wagner), 190
Iron Dawn (Stover), 188
"Iron Shadows in the Moon" (Howard), 108, 109, 132
The Iron Wars (Kearney), 189
Jack Dempsey's Fight Magazine, 30
Jackson, Peter, 190
Jakes, John, 47
James Allison series (Howard), 34-35
Jericho Moon (Stover), 188
The Jungle Book (Kipling), 25
The Junto, 28
Jordon, Robert, 47
Joshi, S.T., 7
Joyce, Patrick Weston, 83
Kay, Guy Gavriel, 181
Keats, John, 8, 43
Kearney, Paul, 189, 190
"The King and the Oak" (Howard), 126
King Kull (Howard & Carter), 126
Kierkegaard, Soren, 138
King, Stephen, 184
King, William, 190-191
"Kings of the Night" (Howard), 31, 180
Kipling, Rudyard, 24, 26
Kirby O'Donnell series (Howard), 34
Kline, Otis Adelbert, 37, 169
Knight and Knave of Swords (Leiber), 185
Knight, Damon, 181
Kull: Exile of Atlantis (Howard), 190
Kull series (Howard), 31, 32, 125-133
Kuttner, Henry, 47, 182
Lansdale, Joe, 11
The Last Guardian (Gemmell), 184
Last Sword of Power (Gemmell), 184
Legend (Gemmell), 183
Le Guin, Ursula, 8
Lee, D. C., 157-159, 161
Lee, Tanith, 185, 186
Leiber, Fritz, 16-17, 47, 98, 105, 107, 180, 181, 182, 184-185
"The Lion of Tiberias" (Howard), 118-119, 122
London, Jack, 9, 17, 25, 45, 89, 146
"Lord of Samarcand" (Howard), 117-118

The Lord of the Rings (Tolkien), 12, 47
Lord of the Silver Bow (Gemmell), 183
Louinet, Patrice, 172
Lovecraft, H.P., 17, 22, 24, 25, 26, 27, 28, 34, 35, 38, 46, 47, 51-80, 83, 88, 104, 122, 121, 143, 148, 148, 150-152, 163, 164, 169, 175, 176
Lovecraft's Book (Lupoff), 148
Luther, Martin, 136-137, 138
"Lynortis Reprise" (Wagner), 183
MacLeod, Fiona, 52
Malazan Book of the Fallen series (Erikson), 189
"The Mandrakes" (Smith), 166, 167
"Marchers of Valhalla" (Howard), 35
The Mark of Ran (Kearney), 189
Mather, Cotton, 135, 138
Maximinus the Thracian (Roman Emperor), 131
McMurtry, Larry, 11, 14
A Means to Freedom: the Letters of H. P. Lovecraft and Robert E. Howard, 51
Melville, Herman, 11, 17
Memories of Ice (Erikson), 189
"A Memory of Robert E. Howard" (Price), 30n
Merritt, A., 164
Michaelangelo, 68
Midnight Sun: The Complete Stories of Kane (Wagner), 190
Midnight Tides (Erikson), 189
A Midsummer Night's Dream (film), 169
Mignola, Mike, 21
Milius, John, 10
Miller, P. Schuyler, 39
Milman, Dean, 70
The Mines of Behemoth (Shea), 185
Milton, John, 181
"The Mirrors of Tuzun Thune" (Howard), 31, 126, 131, 180
Monarchies of God series (Kearney), 189
"Moon of Skulls" (Howard), 42, 44, 52, 94-95, 135
Moorcock, Michael, 133, 182, 185
Moore, C.L. 47
Morningstar (Gemmell), 184
Mosutha's Magic (Smith), 182
"The Mouser Goes Below" (Leiber), 185
Mundy, Talbot, 24, 31, 34, 184
"Murders in the Rue Morgue" (Poe), 127
The Mystery of Edwin Drood (Dickens), 126
Myths and Legends of Our Own Land (Skinner), 25
Nameless Cults (Von Junzt), 33
Neail, N.J., 53

Necronomicon Press, 18, 144
"Nevermore" (Bischoff & Smith), 149-150
New Worlds, 13
The New York Times, 17
Nifft the Lean (Shea), 185
Night Shade Books, 190
Night Winds (Wagner), 182, 183, 189
Now Let Us Praise Famous Men (Agee), 155
October's Baby (Cook), 190
One Who Walked Alone (Price-Ellis), 19, 145, 149, 170-171
Oriental Stories, 30, 35, 156, 165, 176
Oron (Smith), 182
The Outline of History (Wells), 87
"People of the Black Circle" (Howard), 94, 97, 162, 189
"The Phoenix on the Sword" (Howard), 31, 47, 48, 54, 125, 129-130, 131
Pizarro, Francesco, 25, 47
Playboy Magazine, 44
Poe, Edgar Allan, 17, 42, 149-150
"The Pool of the Black One" (Howard), 109
Poscik, John, 42
Post Oaks and Sand Roughs (Howard), 22, 145-147
Preece, Harold, 28
Presley, Elvis, 12
Price, E. Hoffmann, 143-144, 170, 174, 175
Price-Ellis, Novalyne, 19, 127, 170, 171, 172
Prince of Nothing series (Bakkev), 189-190
Pringle, David, 189
"Queen of the Black Coast" (Howard), 132
The Quest for Kush (Saunders), 192
Quest for Riverworld, (ed. Farmer) 149
Quinn, Seabury, 1964, 1969
The Races of Europe (Coon), 88
"The Rats in the Walls" (Lovecraft), 52
"Raven's Eyrie" (Wagner), 189
Raven's Gathering (Taylor), 186
Ravenheart (Gemmell), 184
"Red Blades of Black Cathay" (Howard & Smith), 115-16, 123
"Red Nails" (Howard), 21, 33, 95, 96, 107, 108, 109, 110, 111, 172
"Red Shadows" (Howard), 29, 42, 45, 47
Red Sonja, 122-123, 150
REHupa, 21, 152
Reinhardt, Max, 169
Renault, Mary, 35
Report on a Writing Man (Smith), 144
"The Return of Liron Wolfbaiter" (McNaughton, 187-188)
The Revenge of the Rose (Moorcock), 185

Riverworld series (Farmer), 148
"The Road of Azrael" (Howard), 120
"The Road of Eagles" ("The Way of Swords") (Howard), 119-120, 123
"Robert E. Howard: A Memorian" (Lovecraft), 143
Robert E. Howard Days (festival), 19
"Robert E. Howard's Hyborian Tales and the Question of Race in Fantastic Literature" (Ditomasso), 88n
"Rogues in the House" (Howard), 108-109
Rohmer, Sax, 24
Roosevelt, Franklin D., 166
The Roots of the Mountains (Morris), 25
Rousseau, Jean-Jacques, 26
Ruber, Peter, 165
Salammbo (Flaubert), 25
Santesson, Hans Stefan, 13
Saunders, Charles, 182, 190
"The Scarlet Citadel" (Howard), 107, 132
Science Fantasy, 13
Science Fiction Adventures, 13
Scott, Sir Walter, 11
The Scroll of Thoth: Tales of Simon Magus (Tierney), 190
The Second Empire (Kearney), 189
Selected Letters (Howard), 51, 88n, 90,
Selected Letters (Lovecraft), 51
Service, Robert W., 65
Severus Alexander, 131
The Shadow (character), 98
"The Shadow Kingdom" (Howard), 31, 47, 136-127, 131, 179, 189
Shadow of Night Falling (Cook), 190
"The Shadow of the Vulture" (Howard), 119, 122, 189
"The Shadow Out of Time" (Lovecraft), 85
Shadows Bend (Barbour & Raleigh), 150
"Shadows in the Moonlight" (Howard), 25
Shelley, Percy Bysshe, 15
Ships from the West (Kearney), 189
Short Stories, 31, 175
Silverberg, Robert, 148-149
"The Sin Eater" (MacLeod), 52
The Skraeling Tree (Moorcock), 185
"Skull-Face" (Howard), 53, 128
Skull-Face and Others (Howard), 17, 143
"The Slave Princess" (Howard), 117
"The Slithering Shadow" (Howard) (see "Xuthal of the Dusk")
Smith, Arthur D. Howden, 24, 31
Smith, Clark Ashton, 46, 47, 90, 151, 163, 164n, 165, 167, 175, 185-186
Smith, David C., 182

Smith, Tevis Clyde, 28, 53, 58, 83, 144, 181
Solomon Kane series, 11, 21, 29-30, 31, 42, 94, 133-138
Sonnotorrek (Skallagrimsson), 40
"Son of the White Wolf" (Howard), 122
The Sorcerer's Shadow (Smith), 182
"Sowers of the Thunder" (Howard), 117
"Spear and Fang" (Howard), 29
Spengler, Oswald, 87
Spicy Adventures, 35
Sprenger, William, 166, 167, 170, 174, 176
Starrett, Vincent, 165
The Star Rover (London), 45
Steinbeck, John, 15
Steve Costigan series, 30, 37
Stevenson, Robert Louis, 11, 22, 24
Stoddard, Solomon, 137
The Storm Lord (Lee), 186
Stormrider (Gemmell), 184
Stover, Matthew Woodring, 188, 189, 190
Strange Stories, 166
Strange Tales, 166
"The Striking of the Gong" (Howard), 128
"Superman on a Psychotic Bender" (Hays), 17
Sword in the Storm (Gemmell), 184
The Sword of Rhiannon (Brackett), 12
Swords and Sorcery (ed. De Camp), 156
Swords of Night and Day (Gemmell), 183
"Swords of Shahrazar" (Howard), 121
"Swords of the Purple Kingdom" (Howard), 126
"Swords of the Red Brotherhood" (Howard), 24
"The Sword of Welleran" story (Dunsany), 127
The Sword of Welleran collection (Dunsany), 127
Tam, Son of Tiger (Kline), 165
Tarzan Adventures, 13
Tarzan series (Burroughs), 12, 25, 112, 125
Tarzan the Untamed (Burroughs), 26n, 32
The Tattler, 28
Taylor, Keith, 186
Tennyson, Alfred, Lord, 40
Terror Tales, 104
Thais (courtesan), 99
"The Thing on the Doorstep" (Lovecraft), 169
"The Thing on the Roof" (Howard), 33
This Fiction Business (Bedford-Jones), 165
This Forsaken Earth (Kearney), 189
Thomas, Roy, 150

Thompson, Jim, 9, 11
The Thousandfold Thought (Bakker), 189
"Through the Gates of the Silver Key" (Lovecraft and Price), 169
"The Treasures of Tartary" (Howard), 120-121
Thrilling Mystery, 104
The Throne of Bones (McNaughton), 187-188
Tierney, Richard, 190
Time and Chance (de Camp), 17
Tolkien, Christopher, 181
Tolkien, J.R.R., 8, 12-13, 17, 41, 180, 181, 188
Tompkins, Steve, 8
Top Notch, 170
To the Land of the Living (Silverberg), 148
The Tower of Fear (Cook), 187
To Your Scattered Bodies Go (Farmer), 148
"The Tower of the Elephant" (Howard), 25, 97, 132, 182
Toynbee, Arnold, 87
The Trail of Bohu (Saunders), 182
"The Treasure of Tranicos" (Howard), 24
Trollslayer (King), 191
Turloch O'Brien series (Howard), 127, 34, 35
Tyranny of Night (Cook), 189
Us (magazine), 155
"The Valley of the Worm" (Howard), 35
Vandermeer, Jeff, 188
Vance, Jack, 186
Vathek (Beckford), 43
Vetter, John, 174
Vinson, Truett, 28, 171
"The Vultures of Whapeton" (Howard), 37
Wagner, Karl Edward, 181-182, 190
Wandering Star (publisher), 7, 20
War of the Gods (Anderson), 186-187
The Warrior Prophet (Bakker), 189
The Washington Post, 16, 18
Weber, Ione, 162
Weird Tales, 9, 13, 17, 20, 29, 30, 31, 32,, 33, 44, 46, 47, 52, 53, 96, 97, 99, 104, 108, 126, 129, 131, 156, 162-176, 180, 182
Weird Tales, anthology (ed. Margolies), 156
Weisinger, Mort, 106
Wellman, Manly Wade, 163
Wells, H.G., 83, 87
Westerfield, Jerry, 164
"A Whim of Circumstance" (Finn), 153
Whitehead, Henry, 5, 47
The White Isle (Schweitzer), 187

White Wolf (Gemmell), 184
The White Wolf's Son (Moorcock), 185
The Whole Wide World (film), 8, 19, 145
Wildside Press, 7, 20, 21
Williams, Paul, 155
Williamson, Jack, 167
Winfrey, Oprah, 19
"Wings in the Night" (Howard), 136
Winter Warriors (Gemmell), 184
"A Witch Shall Be Born" (Howard), 32
With Mercy Toward None (Cook), 189
"Wolfshead" (Howard), 29
Wonder Stories, 106
Worlds of the Weird (ed. Margolies), 156
Wolf in Shadow (Gemmell), 184
The Worm Ouroboros (Eddison), 39, 43
Wright, Farnsworth, 29, 31, 52, 96, 131, 162-176
Wright, Robert, 175
Wright's Shakespeare Library, 169, 176
Writer's Digest, 164
"Xuthal of the Dust" ("The Slithering Shadow") (Howard), 94-113
The Yellow Jacket, 28
Zellweger, Renée, 19

www.ingramcontent.com/pod-product-compliance
Lightning Source LLC
LaVergne TN
LVHW041616070426
835507LV00008B/284